Due Dilligence

Nijhoff Law Specials

VOLUME 73

The titles published in this series are listed at the end of this volume.

Due Diligence and Its Application to Protect Women from Violence

Edited by

Carin Benninger-Budel

MARTINUS NIJHOFF PUBLISHERS

LEIDEN • BOSTON
2008

This book is printed on acid-free paper.

Library of Congress Cataloging-in-Publication Data

Due diligence and its application to protect women from violence / edited by Carin Benninger-Budel.
p. cm.
Includes index.
ISBN 978-90-04-16293-8 (pbk. : alk. paper)
1. Women—Legal status, laws, etc. 2. Sex discrimination against women. 3. Women—Violence against. 4. Women—Crimes against. 5. Women's rights. 6. Human rights. 7. Human trafficking. I. Benninger-Budel, Carin.
K3243.D84 2008
362.88—dc22

2008036006

ISSN: 0924-4549
ISBN: 978 90 04 16293 8

Koninklijke Brill NV incorporates the imprints Brill, Hotei Publishers, IDC Publishers, Martinus Nijhoff Publishers and VSP.

http://www.brill.nl

Printed and bound in The Netherlands.

Table of Contents

Preface

For the past fifteen years, women's human rights have been at the top of the international agenda. We have witnessed the adoption of a series of new instruments to enforce women's human rights globally and the issue of violence against women has increasingly drawn the attention of women's rights activists and lawmakers at both international and domestic levels.

All available research, however, provides few signs of optimism. Women and girls continue to run particularly high risks of becoming the victims of human rights violations. Many abuses involve violence and often the sexual integrity of the victims is targeted. Ignorance and denial are frequently among the reasons for the ineffectiveness of the international legal framework in combating violence against women. States still fail in too many instances to recognise domestic violence as a human rights violation because it is predominantly committed in the 'private' sphere, by non-state actors. Or else, such abuse is justified with the reference to culture, tradition and religion. In countries with high immigration levels, this is one of the frequently heard excuses for police inactivity with regard to violence against women in minority communities, which ironically corresponds with parallel efforts by xenophobic circles to exploit such incidents for political purposes.

Trafficking in human beings, furthermore, particularly affects women and girls. So far, international efforts in the prosecution of trafficking have proved fairly ineffective and have not prevented trafficking from developing into a continuing global problem. Moreover, recent armed conflicts have drawn public attention to the horrific levels of violence against women, including genocide, rape, sexual slavery, forced abortion and forced pregnancies. During conflicts, violence against women is often used as specific means of warfare in order to terrorise the women themselves and to break down the families and communities to which they belong.

This situation confronts us with an obvious paradox. Despite growing international awareness of the problem and declared willingness to enforce women's human rights, violence against women does not seem to be in decline. This realisation motivated us to dedicate an international symposium to the question of how the existing international legal and policy framework could be used in a better way to fight violence against women. We decided to focus debate on the responsibility of the state to implement this framework at the national level. The idea to organise a symposium specifically focused on the due diligence concept was inspired by the *Stop Violence against Women Campaign* that Amnesty International launched in 2004. In recent years, the 'due diligence' concept has emerged as a formula to express the state obligation to create conditions to prevent and adequately respond to violence against women perpetrated by non-state actors.

The symposium *Due Diligence: The Responsibility of the State for the Human Rights of Women*, hosted by Amnesty International (Swiss Section), Humanrights.ch/MERS, the Interdisciplinary Centre for Gender Studies (ICFG) at the University of Bern, and the World Organisation Against Torture (OMCT) took place from 21 to 23 September 2005 in Berne, Switzerland. It brought together activists and experts dealing with human rights issues in their daily practice as well as academics specialising in gender studies. We felt the need to engage in the exchange of knowledge and experience to bridge the often deplored gap between theory and practice. And we were surprised by its result; our intention corresponded with a widely shared desire. Many of the 170 participants, women and men from all over the world who participated in the symposium, expressed their wish to strengthen such exchange. This convinced us that the publication of the symposium papers, together with some additional essays focusing on questions not directly addressed by the speakers on the symposium panels, could be a valuable contribution to the campaign for the realisation of women's human rights – for theorists as well as practitioners. Consequently, this essay collection reflects some of the most recent debates on women's human rights and the eradication of violence against women. It is our hope that this book will promote further reflection on the subject and give inspiration for action and novel approaches that have an impact on reality for all women worldwide.

Carin Benninger-Budel
World Organisation Against Torture (OMCT) and the Interdisciplinary Centre for Gender Studies (ICFG), University of Bern

Christina Hausammann
Humanrights.ch/MERS

Stella Jegher
Amnesty International Swiss Section

Regula Ludi
Interdisciplinary Centre for Gender Studies (ICFG), University of Bern/Karman Center for Advanced Studies in the Humanities, University of Bern

Brigitte Schnegg
Interdisciplinary Centre for Gender Studies (ICFG), University of Bern

Acknowledgements

We would like to express our enormous gratitude to the authors of the chapters of this book. They are the ones who made this publication happen.

This book has its origins in the international symposium *Due Diligence: The Responsibility of the State for the Human Rights of Women* which took place at the University of Bern, Switzerland, 21-23 September 2005. The contributions of all participants, either in the form of a presentation or through observations, analysis and exchange of ideas, generated a fascinating information platform. They were the inspiration for the development of the concept and chapters of this publication. We would like to extend our thanks to each participant.

The symposium benefited from the generous support of the involved institutions and organisations, namely Amnesty International (Swiss Section), the Interdisciplinary Centre for Gender Studies (ICFG) at the University of Bern, Humanrights.ch/MERS, and the World Organisation Against Torture (OMCT). The symposium was financially supported by the Max and Elsa Beer Brawand Foundation, the Swiss Academy of Humanities and Social Sciences, Migros-Kulturprozent, and the Political Affairs Division IV of the Federal Department of Foreign Affairs (Switzerland).

Much of the preparatory work and the organisation during the symposium itself were done by volunteers. Gratitude is owed to each volunteer. And without the relentless efforts by Sabrina Büchler, who managed the coordination of the symposium, and Barbara von Rütte, who assisted her in this enormous undertaking, it would not have been possible to organise an event of this size.

We would like to express our deepest appreciation to Martinus Nijhoff, the publisher, and most especially to Lindy Melman and Bea Timmer. The publication of this book was further made possible thanks to the generous financial support from the following foundations and organisations: Avina Foundation and the Swiss Agency for Development and Cooperation (SDC) as well as different foundations through the Swiss Section of Amnesty International.

We are also grateful for the important proofreading assistance by Tanja Rietmann of the Interdisciplinary Centre for Gender Studies (ICFG) at the University of Bern and the language editing provided by Lesley McBain of canyouproofthis.com.

Carin Benninger-Budel
World Organisation Against Torture (OMCT) and the Interdisciplinary Centre for Gender Studies (ICFG), University of Bern

Christina Hausammann
Humanrights.ch/ MERS

Stella Jegher
Amnesty International Swiss Section

Regula Ludi
Interdisciplinary Centre for Gender Studies (ICFG), University of Bern/ Karman Center for Advanced Studies in the Humanities, University of Bern

Brigitte Schnegg
Interdisciplinary Centre for Gender Studies (ICFG), University of Bern

I would like to add my personal thanks to Christina Hausammann, Stella Jegher, Regula Ludi and in particular to Brigitte Schnegg for their constant inspiration and support throughout the preparation of this book. I am very grateful to Joanna Bourke-Martignoni for her invaluable advice and comments during the preparation of the book. I want to thank Mariette Johnson Wharton who has helped me in the final stages of the project with the proof copy of the book. Finally, I want to express my deepest gratitude and love to my husband David for his support and patience and to my sons Tom, Victor and Nicolas for their continuing entertainment throughout the process.

Carin Benninger-Budel

Introduction

Carin Benninger-Budel

As part of addressing violence against women more effectively, women human rights advocates have been developing new tools in order to ensure that international law addresses the specific experiences of women. This book examines such a tool: the due diligence standard, a measure for assessing state responsibility for violations of human rights emanating from non-state actors. The application of human rights law to the 'private' sphere has important implications for the legal protection of women from violence, as it is in this sphere where women are most threatened in the enjoyment of their human rights. This introduction explains some of the background factors that inform the recent developments in human rights law aimed at protecting women from non-state violence, while the contributors to this book focus on explaining where and how the due diligence standard and other tools are being applied to achieve this end.

The Historical Lack of Protection of Women from Violence

The historically unequal position of women in every society in the world has been reflected in many of the formulations and interpretations of international human rights law. Traditionally, human rights law has focused strongly on the protection of the individual from abuse within the 'public' sphere and their relationship with the government. This 'public' focus is a consequence of the fact that women have, until recently, been virtually absent from the process of law-making at every level from the organs of the state, to the composition of delegations defining international human rights norms and international bodies monitoring human rights compliance.[1] At each step of the way it has been male experiences that have been

1 See, e.g., Hilary Charlesworth and Christine Chinkin, *The Boundaries of International Law, A Feminist Analysis* (Manchester: Manchester University Press, 2000) who have underlined this argument throughout their book; Ineke Boerefijn, *De blindoek opzij, Een mensenrechtenbenadering van geweld tegen vrouwen* (Maastricht: Universiteit Maastricht, 2006), 7-9. Historically, the presence of women in prominent

C. Benninger-Budel ed., Due Diligence and Its Application to Protect Women from Violence
 ISBN 978 90 04 16293 8. pp. 1-24

used to define what it is to be 'human' for the purposes of international human rights norms.[2] This focus on the life of men has tended to revolve around human rights violations occurring in the 'public' sphere and the risk of state violence and repression. The resulting construction of the public/private dichotomy has served to marginalise women's experiences in international human rights law.[3] Their concerns have for a long time been ignored in law-making and in practice.

It was, of course, not the intention to exclude women from the protection offered by the general human rights instruments. The Universal Declaration of Human Rights – proclaimed in 1948 by the General Assembly of the United Nations (UN) – provides that everyone is entitled to enjoy human rights without discrimination on grounds of sex.[4] The UN Charter affirms that the 'equal rights of men and women' is among the UN's core principles and objectives.[5] Other multilateral human rights instruments at both the international and regional levels contain rights of non-discrimination on a number of grounds including sex and prohibit distinctions based on sex with respect to the enjoyment of human rights.[6] Thus, in theory the human rights protections and dispute settlement mechanisms con-

positions within the United Nations agencies or bodies has been restricted to those specifically concerned with women's issues, such as the Commission on the Status of Women (CSW), the Committee on the Elimination of Discrimination against Women (CEDAW Committee), the Division for the Advancement of Women (DAW), and the UN Development Fund for Women (UNIFEM). These entities had until recently comparatively limited influence in the international arena. See also Kelly D. Askin, 'Introduction', in *Women and International Human Rights Law*, Volume 1, ed. Kelly D. Askin and Dorean M. Koenig, xxv (Ardsley, New York: Transnational Publishers, Inc, 1999).

2 See also for discussion on this issue, Farida Shaheed, 'Violence against Women Legitimised by Arguments of "Culture" – Thoughts from a Pakistani Perspective', in this book. Further, Elizabeth A. H. Abi-Mershed underscores in her contribution to this book, *Due Diligence and the Fight against Gender-Based Violence in the Inter-American System*, the importance of the fact that the vast majority of delegates and experts who participated in the decisive drafting meetings of the Convention of Belém do Pará were women.

3 See for a discussion on the public/private dichotomy in international human rights Yakın Ertürk in this book, referring to the divide as one of the main obstacles to the protection of women's rights. See, e.g., also Celina Romany, 'State Responsibility Goes Private: A Feminist Critique of the Public/Private Distinction in International Human Rights Law', in *Human Rights of Women: National and International Perspectives*, ed. Rebecca Cook, 85-115 (Philadelphia: University of Pennsylvania Press, 1994).

4 Article 2.

5 Preamble, UN Charter.

6 See, e.g., Articles 2, 3, 26 of the International Covenant on Civil and Political Rights, Articles 2, 3 and 7 of the International Covenant on Economic, Social and Cultural Rights, Article 1 of the American Convention on Human Rights, Articles 2 and 18 (3) of the African Charter on Human and Peoples' Rights, and Article 14 of the European Convention on Human Rights.

tained in these instruments are available to men and women on an equal basis. However, that does not mean that women actually enjoy equal human rights protection in practice.

The following example concerning the right to be free from torture may illustrate the way in which human rights law has a disproportionate impact on the enjoyment of rights by women. There is no legally binding instrument at the international level that specifically deals with violence against women; hence the Convention against Torture and Other Cruel, Inhuman or Degrading Treatment or Punishment, as an instrument exclusively dealing with violence, has the potential to fill certain aspects of this gap.[7] And the widely accepted *jus cogens*[8] status of the prohibition of torture – which means that the norm is absolutely binding on all states, regardless of their treaty obligations and as such cannot be altered by treaty or by a subsequent customary rule but only by the emergence of a new contrary norm of *jus cogens* – may help to give additional value to the assertion that violence against women is a violation of fundamental human rights prohib-

7 Carin Benninger-Budel and Lucinda O'Hanlon, 'Expanding the Definition of Torture', *Human Rights Dialogue*, Carnegie Council on Ethics and International Affairs, series 2, 10 (Fall 2003): 14-15.

8 See for example the European Court of Human Rights, *Al Adsani v UK*, judgment of 21 November 2001, Reports of Judgments and Decisions 2001-XI, para. 60-61; International Criminal Tribunal for the Former Yugoslavia, *the Prosecutor v Anto Furundžija*, Trial Chamber II, case no. IT-95-17/1-T, 10 December 1998; the Human Rights Committee, General Comment no. 24 on Issues Relating to Reservations Made Upon Ratification or Accession to the Covenant or the Optional Protocol thereto, or in Relation to Declarations under Article 41 of the Covenant (4 November 1994), para. 10, states that 'the prohibition of torture has the status of a peremptory norm'. The prohibition of sex discrimination has generally not been understood as a norm of *jus cogens*. Charlesworth and Chinkin have noted that as the substance of human rights law has been developed in accordance with male values this claim can be extended to the norms of *jus cogens*, in Charlesworth and Chinkin (2000), see note 1 above, 120. However, some developments in this area have recently taken place. Ian Brownlie notes: 'there is a considerable support for the view that there is in international law today a legal principle of non-discrimination which applies in matters of race. This principle is based in part, upon the UN Charter, especially Articles 55 and 56, the practice of organs of the UN, in particular resolutions of the General Assembly condemning apartheid, the Universal Declaration of Human Rights, the International Covenants on human rights and the European Convention on Human Rights. There is also a legal principle of non-discrimination in matters of sex, based on the same set of multilateral instruments, together with the Convention on the Elimination of All Forms of Discrimination against Women adopted by the UN General Assembly in 1979.' In Ian Brownlie, *Principles of Public International Law*, 6th ed. (Oxford: Oxford University Press 2003), 546. Moreover, in 2003, the Inter-American Court of Human Rights noted that the principle of equality and non-discrimination, including between men and women, belongs to *jus cogens*. Inter-American Court of Human Rights, *Juridical Condition and the Rights of the Undocumented Migrants*, Advisory Opinion OC-18, 17 September 2003.

ited under international law. A 'traditional' reading of torture, defined in Article 1 of the Convention against Torture, implies that it takes place in the 'public' realm: it must be 'inflicted by or with the consent or acquiescence of a public official.' Although women are also victims of torture at the hands of state officials, given that they more often live and work in the 'private' sphere they are therefore at greater risk of human rights abuses within this 'sphere' of existence. This is a crucial difference in the way in which men and women have traditionally been protected against violence under international human rights law. When women suffer from abuse, it is much more likely to be perpetrated by an intimate partner or a family member than by a state/public actor. Thus since the Convention against Torture offers in the first place protection against state conduct, women clearly benefit less than men from the right to be free from torture.

A formulation and interpretation of the right to be free from torture that also takes into account the specific disadvantages and harms women are facing would, for example, include the right to be free from domestic violence, genital mutilation and sexual abuse by non-state actors. With regard to the protection of other human rights, such redefinitions to encompass the concerns of women would for example entail that the right to life includes the right of women and girls not to be killed in the name of 'honour' by their family members; that the right to be free from slavery and servitude includes the right to be protected against trafficking and forced prostitution; that equal protection under the law means that states investigate, prosecute and punish violence against women; that the right to just and favourable conditions of work also includes the right of women not to be sexually harassed in their workplaces; and that the right to adequate housing includes the right to live in a house free from violence.

The decision not to intervene in or regulate particular areas of 'private' life is also a political decision that serves to maintain unequal gender relations. Violence against women in the 'private' sphere has long been considered as a 'private', 'family' or 'cultural' matter, instead of as a social and structural problem, a human rights violation for which the state can be held responsible. Some states have even argued that addressing violence by non-state actors as a human rights violation would devalue the traditional notion of human rights:[9] the protection of the individual against the abuse of power by the state. This argument has been reinforced by the development of rights of privacy and protection of the family embodied in both national and international human rights laws.[10] While these rights are obviously very important, the fact that they have been frequently upheld at the expense of other rights has meant that in many parts of the world the protection

9 See Charlesworth and Chinkin (2000), note 1 above, 235-236, when discussing why the UN Declaration on the Elimination of Violence against Women, which, apart from a reference to human rights in the Preamble, does not explicitly present violence against women as a general human rights concern.

10 Amnesty International, *It's in Our Hands, Stop Violence against Women* (London: Amnesty International Publications, 2004), 67.

of human rights – in particular, the right of women to bodily security – has not been upheld in the personal, domestic sphere.[11]

On the other hand, the question of whether conduct by non-state actors in the private sphere may give rise to violations of international human rights law is not a new one and it is one that has largely been discussed outside of issues concerned exclusively or primarily with women. Slavery, for example, was recognised a long time ago as a human rights violation and it is mainly non-state actors who have traditionally engaged in this form of human trafficking. States are under a duty to protect non-state actors from one another under the 1965 Convention on the Elimination of Racial Discrimination.[12] The activities of influential non-state actors, such as multinational corporations, financial institutions, international organisations and illegal networks, are increasingly being scrutinised from a human rights perspective and have put the question of how to deal with the conduct of non-state actors high on the present-day human rights agenda. As Yakın Ertürk, the UN Special Rapporteur on violence against women, noted during the symposium on due diligence in Bern, state intervention in the form of defining a framework for marriage or having a say in how children are brought up and educated has long been accepted, while state intervention to protect women's rights is still viewed with great suspicion.[13] The fact that it is *women* who are the primary victims of violence perpetrated by non-state actors has played a major role in the historic refusal to view such violence as a human rights violation.[14]

Towards Addressing Violence against Women as a Human Rights Violation

Recent developments in women's human rights have resulted in a review of the way in which the ideological separation of the 'public' and 'private' spheres has been constructed. The dismantling of the public/private divide is one of the most important achievements of the movement to end violence against women, in terms of mindset and in paving the way in understanding violence against women as a human rights issue. A number of important developments in this area are highlighted in the following section, which demonstrates how the women's movement has been able to shift the accentuation of human rights law to issues

11 See Yakın Ertürk in this book. See also Rikki Holtmaat in this book for a discussion on the right of privacy of the home or of family life in relation to Article 5a of the Convention on the Elimination of All Forms of Discrimination against Women.

12 See article 2 of the Convention on the Elimination of Racial Discrimination, which states: 'd) Each State Party shall prohibit and bring to an end, by all appropriate means, including legislation as required by circumstances, racial discrimination by any persons, group or organization.' According to Article 4 of this Convention, certain racist groups or activities are to be penalised. And Article 6 requires the state parties to assure effective protection from racial discrimination and to assure the individual's right to seek damages if it nevertheless occurs.

13 Text available at http://www.izfg.unibe.ch/duediligence/e/index_e.htm.

14 Boerefijn (2006), see note 1 above, 8.

of concern to women including domestic violence, rape and other forms of sexual abuse, trafficking, certain unfair labour conditions, cultural practices and violence against women in armed conflict.

The adoption of the Convention on the Elimination of All Forms of Discrimination against Women (CEDAW Convention) on 18 December 1979 by the United Nations General Assembly signified an important step to advance women's human rights as such. It sets out a series of obligations for states to guarantee both *de facto* and *de jure* equality for women and identifies areas where the human rights of women were either not protected or not well developed in existing instruments, or not properly implemented.[15] The CEDAW Convention addresses the protection of women's human rights in the 'public' sphere as well as in the 'private' sphere, e.g., by explicitly affirming women's rights to equality within the family.[16] However, the CEDAW Convention does not include a provision explicitly dealing with violence against women. In order to compensate for this omission, the Committee on the Elimination of Discrimination against Women (CEDAW Committee) issued at its eleventh session in 1992 General Recommendation no. 19 on Violence against Women.[17] The Recommendation describes gender-based violence[18] as a form of discrimination against women, and in so doing emphasises the importance of the private sphere where women are most often subjected to oppression. Gender-based violence is understood as encompassing violence against women, violence against men in certain circumstances as well as violence against women and men on the basis of sexual orientation or gender identity.[19]

15 See in respect to the various obligations under the CEDAW Convention, e.g., Rebecca Cook, 'State Accountability Under the Convention on the Elimination of All Forms of Discrimination Against Women', in *Human Rights of Women. National and International Perspectives,* ed. Rebecca Cook, 228-256 (Philadelphia: University of Pennsylvania Press, 1994); Andrew Byrnes and Jane Connors, 'Enforcing the Human Rights of Women: A Complaints Procedure for the Women's Convention?', *21 Brooklyn Journal of International Law* 697 (1995-1996): 679-797.

16 Article 16 of the CEDAW Convention. Some general human rights instruments consider the family as a unit entitled to protection by society and state. See, e.g., Article 16 of the Universal Declaration of Human Rights and Article 23 of the International Covenant on Civil and Political Rights.

17 Committee on the Elimination of Discrimination against Women, General Recommendation no 19, Violence against Women, eleventh session, 1992, UN Doc. A/47/38. The Committee is mainly composed of women who are specialists in the field of women's human rights.

18 The distinction between the terms gender and sex is widely accepted. The term gender refers to the way in which the roles, attitudes, values and relationships regarding men and women are constructed without foundation in biological necessity. The term is contingent on a particular socio-economic, political and cultural context and is affected by other factors such as age, race, class, sexuality or ethnicity. Sex typically refers to biological differences between men and women.

19 See, e.g., the first UN Special Rapporteur on violence against women, Radhika Coomaraswamy, who observed that: 'Gender-based violence is also related to the social

General Recommendation no. 19 specifies the nature of governments' obligations to take comprehensive action to combat violence against women. It notes that it applies to violence by public authorities but underlines that governments are responsible for eliminating discrimination against women by any person, organisation or enterprise and that governments are required to prevent violations of rights by any actor, punish these acts and provide compensation.[20]

The relatively new individual complaints and inquiry procedures established under the Optional Protocol to the CEDAW Convention, in force since 2000, provide the CEDAW Committee with additional tools to further develop jurisprudence in the area of violence against women perpetrated by private individuals and to interpret the obligations of states in different socio-cultural contexts. In 2005, the CEDAW Committee decided a case under the Optional Protocol that concerned domestic violence and found that the state party had failed to fulfil its obligations under articles 2, 5, and 16 of the Convention.[21]

While the CEDAW Convention is an important and effective instrument to improve the position of women, its creation has also resulted in the marginalisation of women's rights within the 'mainstream' system for the promotion and protection of human rights. These general human rights institutions appeared for a long time to believe that it was unnecessary to apply human rights norms contained in human rights instruments to women's concerns due to the fact that there was a specific treaty dealing with women. The failure to address human rights from a woman's perspective by institutions including the different UN human rights treaty monitoring bodies and the special procedures of the UN Commission on Human Rights (now the Human Rights Council) increasingly attracted criticism from women's rights advocates. This neglect of women's human rights was powerfully articulated by groups at the World Conference on Human Rights, held in Vienna in 1993. Recognising that women's human rights form 'an inalienable, integral and indivisible part of the universal human rights',[22] the Vienna Declaration and Programme of Action stresses the importance of working towards the elimination of violence against women in all its forms in public and

construct of what it means to be either male or female. When a person deviates from what is considered "normal" behaviour they are targeted for violence. This is particularly acute when combined with discrimination on the basis of sexual orientation or gender identity,' in her statement to the 58th session of the UN Commission on Human Rights, 10 April 2002.

20 Para. 9.

21 Committee on the Elimination of Discrimination against Women, *Ms A.T. v Hungary*, Communication no. 2/2003, View adopted on 26 January 2005, para. 9.4.

22 UN Doc. A/CONF.157/23, Vienna Declaration and Programme of Action, Part I, para. 18.

private life[23] and calls on all of the UN organs to integrate a gender perspective into their work.[24]

The UN General Assembly adopted the UN Declaration on the Elimination of Violence against Women in December 1993. It sets out a mandate for addressing violence against women and defines violence against women in a broad manner as 'any act of gender-based violence that results in, or is likely to result in, physical, sexual or psychological harm or suffering to women, including threats of such acts, coercion or arbitrary deprivation of liberty, whether occurring in public or in private life'.[25] The cause of violence against women is analysed in the Declaration as '...a manifestation of historical unequal power relationships between men and women, which have led to the domination over and discrimination against women by men...'.[26] The Declaration highlights the different sites where violence against women takes place – violence in the family, violence in the community and violence perpetrated or condoned by the state – and further recognises the fact that particular groups of women are especially prone to be targeted for violence, including minority, indigenous and refugee women, destitute women, women in institutions or in detention, girls, women with disabilities, older women and women in situations of armed conflict.

With the encouragement of the World Conference on Human Rights, in 1994 the UN Commission on Human Rights appointed a Special Rapporteur on violence against women, its causes and consequences.[27] The appointment of a Special Rapporteur on violence against women under the special procedures of the UN Commission on Human Rights constitutes a recognition by the international community of the need to address violence against women within a human rights framework.

The Beijing Declaration and Platform for Action, adopted at the Fourth World Conference on Women in Beijing in 1995, reinforced the achievements brought about through the lobbying efforts of networks of women's groups around the world over the years by underscoring that violence against women is both a violation of women's rights and an impediment to the full enjoyment by women of all human rights. The focus shifted to calling for state responsibility to prevent and address violence against women. The Beijing Platform for Action identifies 12 critical areas of concern that require urgent action to achieve the goals of equality, development and peace; one of these areas is specifically about violence against women while several other critical areas of concern also recognise and address

23 UN Doc. A/CONF.157/23, Vienna Declaration and Programme of Action, Part II, para. 38.

24 Ibid., para. 37.

25 General Assembly Resolution 48/104, Article 1.

26 Ibid., Preamble.

27 The mandate of the Special Rapporteur on violence against women, its causes and consequences, was established by the Commission on Human Rights in 1994 (Resolution 1994/45) and was extended in 1997, 2000 and 2003 (Resolutions 1997/44, 2000/45 and 2003/45).

the problem.[28] At the five-year review of the Beijing Platform for Action, states stipulated that violence against women and girls, whether occurring in public or private life, is a human rights issue and highlighted state responsibility in addressing such violence.[29]

Regional human rights institutions have also adopted instruments aimed at the eradication of violence against women. Within the inter-American human rights system, the Inter-American Convention on the Prevention, Punishment and Eradication of Violence against Women was adopted in 1994. This instrument is the first multilateral treaty to explicitly address violence against women and details the obligations of states to guarantee that women are free from violence in both the public and private spheres.[30]

On 11 July 2003, the Protocol to the African Charter on Human and Peoples' Rights on the Rights of Women in Africa was adopted by the Assembly of the African Union at the second summit in Maputo Mozambique. This protocol requires states parties to take measures to suppress all forms of violence against women, identify the causes, punish the perpetrators and ensure effective rehabilitation and reparation for victims.

Other significant efforts have been applied to afford women better protection against violence. For example, the Rome Statute of the International Criminal Court establishes jurisdiction to try crimes of sexual violence, such as rape, sexual slavery, enforced prostitution, forced pregnancy and enforced sterilisation, as crimes against humanity and as war crimes.[31] The Statute categorises trafficking in persons as a form of enslavement and for the first time recognises the crime of sexual slavery. The Rome Statute also contains progressive provisions on women's participation in the International Criminal Court as judges, prosecutors and staff. The UN Security Council Resolution 1325 on women, peace and security, adopted in 2000, is another important achievement in addressing violence against women in times of armed conflict.[32] The Resolution calls on all parties to armed conflict 'to take special measures to protect women and girls from gender-based violence, particularly rape and other forms of sexual abuse' and 'emphasises the responsibility of all States to put an end to impunity and to prosecute those responsible for genocide, crimes against humanity and war crimes, including those relating to sexual and other violence against women and girls…'. The Resolution also stresses

28 Report of the Fourth World Conference on Women, Beijing, 4-15 September 1995 (UN Publication, sales no. E.96.IV.13).

29 See General Assembly Resolution S-23/3, annex, para. 13.

30 See the contribution of Elizabeth A.H. Abi-Mershed, 'Due Diligence and the Fight against Gender-Based Violence in the Inter-American System', in this book for a discussion on a number of cases relating to violations of the Convention of Belém do Pará have been decided by the Inter-American Commission on Human Rights.

31 Rome Statute of the International Criminal Court, A/CONF.183/9, adopted on 17 July 1998, entered into force on 1 July 2002.

32 UN Security Council Resolution 1325 on Women, Peace and Security, UN Doc. S/RES/1325 (2000), 31 October 2000.

the need to ensure the representation of women at all levels of decision-making in national, regional and international institutions that deal with conflicts.

The recognition of violence against women as a human rights violation has also had an impact on the interpretation of provisions under the various human rights treaties, going beyond violations by the state in the public sphere. While the extent to which this is the case remains variable, international human rights treaty monitoring bodies have increasingly become more gender-sensitive – a fact which can be observed in their concluding observations and recommendations in the state party reporting procedures, the individual complaints procedures and in their general comments/recommendations interpreting certain rights under the treaty they monitor. For example, the Human Rights Committee, Committee on Economic Social and Cultural Rights and the Committee on the Elimination of Racial Discrimination have adopted General Comments and General Recommendations on the equality of rights between men and women and gender-related dimensions.[33] The Committee on the Rights of the Child has dealt intensively with the question of violence against children, girls and boys, by non-state actors, e.g., within the family, and the role of the state in relation to such cases.[34] Also the Committee against Torture, which historically adopted a 'traditional' reading of torture, based on the public/private divide, has started to pay attention to violence against women by non-state actors in its examination of reports by states parties to the Convention against Torture. In 2001, for the first time, the Committee against Torture expressed its concern about trafficking in women and domestic violence in its concluding observations and recommendations.[35] Since then, this Committee has expressed concern in its concluding observations and recommendations about issues of violence emanating from non-state actors including complaints of threats and attacks against sexual minorities and transgender activists,[36] and has, for example, recommended to end exemption from

33 Human Rights Committee, General Comment no. 28, The Equality of Rights Between Men and Women (2000), UN Doc. CCPR/C/21/Rev.1/Add.10, 29 March 2000; Committee on the Elimination of Racial Discrimination, General Recommendation no. 25, Gender-related Dimensions of Racial Discrimination, 20 March 2000, contained in UN Doc. A/55/18, annex V; Committee on Economic Social and Cultural Rights, General Comment no. 16, The Equal Right of Men and Women to the Enjoyment of All Economic, Social and Cultural Rights, UN Doc. E/C.12/2005/4, 11 August 2005.

34 See, e.g., the General Comment no. 8 of the Committee on the Rights of the Child, The Right of the Child to Protection from Corporal Punishment and Other Cruel or Degrading Forms of Punishment, UN Doc. CRC/C/GC/8, 2 March 2007, adopted in 2006.

35 Committee against Torture, Concluding Observations of the Committee against Torture: Greece, 8 May 2001, UN Doc. A/56/44, paras. 83-88 and Concluding Observations of the Committee against Torture: Georgia, 7 May 2001, UN Doc. A/56/44, paras. 77-82.

36 Committee against Torture, Conclusions and Recommendations of the Committee against Torture: Venezuela, 21 November 2002, UN Doc. CAT/C/CR/29/2.

punishment of a rapist if he subsequently marries the victim and to enact legislation to ban female genital mutilation.[37]

State Responsibility to Prevent and Address Violence against Women and the Due Diligence Standard

It is now generally accepted that international human rights instruments impose several layers of obligation for states and these obligations may be typified as obligations to *respect, protect* and *fulfil* human rights.[38] States are obliged to respect human rights by refraining from violating human rights themselves through their state agents and apparatus. States have a further duty to protect human rights that requires them to take measures to prevent non-state actors from interfering with the human rights of individuals, as well as a duty to fulfil these rights, which requires states to adopt appropriate positive measures such as laws, policies and promotional measures in order improve the full realisation of human rights. As it is today well recognised that violence against women is a human rights violation under international law, states' obligations to respect, protect and fulfil human rights include the binding obligation to prevent, investigate and punish violence against women and to provide redress for such acts of violence, wherever they take place. This is true where the state or any of its agents perpetrates violence, but also when non-state actors in the private sphere perpetrate violence. If a state fails to comply with these obligations, it can be held accountable on the international plane.

The determination of state responsibility for human rights violations when the perpetrator of the abuse is a non-state actor differs from the manner in which responsibility is attributed when it is the state that directly violates the human rights of women.[39] A state is responsible under international law for its own con-

37 Committee against Torture, Conclusions and Recommendations of the Committee against Torture: Cameroon, 20 November 2003, UN Doc. CAT/C/CR/31/6.

38 The Special Rapporteur of the Sub-Commission on the right to adequate food as a human right initially developed this jargon, UN Doc. E/CN.4/Sub.2/1987/23, paras. 66-69, which was subsequently elaborated on by the Committee on Economic, Social and Cultural Rights in its General Comment no. 14, the Right to the Highest Attainable Standard of Health, UN Doc. E/CN.12/2000/4. 11 August 2000. See also General Recommendation no. 24 of the CEDAW Committee, Article 12, Women and Health (1999) which provides that the state's duty to respect, protect and fulfil rights in relation to health care and 'requires States Parties, their agents and officials to take action to prevent and impose sanctions for violations of rights by private persons and organisations', UN Doc. HRI/GEN/Rev.8, 329 paras. 13 and 15. See, e.g., for a further explanation of these obligations Judith Wyttenbach and Susana T. Fried in this book.

39 With regard to the principles respectively of responsibility due to attribution and responsibility based on the failure to protect with due diligence: see Jan Arno Hessbruegge, Human Rights Violations Arising from Conduct of Non-State Actors, *11 Buff. Hum. Rts. L. Rev* (2005): 21-88.

duct – through any of its organs or officials – when the conduct constitutes a breach of an international obligation of the state, since such acts or omissions are attributed to the state even if they exceed their authority or contravene instructions.[40] For example, the state is responsible for the rape of a woman in the power or custody of a state agent, an act which constitutes torture,[41] due to attribution. Also other sexual, physical or psychological violence against women by state actors, such as virginity testing, forced abortion or sexually degrading or humiliating language, constitutes torture or ill-treatment for which the state is responsible.[42] State responsibility arises not only from actions but also from omissions, including the failure to take positive measures such as law reform or law enforcement as well as the failure to take measures to protect or ensure human rights.[43] States are, for example, under a positive treaty obligation to protect against non-state interference under article 2 (e) of the CEDAW Convention which requires state parties 'to take all appropriate measures to eliminate discrimination against women by any person, organisation or enterprise.'

40 The International Law Commission of the United Nations has researched the principle of attribution at great length and has adopted a set of Articles on state responsibility. International Law Commission, *Responsibility of States for Internationally Wrongful Acts*, Text adopted by the Commission at its fifty-third session in 2001, Annexed to UN General Assembly Resolution 56/83 of 12 December 2001. Article 1 provides that every internationally wrongful act entails the responsibility of the state. Article 2 describes the elements of an international wrongful act of a state: '[t]here is an internationally wrongful act of a state when conduct consisting of an act or omission: (a) is attributable to the state under international law; and (b) constitutes a breach of an international obligation of the state.' See Articles 4-11 on the criteria for attributing conduct to a state.

41 Peter Kooijmans, the first Special Rapporteur on torture, stated in his oral introduction to the 1992 session of the Commission on Human Rights that '[s]ince it was clear that rape or other forms of sexual assault against women in detention were a particularly ignominious violation of the inherent dignity and the right to physical integrity of the human being, they accordingly constituted an act of torture', UN Doc. E/CN.4/1992/SR.21, para. 35, quoted in the Report of the Special Rapporteur on torture, Nigel S. Rodley, UN.Doc. E./CN.4/1995/34, 12 January 1995, para. 16.

42 The Special Rapporteur on torture has referred to acts of rape, sexual abuse and harassment, virginity testing, forced abortion or forced miscarriage as gender-specific forms of torture in his interim report to the General Assembly in 2000, UN Doc. A/55/290, para 5. Moreover, the Special Rapporteur on torture has pointed out that the fear of physical torture may constitute mental torture, in: *Report on his visit to Azerbaijan*, UN.Doc. E./CN.4/2001/66, Add.1, 14 November 2000, para. 115.

43 See, e.g., Danwood Mzikenge Chirwa, 'The Doctrine of State Responsibility as a Potential Means of Holding Private Actors Accountable for Human Rights', *Melbourne Law Journal*, vol. 5 (2004): 5. In determining the responsibilities of states for the harm of trafficking, see the contribution of Anne Gallagher in this book.

Although acts or omissions at the hands of non-state actors are generally not attributable to the state,[44] under human rights law state responsibility may arise, not because of a particular action or omission itself, but because the state has failed to take reasonable and adequate measures to prevent or address the violation. In order to determine whether a state has undertaken the necessary measures, the concept of due diligence has been introduced into human rights law in order to legally establish the state's responsibility for acts of violence by non-state actors. The standard of due diligence constitutes an obligation for the state to take all appropriate measures which, taking into account the circumstances, ought reasonably to be taken in order to prevent, investigate, punish and redress a human rights violation. As such it is a way to measure whether a state has fulfilled or failed to implement international human rights obligations in a particular situation.

Due diligence is not a new concept and has its roots in other areas of law. But it is only over the last decades that it has been applied in the human rights context.[45] Since women experience much of the violence against them at the hands of non-state actors, it is not surprising that the standard of due diligence has special value in the area of women's human rights and this importance is reflected in women-specific instruments relating to violence. The standard is among others developed in the context of the CEDAW Convention in General Recommendation no 19 on Violence against Women, which notes that '[u]nder general international and specific human rights covenants, States may also be responsible for private acts if they fail to act with due diligence to prevent violations of rights or to investigate and punish acts of violence, and for providing compensation.'[46] The Declaration on the Elimination of Violence against Women calls in Article 4(c) on states to '[e]xercise due diligence to prevent, investigate and, in accordance with national legislation, punish acts of violence against women, whether those acts are perpetrated by the State or private persons.' This provision was reiterated in paragraph 125 (b) of the Beijing Platform for Action. At the regional level, article 7 (b) of the Inter-American Convention on the Prevention, Punishment and Eradication of Violence against Women requires that states 'apply due diligence to prevent, investigate and impose penalties for violence against women.' The UN

44 The International Law Commission has pointed out that '[a]s a general rule the conduct of private persons or entities is not attributable to the state under international law.' International Law Commission, *Draft Articles on State Responsibility for Internationally Wrongful Acts with Commentaries,* Yearbook of the International Law Commission, 2001, vol. 2, Part Two, Commentary to Article 8, 103.

45 For a comprehensive overview on the history and development of the due diligence standard in international human rights law in general and in the Inter-American System, see the chapters by respectively Joanna Bourke-Martignoni and Elizabeth A. H. Abi-Mershed in this book.

46 Committee on the Elimination of Discrimination against Women, General Recommendation no 19, Violence against Women, eleventh session, 1992, UN Doc. A/47/38, para. 9.

Special Rapporteur on violence against women devoted a whole report to the subject in 2006.[47]

A question which arises is whether the due diligence standard should also play a role in determining state responsibility when the harm is caused by the state's own activities and those of their agents. Ineke Boerefijn asserts that the use of the due diligence standard should be reserved for the assessment of the responsibility of the state for acts by non-state actors.[48] The violations of concrete international obligations to act or to refrain from acting by a state, such as an act of torture or inhuman or degrading treatment by a state official or the passing or maintenance of discriminatory laws,[49] result in international responsibility and accountability. An assessment to establish whether a state has exercised due diligence in complying with these obligations in order to determine state responsibility would not be strict enough and should therefore not be attempted.[50] The application of the due dilligence standard would in such cases waken the human rights of women instead of strengthening them.

In the context of the application of the CEDAW Convention in respect of the acts of private persons, Andrew Byrnes and Jane Connors have observed that the recognition that many of the violations of women's rights occur at the hands of individuals should not distract attention from violations by the state: states violate the human rights of women directly and, by maintaining discriminatory laws and practices, also violate these rights by discrimination.[51] The so-called 'honour' defence, for example, is accepted in different parts of the world as an exonerating or mitigating circumstance embodied in law. Perpetrators of crimes against women committed in the name of 'honour' go unpunished, receive reduced sentences or are exempted from prosecution because of the justification of 'honour'. A crime committed in the name of 'honour' by a non-state actor is a human rights violation for which the state can be held responsible under international law

47 Report of the Special Rapporteur on violence against women, UN Doc. E/CN.4/2006/61, 20 January 2006.

48 Boerefijn (2006), see note 1 above, 16, 19-23.

49 The Committee on Economic, Social and Cultural Rights stated in its General Comment no. 16, The Equal Right of Men and Women to the Enjoyment of All Economic, Social and Cultural Rights, that '[t]he obligation to respect requires States parties to refrain from discriminatory actions that directly or indirectly result in the denial of the equal right of men and women to their enjoyment of economic, social and cultural rights. Respecting the right obliges States parties not to adopt, and to repeal laws and rescind, policies, administrative measures and programmes that do not conform with the right protected by article 3.' UN Doc. E/C.12/2005/4, 11 August 2005, para. 18.

50 Boerefijn (2006), see note 1 above, 16, 19-23.

51 Byrnes and Connors (1995-1996), see note 15 above, 734, referring to Dorothy Q. Thomas, 'Acting Unnaturally: In Defense of the Civil and Political Rights of Women', in *From Basic Needs to Basic Rights: Women's Claims to the Human Rights 41*, ed. Margaret A. Schuler (Washington, DC: Women, Law & Development International, 1995).

when it has failed to exercise due diligence to take adequate preventive, punitive or remedial measures. At the same time, the state is also directly involved in the harm. The maintenance of discriminatory laws is an explicit violation of Article 2 (g) of the CEDAW Convention that requires states parties to repeal all national penal provisions that constitute discrimination against women. The obligation is phrased as a concrete obligation of immediate effect.[52] Non-compliance by a state party leads directly to international state responsibility and should not require further justification through arguments grounded upon the due diligence standard. This book will focus on states' obligation to act with due diligence in cases of violence against women by non-state actors.

Aims and Structure

While the due diligence standard as a mechanism for promoting greater state accountability for failures to prevent and respond to violence against women by non-state actors is now widely accepted, there remains a lack of clarity with regard to both the content and scope of due diligence obligations. International human rights law provides that a state is obliged to prevent, investigate, punish and provide redress with due diligence for acts of violence against women. But what are the actions that need to be taken by a state in order to fulfil its due diligence obligations? What are the criteria that should be used to determine whether a state has met or failed to meet these obligations to prevent and respond to violence against women? Should a minimum due diligence standard be established, or can it only be determined and applied on a case-by-case basis? What are the limits on the state's obligations to protect one individual from another, as the protection for the benefit of the former may reduce the freedom to act of the latter? What factors determine whether a state has to intervene in order to protect non-state actors from non-state conduct? This book intends to offer constructive analysis of the due diligence standard, to clarify its scope, and where possible and reasonable provide some practical suggestions concerning the steps that a state must take in order to give real effect to due diligence obligations.

The contributors to this book explore the history and development of the due diligence standard in human rights law and the ways in which the standard has been and can be applied in the protection of women against violence by non-state actors – individuals and groups acting outside the state including intimate partners and other family members, acquaintances and strangers, neighbourhood and community institutions, religious groups, criminal organisations and business and other private sector institutions. They address how and to what extent violence against women by non-state actors may result in state responsibility by looking at international and regional human rights law, jurisprudence and other developments and efforts in the international, regional and national arenas. As the jurisdiction of international and regional human rights bodies is restricted to complaints against states, an extensive body of jurisprudence has been de-

52 Byrnes and Connors (1995-1996), see note 15 above, 724.

veloped in relation to due diligence or similar standards concerning the positive obligations of states to protect non-state actors from human rights abuses by other non-state actors.[53] While it is true that human rights jurisprudence has not developed a set of detailed principles for the determination of when the duty of due diligence to implement rights has been met, it does illustrate, for example, which human rights can give rise to obligations to protect human rights from infringement by non-state actors. Although it is now widely accepted that states have such obligations, certain human rights are not – in the words of the Human Rights Committee – 'amenable to application between private persons or entities'.[54] Jurisprudence from international and regional human rights bodies shows that many rights do seem to give rise to obligations to protect individuals from harm by other private persons. Jurisprudence also illustrates how these rights are applied in the context of a human rights violation by non-state actors; how the countervailing human rights, individual human rights or collective human rights, of non-state actors against whom the state should provide protection are taken into consideration; and, once the obligation to protect is established, when the responsibility of the state is engaged in the context of concrete facts.

The contributors also consider the effectiveness of the due diligence standard to combat violence against women against the backdrop of contemporary problems that pose threats to women's rights. They discuss the current international developments with which the due diligence standard is confronted, such as the public/private divide, identity politics, gender stereotypes, armed conflicts and aspects of globalisation. They address questions such as: Is a state that functions according to patriarchal principles in any position to protect women from violence? Should the due diligence standard be directly applicable to quasi-formal legal structures or should the responsibility in the case of discriminatory decision-making by these alternative justice mechanisms rest with the state? Is a state whose ability to protect women is weakening due to a power shift from national governments to other actors in the non-state sphere, including international organisations, multinational corporations and armed opposition groups, in any position to protect women effectively from the conduct of these powerful actors?

The due diligence standard as an answer to protect women from violence by non-state actors is in itself also challenged by the contributors. While the stand-

53 See Andrew Clapham, *Human Rights Obligations of Non-State Actors* (Oxford: University Press, 2006), 347-348.

54 The Human Rights Committee in General Comment 31 on Article 2 of the International Covenant on Civil and Political Rights, setting out the nature of the general legal obligation imposed on states parties to the Covenant, stated: '[t]he positive obligations on States Parties to ensure Covenants rights will only be fully discharged if individuals are protected by the State, not just against violations of Covenant rights by its agents, but also against acts committed by private persons or entities that would impair the enjoyment of Covenants rights *in so far as they are amenable to application between private persons or entities* [emphasis added]', Human Rights Committee, General Comment 31, Nature of the General Obligation Imposed on States Parties to the Covenant, CCPR/C/21/Rev. 1/Add 13, 26 May 2004, para. 8.

ard has on the one hand helped to dissolve the public/private divide, contributors also consider the question of whether the distinct methods used in the examination and establishment of international responsibility with regard to conduct by state actors and non-state actors has on the other hand entrenched this division. They examine whether working with two separate regimes of responsibility for 'private' as opposed to 'public' acts has an effect on accountability for protection of human rights. They discuss the traditional approaches to human rights, under which states are considered to be the primary subjects of international law and therefore the sole bearers of human rights obligations, while non-state actors are not regarded as being directly bound by international human rights law. They analyse some of the various initiatives taken in the past few years that aim at entrenching the direct responsibility of non-state actors under international human rights law, breaking down the public/private divide, and ensuring accountability for violations of women's human rights.[55]

The book discusses the questions raised by the due diligence standard from an inter-disciplinary perspective and aims to assume a broad, holistic approach. Its central theme is on the problem of violence against women as a human rights concern and its focus is on international law and human rights law. As such it includes discussions of housing, education, health, criminal justice, humanitarian and security issues in order to propose measures for the prevention of violence and the protection of women.

The book is divided into two sections. The first section provides essentially theoretical explanations of the due diligence standard under international and regional human rights law. The chapters in this section discuss the different standards, problems and outlook of the relatively new concept for the enforcement of the human rights of women as well as other strategies to eliminate violence against women in light of the various current human rights issues affecting women.

The second section is largely based upon discussions that took place during the working groups at the international symposium in Bern and proposes practical tools for engaging the due diligence standard in different contexts. The chapters focus on how the due diligence concept is or should be used in relation to some of the most common forms of violence against women around the world, namely domestic violence, trafficking in women, violence against women legitimised by arguments of culture and violence in armed conflict. The contributors explain how the recognition of violence against women as a human rights issue has impacted criminal justice systems at the national level with the recognition of 'new' crimes such as domestic violence and trafficking under their criminal laws. They lay out how they use the due diligence concept in their work to combat violence against women, how they use the international legal frameworks that have been developed to combat these forms of violence, and the problems relating to their

55 See, e.g., the contributions of Ineke Boerefijn and Eva Naezer and of Helen O'Connell in this book. On human rights obligations of non-state actors in general see Clapham (2006), note 53 above.

implementation in reality as well as obstacles faced in applying the due diligence standard.

Section I

Due Diligence: Standards, Problems and Outlook

In light of the evolving international agenda on violence against women on the one hand and the prevailing obstacles and challenges in combating such violence on the other, **Yakın Ertürk** explores the potentials of the due diligence standard for expanding the obligation to eliminate violence against women. She emphasises that the major potential for expanding the due diligence framework lies in the obligations of prevention and compensation – while effectively realising the existing practices to protect and punish – and in the inclusion of relevant non-state actors as duty-bearers in relation to violence against women. Yakın Ertürk considers how the due diligence obligation should be implemented so that it responds more effectively to the specificities of violence against women at different levels, namely (i) the level of the individual woman; (ii) the community/societal level; (iii) the state level; and (iv) the transnational level.

Joanna Bourke-Martignoni explains the historical development of the due diligence standard in international law and the way it has been evoked within the international system for the promotion and protection of human rights, and in particular in relation to violence against women. She examines how the standard has advanced our understanding of state responsibility for violence against women perpetrated by non-state actors by discussing human rights standards and jurisprudence and provides clarification of what is expected of states in order to fulfil the due diligence obligation. Joanna Bourke-Martignoni also provides a critical assessment of the due diligence standard. She discusses the question of whether it is worthwhile to insist upon generalised obligations of due diligence in light of the fact that it appears almost impossible to define the parameters of these obligations. She examines the added value of the due diligence standard in relation to the pre-existing positive obligations under international human rights law. And she considers the advantages of holding non-state actors directly responsible for failures to fulfil their human rights obligations under international law instead of through the 'back door' of state responsibility.

Rikki Holtmaat examines the obligations that can be derived from Article 5 (a) of the CEDAW Convention for its state parties. The Article provides that the state parties to this Convention 'shall take all appropriate measures' to modify the social and cultural patterns of conduct of men and women, with a view to achieving 'the elimination of prejudices and customary and all other practices which are based on the idea of the inferiority or the superiority of either of the sexes or on stereotyped roles for men and women.' It is argued throughout the chapters of the current book that in order to prevent violence against women, states parties are required to effectively address the underlying causes of violence against women resting in the social and cultural structures of patriarchy. Rikki Holtmaat looks at the place and role of Article 5 (a) of the CEDAW Convention as well as its meaning and scope. She examines the obligations under Article 5 (a) in relation to the elimination of violence against women and ends her chapter considering whether the due diligence standard is an appropriate tool where general prevention of violence against women by means of combating gender stereotypes is concerned.

Ineke Boerefijn and **Eva Naezer** look at the various initiatives that have been taken in the past decades which aim at formulating human rights obligations for non-state actors under international law. They examine how the conduct of non-state actors can give rise to violations of international human rights law as it presently stands as well as to what extent direct obligations for non-state actors under international human rights law are emerging, i.e., for transnational corporations and other business enterprises as well as for international organisations such as the World Bank and the International Monetary Fund (IMF), all of whose activities can have a major impact on the enjoyment of human rights by women. They give special attention to issues relating to the monitoring of the implementation of emerging norms, as this is of particular relevance for giving effect to the accountability of non-state actors.

Helen O'Connell argues that economic actors, such as multinational companies and financial institutions, need to play their part in the promotion and protection of human rights and have their own due diligence obligations. She provides an overview of the position of women in the global economy and the often harmful impacts of globalisation for women. She discusses the implications of the shift in power from the state to the non-state realm on the accountability for human rights protection and the principle of due diligence. Helen O'Connell also traces the development of international codes and standards on corporate social responsibility. She further considers the role played by civil society in research, campaigning and advocacy and describes how action in the political sphere and a greater engagement of advocates for women's rights are critical to building accountable governance and gender justice.

Elizabeth A.H. Abi-Mershed examines what due diligence means in the context of efforts within the inter-American human rights system to prevent and respond to gender-based violence. She discusses the roots of the due diligence standard in the inter-American system, beginning with the *Velásquez Rodríguez* case decided by the Inter-American Court of Human Rights in 1988, which serves as a key reference on the concept of due diligence in human rights law, followed by the codification of the standard in the Convention of Belém do Pará, and its application in individual cases, and thematic and country reports. Elizabeth Abi-Mershed also looks at what the concept signifies in the context of different types of investigations into human rights violations and how it can contribute to the advancement of the right of women to be free from violence in practice.

Lisa Pusey discusses the application of the due diligence principle in the Asia Pacific region. She describes the context in which violence against women occurs in the Asia Pacific region and examines some of the factors that have a determinative impact on the form, the circumstances and the consequences of violence against women as well as the availability of and accessibility of reparation and redress to women subjected to manifestations of violence including: neo-liberalism, militarism and fundamentalism. She discusses the impact of multiple systems of oppression on the rights of women and what that means for states' compliance with their international obligations. She further provides insight into a number of obstacles which have a particularly negative effect on the fulfilment of the requirements of the due diligence standard in the elimination of violence against women by the states in the region: the impact of dual justice systems; the reconstruction of minority cultural identity by the dominant group; the numerous conflict situations in the region; the lack of responsibility for certain non-state actors; and the vulnerable position of migrant, trafficked, internally displaced women and refugees.

Section II

Due Diligence in Context

Domestic Violence

Dee Smythe examines the extent to which South Africa has responded to domestic violence in accordance with due diligence. She starts by describing the incredibly bleak reality of violence against women in South Africa. She further describes how the country has, on the other hand, made some substantial efforts, in particular in the area of legislative measures, during the past decade in order to meet international standards in addressing violence against women with due diligence. Dee Smythe then clarifies the many challenges which remain. She notes for example that positive duties are restricted to the criminal justice agencies and that no obligations are placed on the health sector, while this is one of the state agencies with which victims of domestic violence are most likely to come into contact. It is also the area most competent to respond to the interrelation between domestic violence and HIV/Aids, of which many women die every year. With regards to resources, she remarks that when we impose standards which are subject to 'available resources' we are positing in fact that different standards of protection apply to women from developed and developing countries and poses the question of whether a global commitment to ending domestic violence with due diligence should not mean a commitment of targeted donor intervention into resource-constrained countries.

Lisa Gormley explains that Amnesty International's work on domestic violence is very similar to much of its long-term work on human rights violations perpetrated by state agents, e.g., securing justice for victims of torture, extrajudicial executions and 'disappearances': campaigning for the establishment of fair and effective laws and procedures for ensuring prompt, efficient, independent and impartial investigations and prosecuting alleged perpetrators. Amnesty International's research and campaigning experience on women's rights not to suffer gender-based violence received new impetus with the launch of its global campaign 'Stop Violence against Women', which began in March 2004. Lisa Gormley clarifies that a significant part of Amnesty International's work on women's rights relates to state obligations of due diligence to prevent, investigate, punish and provide reparations for acts of violence by non-state actors. She discusses the benefits and limitations of the use of the due diligence approach in the combat of domestic violence.

Based on a report of the Spanish Section of Amnesty International 'Spain: More Rights, but the Obstacles Remain', **María Naredo Molero** analyses how Spain's response to gender-based violence has changed since the 'Basic Law in Comprehensive Protection Measures to Tackle Gender-Based Violence' came into force in 2005. In addition to the implementation of Spain's due diligence obligations at the legislative level, she examines whether women's rights have become reality in Spain.

Trafficking in Women

Anne Gallagher provides a legal analysis of the issue of state responsibility and accountability in relation to human trafficking. She researches human rights law as well as the recent developments under international law outside the human rights framework and provides a summary of the legal 'wrong' of trafficking: the primary rules that provide the basis for identifying core obligations of states in trafficking situations, enshrined in and protected by international law. She further examines the responsibility of states for the harm of trafficking in the typical trafficking situation where not the state itself but private actors are the direct agents of the harm by analysing the relevant international legal principles and rules relating to international state responsibility. In the final part of her contribution, Anne Gallagher provides a set of core obligations for states, a 'state accountability index' in relation to human trafficking, which can be used to identify and attach responsibility for acts and omissions to the state.

Shivaun Scanlan describes the different measures to address trafficking that have been taken in countries of origin in South Eastern Europe and the Commonwealth of Independent States (CIS). She summarises the standards of due diligence obligations in trafficking in the different international and regional instruments before turning to the specific situation of transformation and the related root causes of trafficking in the countries of origin with which the Organisation for Security and Co-operation in Europe is concerned. Shivaun Scanlan further examines the effectiveness of measures taken in these countries in the areas of preventative measures, investigation and punishment, and assistance and protection. In conclusion she notes that while progress has been made on paper with regard to due diligence measures in trafficking, real developments are often hindered by competing political agendas such as combating organised crime, controlling immigration or eliminating prostitution.

Nivedita Prasad and **Babette Rohner** portray the sombre situation of women who have been trafficked to Germany. The legislative framework in Germany effectively prevents trafficked women from attempting to escape from conditions of forced labour and/or akin to slavery as they are, due to their illegal situation, at risk of being compelled to leave the country. The authors compare the situation in Germany with the one in Italy, where trafficked people have in their opinion the best legal conditions in Europe. Under Italian legislation, residence permits for trafficked people are kept as separate as possible from their potential status as witnesses in a court case brought against their perpetrators. However, Nivedita Prasad and Babette Rohner observe that in the destination countries of the European Union in general, the debate on trafficking is focused on the migration process rather than on the responsibility to prevent and address human rights violations related to trafficking with due diligence, a situation which needs to be reversed.

Violence against Women Legitimised with Arguments of Culture

Judith Wyttenbach provides an overview of areas of conflict between women's rights, cultural traditions and state interventions and examines the question of whether freedom of religion and minority rights, protected by international and regional human rights treaties, can challenge the universality of women's rights. She examines in particular the question of whether considerations of freedom of religion or cultural minority rights can legitimise violence against women. Judith Wyttenbach lists numerous legal obligations that a state has to implement in order to fulfil its due diligence obligations in combating violence against women legitimised with arguments of culture. She also discusses the achievements and the various challenges for the future at both the state and international levels in preventing and addressing religiously/culturally motivated violence.

Farida Shaheed examines violence against women legitimised by arguments of culture from a Pakistani perspective. She departs from the principle that regardless of the nature of its manifestation or where or when it occurs, violence against women is always legitimised by arguments of culture because no society is devoid of culture. The dominant culture throughout the world is patriarchal and the patriarchal culture inevitably accepts violence as an attribute of masculinity. She considers some of the problems Pakistan is facing today, such as confronting both the 'traditional patriarchal culture' that denies women's rights and the 'new patriarchal culture' that makes political use of religion and identity politics. She further discusses what the concept of due diligence requires in the Pakistani context, for example with respect to women's representation within minorities or subaltern cultures and informal dispute resolution forums challenging women's rights. Farida Shaheed also poses some important questions such as: Which voice should acquire legitimacy as *the* voice of 'the people', when multiple cultures compete to be heard within a society? Is the concept and desire for women's self-determination merely a western construct?

Susana T. Fried describes the serious situation of countless women around the world who are, because of their actual and/or perceived sexual orientation and gender expression, subjected to crimes of violence in both the public and private sphere. She emphasises that to a large extent, the use of violence to control women's (and men's) sexuality is justified as securing social, economic and cultural norms. Susana Fried describes the complicity of states in such violence, either by turning a blind eye to violence against women that takes place in the context of family and community or by maintaining laws and policies that are based on dominant culture(s) to legitimise gender-based violence. She argues that accountability using the due diligence standard is important to make clear that states are responsible under international law to address and prevent gender-based violence perpetrated in the name of culture with the aim of controlling women's sexuality. She examines various measures states are required to take in order to fulfil their due diligence obligations in ending human rights abuses related to gender and sexuality.

Violence in Armed Conflict

Ambassador **Theodor Winkler** discusses the due diligence standard during armed conflicts. He emphasises that the violence against women in conflict situations is part of a *continuum of violence* experienced by women in times of relative peace, through conflict into post-conflict situations. During armed conflict, the state's capacity to exercise due diligence is weak due to eroding or collapsing security structures. In such situations, violence against women is perpetrated by militias opposing or supporting, or tolerated by, the state security services within a climate of impunity. Theodor Winkler argues that the weakness of the state in exercising due diligence to protect women from violence calls for a range of responses from international actors at different stages of the conflict/post-conflict cycle. The responses should focus on substituting for the state or on enabling the state to protect women by building a democratic and participatory security sector. Theodor Winkler underlines that the due diligence standard is not only important for measuring the behaviour of a state in protecting the people under its jurisdiction but also as a measure for the performance of international actors.

Section I

Due Dilligence: Standards, Problems and Outlook

The Due Diligence Standard: What Does It Entail for Women's Rights?

*Yakın Ertürk**

Introduction

The Declaration on the Elimination of Violence against Women (DEVAW) adopted by the United Nations (UN) General Assembly (GA) in 1993 urges states in Article 4 (c) to 'exercise due diligence[1] to prevent, investigate and, in accordance with national legislation, punish acts of violence against women, whether those acts are perpetrated by the state or by private persons'. Accordingly, the concept of due diligence provides a framework for action while at the same time it is a criteria by which to determine whether a state has met or failed to meet its obligations to combat violence against women. However, what it actually means for a state to act with diligence needs to be further explored and operationalised.

Focusing on violence has been a viable entry point to advance women's human rights as it has made particular manifestations of violence visible while at the same time, by linking diverse experiences of different women's groups, it facilitated the augmentation of a transnational movement.[2] However, there has been

* This article is derived from a report I have submitted to the Commission on Human Rights in my capacity as the Special Rapporteur on violence against women (Report of the Special Rapporteur on violence against women, its causes and consequences, *The Due Diligence Standard as a Tool for the Elimination of Violence against Women*, UN Doc. E/CN.4/2006/61, 20 January 2006). I would like to acknowledge and thank Ms Joanna Bourke-Martignoni for her assistance in the preparation of that report.

1 *Merriam-Webster Dictionary of Law* defines due diligence as 'such diligence as a reasonable person under the same circumstances would use' (Merriam-Webster Inc., 1996).

2 This does not represent a commonly held view. Critics of the universal human rights discourse argue that the international women's rights movement by focusing on violence against women has reinforced the victim subject image of women. See Ratna Kapur, 'The Tragedy of Victimization Rhetoric: Resurrecting the "Native" Subject in International/Post-Colonial Feminist Legal Politics', *Harvard Human Rights Journal* 15 (Spring 2002): 1–37.

C. Benninger-Budel ed., Due Diligence and Its Application to Protect Women from Violence

ISBN 978 90 04 16293 8. pp. 27-46

a general tendency in human rights work to treat violence against women largely within a welfare/humanitarian paradigm. As a result, the application of the due diligence standard has tended to be limited to responding to violence when it occurs, i.e., protecting the victims and punishing the perpetrators. There has been relatively less work done on the more general obligation of preventing violence from occurring, including by supporting women's empowerment and engaging in transformative change at the community and societal levels to eradicate patriarchal norms and values that underlie violence and the subordination of women.

The UN mandate for the elimination of violence against women entails tackling the root causes of the problem at all levels, from the home to the transnational arena. Such a call is also inherent in the prevention obligation of the due diligence standard. Therefore, perceived within such a framework, the 'violence against women agenda' intrinsically challenges the taken-for-granted aspects of everyday life and necessitates a shift of focus from the victimisation-oriented approach to one of empowerment. The former sees women as weak, vulnerable and in need of protection; whereas in the latter approach, women are seen to be subjected to violence not because they are vulnerable, but because of a gender order that privileges male violence through the normative and institutional formations of societies. This gender order has historically been resisted and reacted to through women's individual and collective agency and in the process, traditional patriarchy has slowly but systematically been ruptured at a different pace in different parts of the world. Applying a human rights perspective to violence has created a momentum for breaking the silence around violence and for connecting the diverse struggles across the globe. Today a life free of violence is increasingly accepted as an entitlement rather than merely a humanitarian concern.[3]

Identifying women as rights bearers naturally brings with it a corresponding focus on the duty bearer(s) with respect to combating violence, which is defined in international human rights law to be the state. Due to the exclusively state-centric nature of the due diligence obligation, the challenges posed by power dynamics – emanating from competing claims for representation of the individual or from competing regimes in global restructuring – for state compliance with its human rights obligations as well as the new questions they raise about the accountability of non-state actors have not been sufficiently addressed.

The multiplicity of forms of violence against women frequently occurring at the intersection of different systems of discrimination and hegemony warrants a multifaceted strategy to effectively respond to the problem. This article explores the potentials of the due diligence standard for expanding the obligation to combat violence against women in view of the specificities of violation of women's rights and the prevailing challenges. In so doing, the aim is to push the bound-

3 An entitlement can go astray if taken in a vacuum. The Universal Declaration of Human Rights provides a comprehensive framework of rights where negative and positive rights complement one another. Similarly, the Beijing Platform for Action, a holistic understanding of women's empowerment, encompasses a broad range of entitlements and means for their attainment.

aries of the due diligence standard to strongly endorse: (a) the obligation of a state to engage in the root causes of violence against women to prevent violence against women while effectively responding to it when it occurs; and (b) the role of non-state actors as duty bearers with respect to violence and other violations of women's human rights.

Violence against Women as a Human Rights Violation

Evolving International Agenda on Violence against Women

Within the UN gender agenda,[4] the issue of violence against women was a latecomer. During the drafting of the Convention on the Elimination of All Forms of Discrimination against Women (CEDAW Convention) it was not possible to include violence among its provisions, although reference to specific types of violence, mainly in the framework of crime prevention, did exist in various UN documents.[5] The shortcomings of international human rights law with respect to the experiences and needs of women have been widely discussed by feminists.[6] Critiques have drawn attention to the fragmented and individualistic language of the mainstream understanding of rights as well as its male[7] and western[8] model of the 'human'. The international human rights discourse has remained particularly blind to structural inequalities and the complex and intersecting power relations in the public and private life that lie at the heart of diverse manifestations of discrimination on the ground of sex.

Since the 1980s, women's rights activists have worked with the existing human rights framework to expand the vision of rights to respond to the specificities of violations inherent in women's experiences. In this respect, the success of the women's movement in building on the due diligence standard to hold a state accountable for acts of violence against women, whether perpetrated by the state

4 Yakın Ertürk, 'The UN Agenda for Women's Rights and Gender Equality', *Perceptions: Journal of International Affairs* 10, no. 2 (2005): 91–113; Devaki Jain, *Women, Development, and the UN* (Bloomington: Indiana University Press, 2005); Margaret Snyder, 'Unlikely Godmother: The UN and the Global Women's Movement', in *Global Feminism*, ed. Myra Marx Ferree and Aili Mari Tripp, 24–50 (New York: New York University Press, 2006).

5 Jane Connors, 'United Nations Approaches to Crimes of Honour', in *'Honour': Crimes, Paradigms, and Violence against Women*, ed. Lynn Welchman and Sara Hossain, 22–41 (London: Zed Books, 2005).

6 Rebecca Cook ed., *Human Rights of Women: National and International Perspectives* (Philadelphia: University of Pennsylvania Press, 1994); Kelly D. Askin and Dorean M. Koenig ed., *Women and International Human Rights Law* (New York: Transnational Publishers, 1999); Julie Peters and Andrea Wolper ed., *Women's Human Rights, Human Rights: International Feminist Perspectives* (New York: Routledge, 1995).

7 Charlotte Bunch, 'Transforming Human Rights from a Feminist Perspective', in Peters and Wolper (1995), ibid., 11–17.

8 Kapur (2002), see note 2 above.

itself or by private actors, was intrinsically transformative, thus paving the way for many achievements at national, regional and international levels.

In 1992, the Committee on the Elimination of Discrimination against Women (CEDAW Committee) adopted its General Recommendation no. 19 on Violence against Women in which it specified that:

> 'Under general international law and specific human rights covenants, states may also be responsible for private acts if they fail to act with due diligence to prevent violations of rights or to investigate and punish acts of violence, and for providing compensation.'[9]

In 1993, the World Conference on Human Rights in Vienna officially recognised violence against women as a human rights violation and that same year the GA adopted DEVAW. The following year, in 1994, the post of Special Rapporteur on violence against women, its causes and consequences (SRVAW) was created under the Commission on Human Rights (CHR) to monitor the global situation.[10] In 1995, at the Fourth World Conference on Women in Beijing, the international community adopted the Platform for Action containing 12 critical areas of concern, one of which was violence against women.

These are milestone developments in the UN agenda for equality between women and men representing a turning point in the acknowledgment of violence against women, once a private matter, as a public human rights concern. The Platform for Action, by also including women and armed conflict and the human rights of women among its critical areas of concern, placed a priority on the need to respond to these issues for the advancement of women. The Beijing+5 special session of the GA identified further forms of sexual assault on women and culturally legitimated violent practices that were not specifically mentioned in the Platform. It also demonstrated that violence against women had become a priority issue on the agenda of many member states and significant, although insufficient, steps have been taken to address the problem.[11]

The very engagement with the violence against women agenda has not only transformed the human rights discourse but also reflects a shift from a culture of impunity to a culture of accountability in international criminal law. The recognition of crimes specifically targeting women helped build on and broaden the universal jurisdiction evolving since the 1949 Geneva Conventions. The Rome Statute of the International Criminal Court (ICC)[12] includes rape, sexual slavery, enforced prostitution and forced pregnancy in the definition of crimes against

9 Committee on the Elimination of Discrimination against Women, General Recommendation no. 19, Violence against Women (eleventh session, 1992), UN Doc. A/47/38, para. 9.

10 See www.ohchr.org for a description of the mandate with respect to violence against women and the reports of the Special Rapporteur.

11 United Nations, *From Beijing to Beijing+5* (New York: United Nations, 2001).

12 Rome Statute of the International Criminal Court, UN Doc. A/CONF/183/9.

humanity and war crimes. These developments revealed the emergence of a new social contract which acknowledges that the obligation of justice and rights for women goes beyond national and cultural boundaries. They also clearly demonstrated that violence is not an isolated incident targeting vulnerable women but a systematically used tool of patriarchal control to ensure that 'women stay in their place'.

However, the complex negotiation process during Beijing+5 as well as the great difficulty encountered while adopting the Beijing+10 Declaration,[13] which merely reiterated prevailing commitments, were no doubt indications of the fragmentations in identity politics and the emerging new political polarisations and alliances among states and non-state power blocks.[14] It also reflected the backlash that had been building up in response to the gender agenda in many parts of the world. Concern over these trends is further heightened with the growing threats to reproductive and sexual rights and the post-9/11 security environment.[15] These incidents show that consensus among member states on critical issues concerning women's human rights are becoming increasingly difficult at the multilateral level. Nonetheless, while it is important to acknowledge and monitor these threatening trends, there are ample reasons to believe that the women's human rights agenda is moving forward and in the process challenging, modifying and rupturing the foundation of traditional patriarchy.[16]

Hence, transformative impact of recognising violence against women as a human rights issue has particularly been significant in three respects: (i) transformation of conventional understandings of human rights beyond violations perpetuated mainly by state actors in the public sphere; (ii) transformation of the doctrine of state responsibility to include the actions of private individuals, thus, together with the former point, demystifying the public/private dichotomy; and

---

13 It is also important to recall the failure of the UN Commission on the Status of Women in 2003, for the first time in its history, to reach a consensus on the negotiated text on violence against women. Similarly, the same year, the UN General Assembly had to abandon the omnibus resolution on violence against women and substitute it with a narrower one on domestic violence.

14 Yakın Ertürk, 'Identity Politics: Implications for Gender Analysis, Policy and Training', *INSTRAW News*, no. 27 (second semester 1997): 9–15. Samuel Huntington articulated these polarisations in his infamous thesis of the 'clash of civilizations'. Samuel Huntington, 'The Clash of Civilizations', *Foreign Affairs* 72, no. 3 (1993).

15 Since 11 September 2001, national security responses to global terror have become a major threat to the realisation of international human rights norms and this process is highly gendered. See Jan Jindy Pettman, 'Feminist International Relations after 9/11', *Brown Journal of World Affairs* 10, no. 2 (Winter/Spring 2004): 85–96.

16 In the year 2000 the Security Council addressed the issue of women, peace and security and adopted Resolution 1325. The same year, the Optional Protocol of CEDAW entered into force. The UN General Assembly adopted Resolution 57/179 on Working Towards the Elimination of Crimes against Women Committed in the Name of Honour. Moreover, the UN Commission on Human Rights has continued to renew the violence against women mandate.

(iii) transformation of the criminal justice systems with the recognition of new species of crimes, such as domestic violence, marital rape, etc.

As a result, today there are numerous international and regional mechanisms in place to guide efforts to combat violence against women. Moreover, there is the tendency towards a paradigm shift that recognises that violence against women is neither about the vulnerability of women nor simply acts by deviant men or a characteristic of primitive cultures. Instead, the problem is understood to be rooted in a universal patriarchal culture entrenched in our consciousness as women and men, and in the core values and institutions of societies, albeit in diverse forms. This common legacy underlies the diverse ways in which women experience the violations of their rights. Accordingly, the commonalities in the particular manifestations of violence against women as well as the global connectedness of the diverse trajectories of women's local resistances has set in motion the making of an universalising culture for women's rights from within.[17]

Obstacles and Challenges in Combating Violence

The quest for justice and equality between women and men continues to confront diverse challenges. Three main areas are especially pertinent: (a) the public/private dichotomy and the exclusion of the latter from the realm of politics and law; (b) the resurgence of local power blocks appropriating the realm of identity politics and the right to determine the symbols of representation, thus challenging state authority from below; and (c) the emergence of transnational power blocks with the right to command global governance, thus challenging state authority from above.

The public/private dichotomy

One of the main obstacles to the protection of women's rights has been attributed to the role of the public/private dichotomy in international human rights law, which is conventionally premised on the liberal, minimalist conception of the state. This reflected the hierarchical relations experienced by men in the 'public' sphere and left the hierarchical associations in the 'private' sphere off-limits to state intervention. The 'privacy' of the home, therefore, provided the ground for the abuse of rights and use of violence with impunity. 'Such a division of spheres, by ignoring the political character of power unequally distributed in family life, does not recognise the political nature of the so-called private life. Such a division

17 Gender inequality is one of the few common elements of human history cutting across all civilisations. However, particularly with transition to a capitalist mode of production and the struggles of women, deviations from the norm towards greater equality between the sexes has been possible in varying degrees and scopes across the globe. This has required and continues to require major transformations in the culture of many institutions. See Martin Chanock, 'Culture and Human Rights: Orientalising, Occidentalising and Authenticity', in *Beyond Rights Talk and Culture Talk*, ed. Mahmood Mamdani, 15–36 (New York: St. Martin's Press, 2000).

of spheres clouds the fact that the domestic arena is itself created by the political realm, where the state reserves the right to choose intervention.'[18]

The public/private codification in international law has served as an ideological barrier to the development of the human rights discourse in many societies, as the monitoring of human rights 'legitimately' ends at one's doorstep. Yet, as well demonstrated by Althusser, the ideological apparatuses of the state penetrate the most intimate spheres of life. In this regard, the principle of non-intervention is itself an ideological stand. State intervention in private life has perhaps been most manifest and durable in the heteronormal model of matrimony as the basis of the family institution. The regulations of work, taxation, compulsory education, etc. are other ways by which the state has penetrated and shaped private life. What is left for non-intervention is often the domain of male supremacy, which entails limited authority to primarily discipline the members of the household. Therefore, it can be argued that the separation of spheres, far from providing a realm of privacy, has served for the selective penetration of public state hegemony while allowing some autonomous space for the hegemony of the male head of the household.[19] The construction of consent in the private sphere through the privileging of male authority is in fact a means for the liberal state to establish its own hegemony.

The emergence of the 'violence against women agenda' has exposed these inconsistencies in the public/private divide and applying the due diligence standard to women's rights has helped to invalidate the liberal state theory, thereby bringing violations of rights in the private sphere under scrutiny. This has meant that a state, by failing to respond to domestic violence, can be held accountable for not fulfilling its obligation to protect and punish in a non-discriminatory way and can be charged as an accomplice to private violations.[20]

18 Celina Romany, 'State Responsibility Goes Private: A Feminist Critique of the Public/Private Distinction in International Human Rights Law', in Cook (1994), see note 6 above, 85–115. An-Na'im, while agreeing with the need for the state to be proactive in protecting women against abuse by non-state actors, cautions against repudiating the distinction between public/private spheres. According to him, state intervention in private life carries the risk to abuse power to violate rather than protect human rights. Abdullahi A. An-Na'im, 'The Role of "Community Discourse" in Combating "Crimes of Honour": Preliminary Assessment and Prospects', in Welchman and Hossain (2005), see note 5 above, 64–77. It is precisely for this reason that there is merit in exploring the state's due diligence obligation to ensure human rights for all. Human rights standards can enable the state to use its apparatuses to protect citizens against the tyranny of informal intermediary power. Where such political will is lacking the state machinery may become a tool of tyranny itself.

19 Such autonomous space, although privileging male hegemony, is inherently contradictory as it allows for alternative masculine prerogative, thus providing grounds for multiple forms of dissent and resistance as well as solidarity and collaboration within a household.

20 Romany (1994), see note 18 above; Christine Chinkin, 'A Critique of the Public/Private Dimensions', *European Journal of Int'l Law* 10, no. 2 (1999): 387–395.

While demystifying the public/private dichotomy has indeed been a major breakthrough, it can be argued that the individual perpetrator of an act of private violence is still not directly responsible under international human rights law and that separate regimes of responsibility for private and public acts are sustained.[21] Furthermore, despite the many achievements that have been recorded, issues of public violence tends to be met with a more immediate and effective response at both the international and national levels, whereas identity politics entrenched in a cultural relativist discourse dominates the discussions of private violence, thus contesting the universality of human rights standards.

Identity politics

At the local level, identity politics is increasingly shaped by the resurgence of power blocks contesting public state discourse for the legitimate right of representation of individuals. While such claims may be perceived as manifestations of pluralism and multiculturalism and, therefore, as consistent with social and cultural rights, in practice they are a potential obstacle to the universal human rights guarantees of women who are perceived as bearers of their culture.[22] In some instances such claims have been asserted through the confiscation of public power, as in the case of the Taliban in Afghanistan, where public space became cleansed of women in the name of restoring cultural and religious 'authenticity' or protection of women from Western 'corruption'.[23] The private sphere was also totally transgressed as alternative male prerogative over private life became confiscated.[24]

In many parts of the world, right to culture claims provide a reference point for the judicial system to excuse acts of violence against women and girls, thus sustaining parallel normative systems. These parallel systems of justice may sanc-

21 Mahmood Mamdani ed., *Beyond Rights Talk and Culture Talk* (New York: St. Martin's Press, 2000).

22 The Ontario Arbitration Act (1991) in Canada allows parties to resolve civil matters between individuals outside the mainstream legal system. The proposal in 2004 by Muslim leaders in Toronto to form arbitration tribunals that would apply Shari'a law to civil disputes including family law matters was met with concern by women's rights organisations. Muslim women's groups in Canada firmly opposed the proposal. The review of the arbitration process submitted by a government-appointed expert in December 2004 concluded that faith-based family law arbitration does not, in itself, constitute an obstacle to the rights of women. The National Association of Women and the Law responded that the report gives preferentiality to religious freedom, demonstrating a clear refusal to assume responsibilities for the protection of marginalised persons within minority groups, women in particular. See Natasha Bakht, 'Arbitration, Religion and Family Law: Private Justice on the Backs of Women', March 2005 at www.nawl.ca/Documents/Arbitration-Final-0305.doc.

23 Yakın Ertürk, 'Considering the Role of Men in Gender Agenda Setting: Conceptual and Policy Issues', *Feminist Review*, no. 78 (2004): 3–22.

24 Mission Report to Afghanistan of the Special Rapporteur on violence against women, UN Doc. E/CN.4/2006/61/Add.5, 15 February 2006.

tion acts of violence by deeming them acceptable forms of 'traditional' practice or by handing down severe punishments (such as honour killings) for women who allegedly transgress societal norms. The shift of political struggles to the realm of culture has reinforced and further legitimised informal community mechanisms of justice. When such mechanisms are acknowledged or tolerated by state authority, the state is in fact an accomplice to the acts of violence that occur within such a context.

Control over women's sexuality and their reproductive capacity is often at the heart of misogynist interpretations of culture that place the burden of upholding honour, dignity, etc. on the bodies of women. Paradoxically, while male reputation, in many instances, is dependent on their ability to guard the sexuality of women with whom they are affiliated, the violation of other women's sexuality by means such as rape is also a manifestation of the way in which masculine power establishes domination over women. Violence or the threat of violence is a basic tenet of patriarchal gender order where cultures converge in enforcing and sustaining control over women.[25]

Reconciling the duality of culture versus human rights poses a twofold challenge: celebrating and respecting cultural diversity while developing strategies to resist oppressive practices; and promoting universal human rights standards while rejecting orientalist and imperialist biases.[26]

Global restructuring

In the past two decades economic activity and governance has been radically restructured on a global scale. Globalisation has reconfigured the territoriality and sovereignty associated with the Westphalian state. As already established above, the state is no longer the only site of normativity. Aside from actors operating below the state, there are those above the state that are gaining power over many aspects of life. Actors such as multinational corporations, financial institutions, intergovernmental organisations and international non-governmental organisations (NGOs) are emerging as autonomous spheres of influence. Although these developments may open new space for greater liberties, the responsibility of the

25 The forces associated with religious fundamentalist and conservative political trends in the global order, which pose a threat to the efforts to eradicate violence against women, operate at all levels, ranging from the local to the transnational, and may have access to state power. For example, the refusal in recent years by certain bilateral donors to accord grants to organisations advocating for women's reproductive rights or working with women engaged in the sex sector illustrate the convergence of private and state interests targeting women's rights. Human Rights Watch, 'U.S. Restrictive Policies Undermine Anti-AIDS Efforts: Amicus Curiae Brief Highlights Negative Impact on Public Health Interventions by Anti-prostitution Pledge', 9 November 2005, at http://hrw.org/english/docs/2005/11/09/usdom12006.htm.

26 For further elaboration on the culture-based discourses and women's human rights see my report to the Human Rights Council on *Intersection between Culture and Violence against Women*, UN Doc. A/HRC/4/34.

new power blocks vis-à-vis human rights standards have not been subject to sufficient scrutiny.

Today, the transnational arena constitutes a new 'geography',[27] with contradictory implications for the implementation of women's human rights. Women in massive numbers have become suppliers of low-wage and flexible labour for the globalised labour markets through immigration and off-shore production; they find themselves in work environments with little or no monitoring of labour or other standards.[28] The empirical evidence regarding the risk of violence for women involved in deterritorialised space as migrant workers or as members of transnational households is mixed. While this process may give women direct access to international human rights law and potentially empowers them, opposing trends have also been observed. Some local and 'traditional' forms of violence against women have become globalised while others, such as trafficking, have become increasingly ubiquitous.

The response of the international community to transnational issues is still essentially bound by the 'sovereign state' understanding. The approach to human trafficking and the protection of the rights of migrant workers are particularly illustrative of the failure to develop transnational solutions. The Protocol to Prevent, Suppress and Punish Trafficking in Persons, especially Women and Children, supplementing the UN Convention against Transnational Organised Crime (the Palermo Protocol), takes a law-and-order approach to the issue of trafficking rather than being based in human rights. The impact of transnationalism on women, including restrictive immigration and asylum policies, needs to be further examined in terms of types of violence encountered and the multiplicity of normative systems and actors involved within the continuum of space between countries of origin and destination.[29]

Within this context, it is particularly important to reflect on the compatibility of the new transnational legal regimes and regulatory institutions with human rights standards as well as on the implications for the accountability of the various actors, including states. There is growing pressure for responsibility for the protection of human rights to be extended beyond states to include multinational

27 Saskia Sassen, *Globalization and Its Discontents: Essays on the Mobility of People and Money* (New York: The New Press, 1998).

28 Rhacel Salazar Parrenas, *Servants of Globalization* (Palo Alto, CA: Stanford University Press, 2001).

29 It is striking that the International Convention on the Protection of the Rights of All Migrant Workers and Members of Their Families (1990) has not been ratified by any immigrant-receiving state. As a result, the majority of women migrant workers or those accompanying a migrant worker are not covered by its provisions. On the other hand, national legislation in these countries is systematically being reformulated in view of border control and national security concerns rather than rights of immigrants, refugees or trafficking victims.

corporations and, indeed, other actors within the emerging system of global governance such as international economic institutions.[30]

The Potential of the Due Diligence Standard

The due diligence standard has a long history in international law. More recent application of the standard was taken up in 1988 with the *Velásquez Rodríguez v Honduras* case concerning the disappearance of Manfredo Velásquez, which by way of abstraction, provided a basis for the development of general guidelines on its requirements.[31] Human rights bodies such as CEDAW Committee, the Committee on the Elimination of Racial Discrimination (CERD), the Human Rights Committee (HRC) and the various special procedures of the Commission and regional human rights institutions have also elaborated on the requirements of the due diligence standard in relation to specific country situations as well as on a more general level.

Current Applications of the Standard

As mentioned above, the general trend in the way states have dealt with their due diligence obligation with respect to violence against women has been guided by a victim subject perception; therefore, they have responded to violence when it occurred rather than taking preventive action. As a result, there are more measures undertaken within the due diligence obligation to protect and prosecute.

The protective measures consist mainly of provision of services to women such as telephone hotlines, healthcare, counselling centres, legal assistance, shelters, restraining orders and financial aid to victims of violence. However, the implementation of these measures has been inconsistent and in many cases ineffective in their consequence. For example, in September 2005 a district court judge in the United States agreed to lift a protective order that had been placed against a woman's separated husband following an application by the husband for the order to be rescinded. At the hearing in which the order was lifted, the woman involved expressed her fears and indicated that she wanted to file for divorce. Despite her request that the protective order be maintained, the judge dismissed the order. A few weeks later the husband doused her with gasoline and set her on fire, causing grievous injuries to much of her upper body and face.[32] Protection measures are also frequently based on short-term emergency assistance rather than on sustainable solutions to avoid revictimisation. The lack of adequate en-

30 Susan Marks and Andrew Clapham, *International Human Rights Lexicon* (Oxford: Oxford University Press, 2005), 188.

31 Inter-American Court of Human Rights, *Velásquez Rodríguez v Honduras*, Judgment of 29 July 1988, Series C: Decisions and Judgments, no. 04. For a discussion of how the due diligence standard evolved see Romany (1994), note 18 above; and Joanna Bourke-Martignoni in this book.

32 'Deadly Justice', *Washington Post*, 15 October 2005.

forcement by police and the judiciary of civil remedies and criminal sanctions for violence against women and an absence or inadequate provision of services such as shelters are major gaps observed in the current compliance with the obligation to protect. As a result, women often have no choice but to continue living with their abusers.

With respect to their due diligence obligation to investigate and appropriately punish acts of violence against women, states have adopted or modified legislation, particularly in their criminal codes, in order to modify or repeal discriminatory provisions and to ensure that violent acts are criminalised and appropriately punished. Some states have also adopted specific legislation on domestic violence and trafficking, establishing new criminal offences and often providing for the creation of specialised investigatory or prosecutorial units.

There are, nevertheless, numerous examples of states failing in their duty to appropriately investigate and punish acts of violence against women. Women often report being discouraged from filing a complaint because they are intimidated by the authorities. In many instances when a complaint is filed, law enforcement authorities and social services privilege mediation or 'social solutions' over the application of sanctions under criminal or civil law. Available information reveals that many cases get dismissed at the prosecutorial level for lack of sufficient evidence. Even when cases do reach the courts, there are still alarming numbers of instances of judges handing down reduced or inappropriate sentences for these crimes. For example, the criminal code in many countries provides for a suspended sentence in cases of rape if the victim agrees to marry the perpetrator. Many jurisdictions fail to provide women with equal protection, particularly in cases involving sexual assault and domestic violence. As a result women either remain silent or, if they do report the crime, they may become revictimised.

Pushing the Boundaries of the Due Diligence Obligation

The current understanding and application of the due diligence standard as well as the gaps and challenges identified above highlight the need to redefine the standard so that it responds more effectively to the specificities of violence against women. The major potential for expanding the due diligence framework lies in the full implementation of generalised obligations of prevention and compensation – while effectively realising the existing practices to protect and punish – and in the inclusion of relevant non-state actors as duty bearers in relation to combating violence against women.

While international human rights law provides the guiding principles for state action, innovative strategies need to be employed using alternative discourses such as empowerment and 'cultural negotiation' at different levels of intervention in order to challenge the foundations upon which gender hierarchies are constructed and violence and other forms of discrimination against women are justified and sustained. Cost efficiency models have also been developed to demonstrate the cost of violence against women on human resources and the economy at large.[33] Therefore, in exercising due diligence to effectively implement human rights law with regard to violence against women, states and other relevant actors must use multiple approaches in intervening at different levels, including the individual, the community, the state and the transnational arena. It is important to emphasise that these interventions must be designed on the basis of empirical evidence. Therefore, developing indicators and generating systematic and reliable data is an integral part of the due diligence obligation.

(i) The level of individual women

The basic principle inspiring the Beijing Platform for Action is that the realisation of human rights and fundamental freedoms of all women requires their empowerment (para. 9). This is a prerequisite for achieving political, social, economic, cultural and environmental security among all peoples (para. 43). With this in view, the Platform for Action calls on states and other actors to take strategic action in 12 critical areas of concern.

States, in their efforts to combat violence against women, must promote and support women's empowerment as highlighted in the Platform for Action and engrained in the International Covenant on Civil and Political Rights, the International Covenant on Economic, Social and Cultural Rights and the CEDAW. This approach must embrace the progressive realisation of the full range of rights – economic, social, cultural, civil and political. Fulfilment of these rights requires political will and an equitable allocation of limited resources, ensuring that women's access to critical resources are not sacrificed to other priorities.

Empowerment discourse – through interventions ranging from education, skills training, legal literacy and access to productive resources, among others – aims to enhance women's self-awareness, self-esteem, self-confidence and self-reliance. This enables women to: understand that subordination and violence are not a fate; to resist internalising oppression; to develop their capabilities as autonomous beings; and to be able to constantly negotiate the terms of their personal existence in public and private spheres as well as basic tenets of the overall gender order in their societies.

The involvement and provision of legal and financial support to relevant, rights-based civil society organisations in creating the necessary environment to enable individual women to realise their full range of human rights is a crucial element in the empowerment approach. In this context, development interventions, whether supported by the state, multilateral or bilateral donors, must avoid modalities and conditionalities that would disempower women.[34]

33 Report of the UN Secretary-General, *In-Depth Study on All Forms of Violence against Women*, UN Doc. A/61/122/Add.1, 6 July 2006.

34 Interventions at the individual level may also entail programmes to 'rehabilitate' violent men. Such programmes need to be designed strategically bearing in mind that: (i) violence against women is not an attribute of individual men but rather related to the patriarchal construction of masculinity that privileges male violence; (ii) efforts to deal with violent men must not lead to a deviation from the commitment to

Parallel to this, the due diligence obligation of protection at the level of the individual requires states to ensure that women and girls who are victims or at risk of violence have access to justice as well as to healthcare, legal assistance and support services that respond to their immediate needs, protect against further harm and address the ongoing consequences of violence for them. To this end, states are required to develop appropriate legislative frameworks, policing systems and judicial procedures to provide adequate protection for all women, including a safe and conducive environment for women to report acts of violence against them and measures such as restraining or expulsion orders and victim protection procedures. In situations where in particular women and girls are at known risk of violence, law enforcement agencies have an obligation to set up effective and appropriate protective mechanisms with utmost confidentiality to prevent stigmatisation and harm from occurring.

Measures aimed at providing immediate material assistance (shelter, clothing, child maintenance, employment, education) to women who are survivors of violence must be established. Bearing in mind that stigmatisation may be associated with a woman who ends up in a shelter, the state should consider alternative protective measures while at the same time ensuring a safe refuge for women who have no other option. Experience shows that shelters are better operated by NGOs that take a women's rights approach, but their creation, maintenance and provision of safety (for victims as well as for personnel) are part of the state's obligation.

The obligation to provide adequate reparations to women who have encountered violence or to their families involves ensuring the rights of access to both criminal and civil remedies as well as the establishment of effective protection and support services for survivors of violence. Compensation for acts of violence against women may involve the award of financial damages for any physical and psychological injuries suffered, for loss of employment and educational opportunities, for loss of social benefits, for harm to reputation and dignity as well as any legal, medical or social costs incurred as a consequence of the violence. States are also required to ensure that women survivors of violence have access to appropriate rehabilitation and support services. The notion of reparation may also include an element of restorative justice.

(ii) At the community/society level

At the community and society level, the human rights discourse needs to be complemented by an approach based on 'cultural negotiation'.[35] Such an approach complements the empowerment approach discussed above, in that it confronts

---

support women's empowerment and the diversion of resources from women's programmes.

35 Cultural negotiation is a natural part of societal life, where individuals or groups use formal and informal strategies to resist and change the status quo to their benefit. What is suggested here is creating a public discourse through systematic and focused programmes aimed at demystifying and transforming gender-biased values and

the root causes of violence at the societal level and raises awareness of the oppressive nature of certain practices pursued in the name of culture, tradition or religion. This requires: (a) drawing on positive elements within culture to demystify the oppressive elements of culture-based discourses; (b) recognising and supporting local women's struggles to counter patriarchy as well as the human rights movements in the society; (c) demonstrating through the recognition of alternative cultural stands that culture is not a homogenous and immutable entity; and (d) identifying and contesting the legitimacy of those who monopolise the right to speak on behalf of culture and religion.

The notion of 'cultural negotiation' is inspired by Paulo Frerie's[36] concept of critical consciousness and it starts by challenging hegemonic interpretations of culture rather than privileging them as the legitimate representation of culture, thereby giving them and their underlying power dynamics official recognition. The process of cultural negotiation through public campaigns, dissemination of gender-sensitive information and media reporting can create an important counter-discourse for the transformation of discriminatory values, institutions and power structures. In fulfilling its due diligence obligation, the state must engage with and support social movements that challenge the discourses that promote norms and practices that perpetuate discrimination by making them seem part of the national, natural or divinely ordained order of things.[37]

Article 4 (j) of the DEVAW calls on states to take measures to modify the social and cultural patterns of conduct of men and women to eliminate all practices based on the idea of inferiority or superiority of either of the sexes. In this regard, it is particularly important to support awareness-raising campaigns and curricula that challenge sex stereotypes and uncouple masculinity from oppressive uses of power.[38] Gender-sensitive language and a rights-based discourse in public statements, media reporting, and educational material, among others, can demystify the taken for granted 'truths' about gender constructs and break taboos and the silence around violence. Research and data on violence against women and their dissemination in ways that reach all segments of society can empower the state in its cultural negotiation efforts.

A state's failure to exercise due diligence to confront all claims for custom, tradition or religion as justifications for violations of the human rights of women is itself a human rights violation even in the absence of harm. Article 4 of DEVAW urges that '[s]tates should condemn violence against women and should not invoke any custom, tradition or religious consideration to avoid their obligations with respect to its elimination.' It should be borne in mind that it is not culture, per se, that dictates a woman to be beaten, mutilated or killed, but rather those

practices in order that family, group and community cooperation in compliance with human rights standards are ensured.

36 Paulo Frerie, *Education for Critical Consciousness* (New York: A Continuum Book, 1973).

37 Marks and Clapham (2005), see note 30 above, 415.

38 Ertürk (2004), see note 23 above.

who monopolise the right to speak on behalf of culture and interpret it in a misogynistic manner. The assertions of incompatibility between respect for culture and respect for women's rights are a facade, promoted to sustain the patriarchal status quo and/or to serve specific interests at a given historical moment.[39]

(iii) At the state level

State legitimacy today is increasingly determined according to the state's human rights record, which inherently implies that international human rights standards and the rule of law should inform all state policy and practice. The ratification without reservation of all relevant human rights instruments, including the CEDAW Convention and its Optional Protocol, is an essential first step. The incorporation of international law into the domestic legal, judicial and administrative order at every level and the adoption of measures for its implementation are important prerequisites for a state's capacity to meet its due diligence obligations. The different layers of the state apparatuses need to be addressed separately to ensure that the rights of women are protected, respected and fulfilled by all agents of the state at all levels of governance.

Each of the different powers of the state has a role to play in ensuring gender justice. For example, the judiciary and prosecutors working on cases of domestic violence have the potential and the obligation to change the prevailing balance of power by taking a strong stance to disempower patriarchal norms. Interventions at this level may have both *consequential* effects, in that condemnations of patriarchy can lead to changes in socio-cultural norms, as well as *intrinsic* effects, in that prosecutors or judges can be considered as the opinion leaders of society, and consistent statements condemning violence against women made through the judiciary or prosecutorial services will make that society less patriarchal.[40] While the above-cited case on the grave violence that took place after the lifting of a protection order clearly has the effect of empowering patriarchy, the 2004 decision of the First Aggravated Felony Court in Şanlıurfa, Turkey that gave a life sentence to the perpetrator and 16 years imprisonment for each of the eight in-

39 The Italian Penal Code (The Rocco Code of 1931), repealed in 1981, is illustrative. Article 587 of the Rocco Code distinguished killing or injuring for the cause of honour as a separate crime and provided for reduced sentence in cases of adultery. Analysts have explained the existence of Article 587 by the strict gender discriminatory norms to support the demographic policies of the fascist period, which promoted women's reproductive roles and high fertility rates. 'Article 587 effectively gave a "licence to kill" to the heads of families whose "honour" had allegedly been tarnished.' Maria Gabriella Bettiga-Boukerbout, 'Crimes of Honour in the Italian Penal Code', in *'Honour': Crimes, Paradigms, and Violence against Women*, ed. Lynn Welchman and Sara Hossain, 235 (London: Zed Books, 2005).

40 Michelle M. Dempsey, 'What Counts as Domestic Violence? A Conceptual Analysis', *William and Mary Journal of Women and the Law* 12, no. 2 (2006).

stigators of an honour-related murder demonstrates that judicial authorities, by adopting a gender-sensitive approach, can play a disempowering role.[41]

Public statements made by government leaders have a similar impact. Since 2004, the government of Australia has conducted a campaign entitled 'Violence against women: Australia says no' and members of the government, including the prime minister, have stated publicly that violence against women is unacceptable and 'tarnishes any community that tolerates it'.[42] Conversely, a comment made by a government leader in another country that rape is a 'money-making concern' and an easy way to get asylum is illustrative of a failure by the highest state authority to act with due diligence in challenging oppressive patriarchal norms.

The state has an obligation to send an unequivocal message that violence against women is a serious criminal act that will be investigated, prosecuted and punished. In this regard, the police and judiciary need to be given appropriate training in dealing with cases of violence against women in a gender-sensitive manner. Depending on the circumstances, counselling and rehabilitation programmes for perpetrators of violence, preferably at their own cost, may need to supplement criminal procedures. The re-victimisation of women who have reported violence must be avoided and procedural rules regarding the rule of evidence as well as protection for victims and witnesses must ensure that women are not subjected to further harm.

Focusing on violence against women provides states with a critical entry point for achieving good governance and the effective implementation of their human rights obligations. Gender analysis, gender-sensitive research, sex-disaggregated data and gender budgeting are useful tools to ensure that efforts don't go astray.

(iv) At the transnational level

At the transnational level there is a need to rethink the boundaries of 'geography' as well as duty bearers in relation to the promotion, protection and fulfilment of human rights standards. Given the deterritorial nature of movements and activities, the need to develop transnational solutions to transnational problems such as the regulation of migration and trafficking of women and the role of transnational corporations and international organisations has become urgent. Entities with power need to be held accountable for failures to adhere to international

41 The Criminal Code in force at the time allowed for a reduced sentence on the grounds of grave provocation for murder of women who allegedly transgressed acceptable cultural norms. This law perceived sexual assaults as crimes against the public morale or the family rather than an assault on the bodily integrity of women. Chief Judge Akartuna, who presided over the above-mentioned case, told me later that the public debates and the claims of women's groups during the Criminal Code reform process had a significant effect on his assessment of the case. The debates also resulted in a paradigm shift in the law by placing the rights of the individual at the center of law-making. As such, this represents a good example of the effectiveness of cultural negotiation.

42 See www.australiasaysno.gov.au.

standards and, in some cases, new regimes for monitoring these responsibilities will have to be established.

In relation to migrants, refugees and victims of trafficking,[43] states and international organisations will need to cooperate in order to develop sustainable solutions firmly grounded in international human rights law. This will require rethinking the existing restrictions on legal migration opportunities for women workers as well as ensuring that all workers receive adequate legal protection under national and international labour legislations regardless of their legal status. The current gender biases in national migration laws, whereby the immigration status of a woman is contingent on her being a 'dependent' spouse, also needs to be addressed.[44]

Global restructuring has increased the power of transnational corporations. The fact that this power comes with certain responsibilities, particularly in observing human rights standards, is still not central to discussions on due diligence obligations. While the gender aspect is not emphasised, there are a number of limited initiatives addressing corporate responsibility. These include the Global Compact launched by the UN Secretary-General in 2000, the OECD (Organisation for Economic Co-operation and Development) Guidelines for Multinational Enterprises and the Draft Norms on the Responsibilities of Transnational Corporations and other Business Enterprises with Regard to Human Rights approved by the UN Sub-Commission on the Promotion and Protection of Human Rights at its 55th session in 2003. In addition, large corporations are adopting codes of conduct to respect human rights standards. While more needs to be done to hold corporations accountable for acts of violations of human rights, states must apply the rule of law diligently upon corporations operating within their territory, particularly in the poorly monitored sectors predominantly employing women.

International financial organisations also have obligations of due diligence in relation to preventing and responding to violence and other forms of discrimination against women. The adverse impact of macro-economic policies promoted by such organisations is well documented.[45] In recent years the World Bank responded to such concerns by identifying violence against women as an 'inequality trap' to consider in its development framework. In this regard, while the World Bank undertakes country gender assessments, it does so at the request of the

43 The full implementation of human rights guarantees in the area of human trafficking along the lines suggested in the Office of the High Commissioner for Human Rights (OHCHR) *Recommended Principles and Guidelines on Human Rights and Human Trafficking*, UN ECOSOC, UN Doc. E/2002/68 Add.1, is an essential process for ensuring that women's human rights remain at the centre of anti-trafficking policies and programmes.

44 For a discussion of the related problems within specific national contexts see my mission reports to Sweden (UN Doc. A/HRC/4/34/Add. 3) and the Netherlands (UN Doc. A/HRC/4/34/Add. 4).

45 United Nations, *World Survey on the Role of Women in Development: Globalization, Gender and Work* (New York: United Nations, 1999).

host government. In countries where women's rights are not a priority there is little likelihood that such a request will be made. Therefore, gender assessments should be an integral component of the Bank's programmes so that the results can guide the design and monitoring of all phases.

Similarly, the UN system is obligated to respect and uphold the principles of the organisation. While international organisations clearly have direct obligations not to commit or contribute to acts of violence against women through their programming or funding decisions, they also have additional duties to co-operate and to establish coherent inter-agency strategies to work towards the elimination of violence against women in close collaboration with local communities and relevant civil society groups. The responsibilities of these organisations are in addition to the individual responsibilities of the states that are members of such organisations.[46]

Last but not least, where states and/or intergovernmental bodies are deploying military, peace-keeping or civilian policing operations abroad, they must also act with due diligence to ensure that these personnel do not commit acts of violence against women. For this purpose, the sending authority must adopt the necessary legislation and procedures to prevent and respond to such acts, as receiving states may lack the capacity to do so.

Conclusion

Violence against women is a universal phenomenon with diverse and multiple local manifestations. It is intimately embedded in the history of patriarchal gender relations which is common to all known civilisations and cultures. The normative framework that has allowed domination over and discrimination against women in all parts of the world has been a site of contestation and resistance by women individually and collectively. A focus on violence against women provided a viable entry point for the women's movement to challenge and transform international human rights discourse to be inclusive of women's experiences and the application of the due diligence standard to combat violence offered a possibility to expand the boundaries of state obligation as well as to move beyond the state in holding non-state actors accountable for their acts.

However, state response to the emerging obligation to end violence has tended to be fragmented and treated in isolation from the wider concern for women's rights, empowerment and equality. As a result, until recently the violence against women agenda was dominated by a narrow welfare/humanitarian approach, perceiving women as vulnerable victims

A welfare/humanitarian approach to the problem inherently results in stigmatising women and fails to recognise the underlying factors that systematically reproduce violence. As argued in this article, women are subjected to violence not because they are vulnerable or weak, but because of a discriminatory gender

46 *Montreal Principles on Women's Economic, Social and Cultural Rights*, 2002, principle 20.

order that privileges the use of patriarchal violence to subordinate women. In this regard, it is essential that the violence against women agenda be approached within an empowerment rather than a victimisation framework. This means that the problem must be placed as part and parcel of the wider agenda for equality between women and men as elaborated in the Beijing Platform for Action.

Therefore, the potential of the due diligence standard to effectively respond to the phenomenon of violence against women lies in the renewed interpretation of the obligation to prevent violence from occurring in the first place by addressing all dimensions of gender relations, including its intersections with other systems of inequality. This requires mapping out the parameters of responsibility for state and non-state actors alike and complementing the human rights discourse with other approaches such as empowerment and cultural negotiation, among others. It can be concluded that a broadened understanding of the due diligence obligation of states to address the root causes of violence against women and to hold non-state actors accountable for their acts will enhance the realisation of human rights beyond rhetoric and double standards towards one that is compatible with aspirations for a just world free of violence.

Precisely what is required to meet the standard of due diligence will necessarily vary according to the domestic context, internal dynamics, nature of the actors concerned, international conjuncture and, most importantly, political will at all levels. The progress achieved so far in the struggle to eliminate violence against women, although uneven and with notorious exceptions, has verified the conviction that oppressive values, institutions and relationships can be transformed.

Transformative change in gender structures is not an easy task, particularly in view of how deeply patriarchy is embedded. Furthermore, such change is inherently disruptive of the comfort offered by the status quo, as oppressive as it may be. While such change may hold risks, it also promises a step forward in greater emancipation not only for women, but for everyone. Eradicating violence against women and ensuring that human rights are universally enjoyed is, therefore, a shared interest and obligation. States and non-state actors alike have a stake in exercising due diligence to prevent violence against women from occurring and in effectively responding when it does occur.

The History and Development of the Due Diligence Standard in International Law and Its Role in the Protection of Women against Violence

Joanna Bourke-Martignoni

Introduction

The due diligence standard constitutes a yardstick against which the efforts of states to prevent and respond to violence against women may be measured. Under the standard, states are required to 'exercise due diligence to prevent, investigate and, in accordance with national legislation, punish acts of violence against women, whether those acts are perpetrated by the State or by private persons'.[1] Over the last decade, the concept of due diligence obligations has become a central cog in many campaign strategies on women's human rights. However, despite its popularity as a mechanism for promoting greater state accountability for failures to prevent and respond to violence against women in the so-called private sphere, both the content and scope of due diligence obligations remain vague.

This chapter will examine the historical development of the due diligence standard in international law and the way in which it has been applied to the issue of violence against women. The second part of the chapter will highlight some of the important questions and contemporary challenges related to the due diligence standard such as: Is it really possible to develop a generalised standard of diligence or is it a legal concept that is relevant only on a case-by-case basis? Does the standard of due diligence add anything new to pre-existing positive obligations under international human rights law? Does the reliance upon the state as a filter through which acts of private violence must pass prior to becoming actionable at the international level further entrench the public/private distinction? Can non-state actors be held directly responsible for failures to fulfil their human rights obligations under international law with due diligence? Is it relevant to insist that women's rights be protected, respected and fulfilled within the current human rights paradigm when, according to some, this framework itself does little more than replicate existing patterns of subordination and exclusion?

1 Declaration on the Elimination of Violence against Women, UNGA Res. 48/104 of 20 December 1993, Article 4 (c).

C. Benninger-Budel ed., Due Diligence and Its Application to Protect Women from Violence

ISBN 978 90 04 16293 8. pp. 47-61

The History and Development of the Due Diligence Standard in International Law

The standard of due diligence has a relatively long history in international law. The writings of seventeenth-century jurists including Hugo Grotius, Richard Zouche and Samuel Pufendorf made mention of the responsibility of the sovereign to prevent injury to foreign nationals, to punish private persons who commit acts of violence against foreigners and to ensure that reparations are made.[2] This notion of the standard of diligence that must be exercised by the state authorities was extended and developed during the eighteenth, nineteenth and early twentieth centuries, particularly in the context of international arbitral awards concerning responsibility for protection failures in relation to injuries to foreigners and their property as a result of private violence.[3]

While each of these arbitral awards examined the factual circumstances of the specific case and made a determination as to whether the state had exercised the requisite level of diligence with regards to the prevention of harm to the person or property, no consensus emerged as to what constitutes the defining characteristics of due diligence. As Ian Brownlie notes in relation to the principles applicable to state responsibility for damages to the person or property of foreign nationals arising out of mob violence and insurrection:

> 'There is general agreement among writers that the rule of non-responsibility cannot apply where the government concerned has failed to show due diligence. However, the decisions of tribunals and the other sources offer no definition of "due diligence". Obviously no very dogmatic definition would be appropriate, since what is involved is a standard which will vary according to the circumstances. And yet, if "due diligence" be taken to denote a fairly high standard of conduct the exception would overwhelm the rule.'[4]

Clearly, these situations are not directly analogous to state responsibility for failures to protect, respect and fulfil the human rights of women. It is telling, nevertheless, that no agreement has been reached on a general definition of due diligence within the framework of diplomatic protection, given that this is the area in which the modern articulation of the standard originated. The question of whether it is worthwhile to insist upon generalised obligations of due diligence

---

2 Jan Hessbruegge, 'The Historical Development of the Doctrines of Attribution and Due Diligence in International Law', *New York University Journal of International Law* 36 (2004): 265–306.

3 *Alabama* Claims (1871), Treaty of Washington; *Kummerow* case (Germany/Venezuela Mixed Claims Commission) 1903, RIAJ, vol. 1, 37; Huber, *Spanish Zone of Morocco* Claims (1924), RIAA ii. 615 at 642; *Youmans* Claim (U.S.A. v Mexico, 1926), RIAA iv. 110.

4 Ian Brownlie, *Principles of Public International Law*, 6th ed. (Oxford: University Press, 2003), 438.

in light of the fact that it appears almost impossible to define the parameters of these obligations will be revisited in the second part of this chapter.

Before turning to the way in which the standard of due diligence has been used in relation to human rights obligations in general and to the question of violence against women in particular, it is important to situate the standard within the context of general principles of state responsibility under international law.

The International Law Commission (ILC) has adopted a set of Articles on state responsibility that specifies the consequences that flow from violations of international law by states.[5] Under the Articles, omissions and other failures by states to take positive measures to fulfil their international obligations will, if these breaches are attributable to the state, amount to internationally wrongful acts. The criteria for attributing conduct to a state are listed in Articles 4 to 11, which provide that the state is responsible for the actions of all those organs identified under either internal or international law as forming part of the state as well as for the acts of organs that exceed their authority, for conduct carried out in the absence or default of official authorities and for conduct that is adopted by the state as its own. The Commentary to the Articles notes that standards such as due diligence 'vary from one context to another for reasons which essentially relate to the object and purpose of the treaty provision or other rule giving rise to the primary obligation.'[6] In brief, under the general framework of state responsibility as described in the ILC Articles, the due diligence standard constitutes one means of determining whether or not a primary obligation under international law has been breached. If it is found that state authorities have failed to act with due diligence to protect, respect and fulfil the human rights of people within their jurisdiction, then the state becomes responsible at the international level and will be required to implement its obligations, guarantee that it will not repeat the wrongful conduct and provide reparations.

From its origins in early doctrine and jurisprudence on the duties of states to prevent and respond to harm to foreign nationals, the due diligence standard or variants thereof can now be found across a broad range of different fields of international law, ranging from international corporate law and the regulation of investment disputes, to international environmental law and the legal framework applicable to the trade in stolen or illegally exported cultural objects. The use of due diligence 'checklists' forms part of company law in many national jurisdictions and it is in this context that the term has become most well known. The application of the standard to human rights issues is relatively new.

5 International Law Commission, *Responsibility of States for Internationally Wrongful Acts*, Text adopted by the Commission at its fifty-third session in 2001, Annexed to UN General Assembly Resolution 56/83 of 12 December 2001.

6 International Law Commission, *Draft Articles on Responsibility of States for Internationally Wrongful Acts with Commentaries*, Yearbook of the International Law Commission, 2001, vol. 2, Part Two, Commentary to Article 2, para. 3, 70.

Due Diligence Comes to Human Rights

The due diligence standard was first evoked within the international system for the promotion and protection of human rights in the late 1970s in connection with cases of forced disappearances, particularly in Latin America.

In his 1979 report to the UN General Assembly on the situation of human rights in Chile, independent expert Abdulaye Dieye of Senegal outlined the responsibility of states for acts of violence committed by private individuals. In the report, he noted that a state is responsible in international law for a range of acts or omissions in relation to forced disappearances if *inter alia,* the authorities do not react promptly to reliable reports, the relevant legal remedies are ineffective or non-existent, or it takes no action to punish the perpetrators.[7]

The content and scope of due diligence obligations was examined by the Inter-American human rights system in 1988 in the landmark decision of the Inter-American Court of Human Rights in *Velásquez Rodríguez v Honduras.*[8] In this case, which concerned the disappearance of Manfredo Velásquez, the Court held that Honduras had failed to fulfil its duties under Article 1 (1) of the American Convention on Human Rights. In a now well-cited passage, the Court said:

> 'An illegal act which violates human rights and which is initially not directly imputable to a State (for example, because it is the act of a private person or because the person responsible has not been identified) can lead to international responsibility of the State, not because of the act itself, but because of the lack of due diligence to prevent the violation or to respond to it as required by the Convention.'[9]

The Court went on to note that the state has a legal duty to take 'reasonable steps' to prevent human rights violations, to use the means at its disposal to thoroughly investigate any violations occurring within its jurisdiction, to identify the perpetrators, impose appropriate punishment and to ensure that the victim receives adequate compensation.[10] In relation to the duty to prevent human rights violations, the Court stated that this 'includes all those means of a legal, political, administrative and cultural nature that promote the protection of human rights and ensure that any violations are considered and treated as illegal acts'.[11] The Court noted that the preventive measures that need to be taken would vary depending on the legal, social and political environment of the state concerned.

It is nevertheless a little incongruous that the decision in *Velásquez Rodríguez* has been used as the basis for the development of doctrine related to the obliga-

7 Report of the Special Rapporteur on extrajudicial, summary or arbitrary executions, UN Doc. E/CN.4/2005/7, 22 December 2004, para. 73.

8 Inter-American Court of Human Rights, *Velásquez Rodríguez v Honduras,* Judgment of 29 July 1988, Series C: Decisions and Judgments, no. 04.

9 Ibid., para. 172.

10 Ibid., para. 174.

11 Ibid., para. 175.

tions of states to act with due diligence to prevent and punish acts of violence committed by non-state actors. It was widely acknowledged at the time of the case that Manfredo Velásquez, as with many other victims of forced disappearance in Honduras and elsewhere in Latin America during that period, was almost certainly executed by security forces acting on behalf of the state.[12] Nevertheless, the reasoning of the Inter-American Court in the case constitutes an important precedent that has been taken up and applied particularly in the field of women's human rights.

The European Court of Human Rights has also developed a body of jurisprudence in relation to the positive obligations of states parties to the European Convention on Human Rights to effectively prevent, investigate, prosecute, punish and provide remedies for acts of violence perpetrated by private persons or entities.[13] While the Court has never used the term due diligence in its decisions, in practice it has developed similar standards. In cases such as *Osman v United Kingdom*, the Court established various tests for assessing whether a state's authorities had fulfilled their positive obligations under the European Convention to secure the 'practical and effective protection of the rights and freedoms laid down therein'.[14] According to the Court in *Osman v United Kingdom* and subsequent decisions, the scope of the duty of the state to prevent and to offer protection against violence at the hands of non-state actors will depend on what actions should reasonably be taken in a given context.

The African Commission on Human and Peoples' Rights has also examined the concept of state obligations with regard to human rights violations by non-state actors. In its communication on Burkina Faso in 1997, the Commission emphasised that: '...if a State Party fails to ensure respect of the rights contained in the African Charter, this constitutes a violation of the Charter. Even if the State or its agents were not the perpetrators of the violation'.[15]

Drawing upon the work done in the area of violence against women, the 'mainstream' international human rights treaty monitoring bodies have also begun to interpret their instruments as including the obligation of states to ensure that human rights violations by non-state actors are prevented and responded to with due diligence.[16] In its General Comment no. 31 adopted in 2004, the Hu-

12 Rachel Sieder ed., *Central America: Fragile Transition* (New York: St. Martin's Press, 1996).

13 Andrew Clapham, *Human Rights Obligations of Non-State Actors* (Oxford: University Press, 2006), chapter 9.

14 *Osman v United Kingdom* (2000), 29 EHRR 245, para. 115.

15 Comm. 204/97, *Mouvement Burkinabé des Droits de l'Homme et des Peuples v Burkina Faso*, cited in Clapham (2006), see note 13 above, 434.

16 Human Rights Committee, General Comment no. 31, The Nature of the General Legal Obligation Imposed on States Parties to the Covenant (29 March 2004), UN Doc. CCPR/C/74/CRP.4/Rev.6, para. 8; Committee on the Rights of the Child, General Comment no. 5, General Measures of Implementation for the Convention on the Rights of the Child (2003), UN Doc CRC/GC/2003/5, para. 1; Committee on Eco-

man Rights Committee stated that while the obligations under the International Covenant on Civil and Political Rights are only directly applicable to states, these obligations will not be fully discharged unless individuals are protected against rights violations committed by private persons or entities. The Committee went on to say:

> 'There may be circumstances in which a failure to ensure Covenant rights as required by article 2 would give rise to violations by States Parties of those rights, as a result of States Parties' permitting or failing to take appropriate measures or to exercise due diligence to prevent, punish, investigate or redress harm caused by such acts by private persons or entities.'[17]

As can be seen in the jurisprudence of the regional human rights institutions and in the general comments by the UN treaty monitoring bodies, the positive obligations to protect, respect and fulfil human rights that are contained in human rights treaty law imply a duty to act with due diligence to protect individuals against human rights violations by private persons or entities.

Applying the Due Diligence Standard to Violence against Women

Since the early 1990s, the due diligence standard has been invoked in order to demand that states be held accountable for failures to prevent and adequately respond to violence against women whether the violence is perpetrated by state or by non-state actors. This use of the standard by the women's movement has been crucial to the advancement of our understanding of state responsibility for violence perpetrated by non-state actors.

In its General Recommendation no. 19 which was adopted in 1992, the Committee on the Elimination of Discrimination against Women (CEDAW Committee) noted that under general international law and as a result of specific treaty obligations: 'States may also be responsible for private acts if they fail to act with due diligence to prevent violations of rights or to investigate and punish acts of violence, and for providing compensation.'[18] The Declaration on the Elimination of Violence against Women, which was adopted the following year, urges states to exercise due diligence to 'prevent, investigate and, in accordance with national legislation, punish acts of violence against women whether those acts are perpe-

nomic, Social and Cultural Rights, General Comment no. 14, The Right to the Highest Attainable Standard of Health (2000), UN Doc. E/C.12/2000/4, para. 33.

17 Human Rights Committee, General Comment no. 31, ibid., para. 8.

18 Committee on the Elimination of Discrimination against Women, General Recommendation no. 19, Violence against Women (eleventh session, 1992), UN Doc. A/47/38, para. 9.

trated by the State or by private persons.'[19] This provision was repeated in paragraph 124 (b) of the 1995 Beijing Platform for Action.

The 1994 resolution of the Commission on Human Rights which created the mandate of the UN Special Rapporteur on violence against women, its causes and consequences, also refers to due diligence in its paragraph 2 which emphasises the duty of Governments to 'take appropriate and effective action concerning acts of violence against women, whether those acts are perpetrated by the State or by private persons, and to provide access to just and effective remedies and specialized assistance to victims.'[20]

At the regional level, Article 7 (b) of the Inter-American Convention on the Prevention, Punishment and Eradication of Violence against Women (1994) provides that states shall undertake to: 'apply due diligence to prevent, investigate and impose penalties for violence against women.'[21] The Protocol on the Rights of Women in Africa (2003) requires states parties to enact and enforce laws to prohibit violence against women whether this takes place in public or in private and to adopt such 'legislative, administrative, social and economic measures, to ensure the prevention, punishment and eradication of all forms of violence against women.'[22]

As discussed above, judicial and quasi-judicial human rights bodies have provided important insights into the concrete measures that states must take in order to ensure that they meet their due diligence obligations. Several of the most important decisions relating to state responsibility for acts of violence against women perpetrated by private persons are discussed below. It is important to note that even if they do not explicitly use the due diligence standard as a measure, the institutions responsible for deciding these cases have frequently drawn attention to the systemic failures that have resulted in inadequate prevention and responses to violence against women and have made recommendations as to how to remedy these.

The entry into force of the Optional Protocol to the CEDAW Convention has created an additional source of jurisprudence in relation to state responsibility for violence against women. In the case of *Ms A.T. v Hungary* (2005), the CEDAW Committee found that due to deficiencies in its legal and institutional arrangements, the state party had failed to fulfil its obligations to protect Ms A.T. from her violent former partner. The Committee noted that the obligations of the state party with respect to the measures to be taken to eliminate discrimination as set out in Article 2 (a), (b) and (e) of the CEDAW Convention 'extend to the prevention of, and protection from violence against women and, in the instant case, remain unfulfilled and constitute a violation of the author's human rights and

19 Declaration on the Elimination of Violence against Women, UN General Assembly Resolution 48/104, 20 December 1993, Article 4 (c).

20 UN Commission on Human Rights, Resolution 1994/45.

21 Inter-American Convention on the Prevention, Punishment and Eradication of Violence against Women, 'Convention of Belém do Pará', A-61, 1994.

22 Protocol on the Rights of Women in Africa, 2003, Article 4 (2) (b).

fundamental freedoms, particularly her right to security of person.'[23] The Committee further found that Hungary had violated Articles 5 and 16 of the CEDAW Convention in that it had failed to take adequate measures to combat entrenched stereotypes and to address gender inequality in matters relating to marriage and family relations. The Committee's finding recalls its General Recommendation no. 19 on Violence against Women which refers to the duty of states to act with due diligence to prevent and respond to violence and the standard clearly informed its analysis of Hungary's compliance with its obligations to prevent, protect and respond to violence against women.

In 2004, in its first ever inquiry under Article 8 of the Optional Protocol to the CEDAW Convention, the CEDAW Committee expressed its grave concern at the lack of due diligence shown by the state and municipal authorities in the Ciudad Juarez area of Chihuahua State in Mexico. The authorities systematically failed to prevent, investigate, prosecute, punish or provide reparations for hundreds of cases of violence against women including disappearances, murder, rape and trafficking.[24] In its recommendations, the CEDAW Committee pointed to serious gaps in Mexico's application of the CEDAW Convention as evidenced in widespread and systematic violence against women.

In 2001, the Inter-American Commission on Human Rights found that Brazil had failed to exercise due diligence with respect to preventing and responding to acts of domestic violence. Ms Maria da Penha Maia Fernandes was the victim of domestic violence throughout her married life and this violence culminated in 1983 with her husband's attempt to murder her that left her a paraplegic. Despite the clear evidence against the accused and the seriousness of the charges, the Brazilian authorities failed to take adequate steps to investigate or prosecute the crime and the victim received no compensation during the 17-year interval between the attempted murder and her petition to the Inter-American Commission. The Commission found that the case could be viewed as 'part of a general pattern of negligence and lack of effective action by the State in prosecuting and convicting aggressors' and that it involved 'not only failure to fulfil the obligation

23 Committee on the Elimination of Discrimination against Women, Communication no. 2/2003, *Ms A.T. v Hungary*, View adopted on 26 January 2005, para. 9.4. It is important to note that the CEDAW Convention does not explicitly refer to violence against women. In its General Recommendation no. 19 the CEDAW Committee interpreted the prohibitions on discrimination within the Convention as implicitly including acts of gender-based violence and stated that 'Gender-based violence may breach specific provisions of the Convention, regardless of whether those provisions expressly mention violence.'

24 Committee on the Elimination of Discrimination against Women, *Report on Mexico Produced under Article 8 of the Optional Protocol to the Convention*, UN Doc. CEDAW/C/2005/OP.8/MEXICO, 27 January 2005.

with respect to prosecute and convict, but also the obligation to prevent these degrading practices.'[25]

In the case of *M.C. v Bulgaria* (2003), the European Court of Human Rights held that the state had not fulfilled the positive obligations contained in Articles 3 and 8 of the European Convention on Human Rights.[26] This case involved the failure of the authorities to pursue an investigation into the rape of a 14-year-old girl due to the fact that there was a perceived lack of evidence that the applicant had been 'compelled' as understood in the definition of the crime of rape in Bulgarian law. The Court reiterated its established interpretation that Article 3 'requires States to take measures designed to ensure that individuals within their jurisdiction are not subjected to ill-treatment, including ill-treatment administered by private individuals.' In its conclusions, the European Court of Human Rights noted that:

> '...the effectiveness of the investigation of the applicant's case and, in particular, the approach taken by the investigator and the prosecutors in the case fell short of the requirements inherent in the States' positive obligations – viewed in the light of the relevant modern standards in comparative and international law – to establish and apply effectively a criminal-law system punishing all forms of rape and sexual abuse.'[27]

In her thematic report on due diligence, the UN Special Rapporteur on violence against women evaluated current government practice in relation to the measures that are being taken to discharge due diligence obligations with regard to preventing and responding to violence against women.[28] The Special Rapporteur noted that few of the states that responded to her note verbale were engaging in preventive programmes that adequately addressed the primary cause of violence against women, namely, gender inequality. The report also found that while most states do provide services to women who are victims of violence, there is a lack of coordination amongst these as well as a failure to go beyond the provision of emergency assistance in order to empower women and avoid re-victimisation. Many states have adopted specific legislation and developed particular law enforcement practices as a way of discharging their obligations to investigate and appropriately punish violence against women. The Special Rapporteur concluded that despite this legislative activity, 'failures by law enforcement authorities to seriously investigate crimes of violence against women appear to be common'

25 Inter-American Commission on Human Rights, Report no. 54/01, Case 12.051, *Maria da Penha Maia Fernandes* (Brazil), 16 April 2001, para. 56.

26 European Court of Human Rights, *M.C. v Bulgaria*, Application no. 39272/98, 4 December 2003. Article 3 of the European Convention on Human Rights provides that 'no one shall be subjected to torture or to inhuman or degrading treatment or punishment.' Article 8 deals with the right to respect for private and family life.

27 Ibid., para. 185.

28 Report of the Special Rapporteur on violence against women, UN Doc. E/CN.4/2006/61, 20 January 2006, paras. 38–55.

and that 'even when cases of violence against women do reach the judicial system, there are still alarming numbers of instances of judges handing down reduced or inappropriate sentences'.[29] The obligation to provide reparations for violence against women was highlighted as an area in which much more needs to be done by states in order to fulfil the requirements of the due diligence standard.

The decisions by judicial and quasi-judicial bodies and the assessment of state practice by the Special Rapporteur and other experts assist in the definition of the basic requirements of the due diligence standard. These include measures to prevent violence against women, to investigate and prosecute acts of violence, to punish perpetrators appropriately and to provide access to effective remedies.

The Content and Scope of Diligence Obligations in Relation to Violence against Women

As can be seen from the preceding discussion of the consideration of positive obligations to prevent and respond to violence against women by judicial and quasi-judicial bodies, there are certain basic obligations that should be implemented with due diligence in all contexts. These different strands of the obligation can be broken down into a kind of 'checklist' in a way that is similar to the application of due diligence in the context of domestic corporate law.

In her 1999 report on domestic violence, the former Special Rapporteur on violence against women, Radhika Coomaraswamy, developed a list of considerations against which state compliance with due diligence obligations may be assessed. These included; ratification of international human rights instruments, constitutional guarantees of equality for women, the existence of national legislation and/or administrative sanctions providing adequate redress for women victims of violence, executive policies or plans of action that attempt to deal with the issue of violence against women, the gender-sensitivity of the criminal justice system and police, accessibility and availability of support services, the existence of appropriate measures in the field of education and the media to raise awareness of violence against women and to modify discriminatory practices and the collection of data and statistics concerning violence against women.[30]

The UN Secretary-General's In-Depth Study on All Forms of Violence against Women also examines the international responsibilities of states to act with due diligence to prevent and respond to violence.[31] The study highlights the general duty of states to 'promote de facto equality between women and men and to develop and implement effectively a legal and policy framework for the full protection and promotion of women's human rights'.[32] Other areas that are identified as

29 Ibid., para. 54.

30 Report of the Special Rapporteur on violence against women, UN Doc. E/CN.4/1999/68, 10 March 1999, para. 25.

31 Report of the UN Secretary-General, *In-Depth Study on All Forms of Violence against Women*, UN Doc. A/61/122/Add.1, 6 July 2006.

32 Ibid., para. 261.

forming part of state responsibility under international law include: requirements to enact, implement and monitor legislation and policy covering all forms of violence against women; to conduct prompt, thorough and serious investigations of allegations of violence; to effectively prosecute and punish perpetrators of violence; to provide just and effective remedies to victims of violence; to ensure access to support services including shelters, medical, psychological and legal aid; to address social and cultural patterns of conduct that lead to discrimination and stereotyped roles for women and men; to promote and guarantee education and training of all public officials involved with gender-based violence; to conduct research, collect data and compile accurate statistics.

Based on international legal instruments and state practice, it is possible to draw together a number of general principles that can be said to constitute the basic requirements of the due diligence standard. These general principles, as explained by the Special Rapporteur on violence against women in her 2006 report to the Commission on Human Rights, include; the non-delegable nature of obligations to exercise diligence, the principle of non-discrimination, the principle of good faith, the duty not to invoke custom, tradition or religious considerations to avoid obligations with respect to the elimination of violence against women and the duty to base strategies and programmes for ending violence against women on verified quantitative and qualitative research.[33]

The principle of non-discrimination requires that states undertake to devote the same levels of effort and resources to preventing and responding to violence against women as they do to other forms of violence and discrimination. The principle of good faith implies that states must go beyond the 'mere enactment of formal legal provisions' and take positive measures to fully implement their obligations to prevent, protect, investigate, punish and provide redress for violence against women.[34]

It therefore appears to be possible to distil certain features of the positive obligations of states in relation to preventing and responding to violence against women into universally applicable standards. Nevertheless, leaving aside the basic structural considerations such as the requirement that states establish a comprehensive legislative and policy framework on violence against women, the determination as to whether a particular state has acted with the required level of diligence in a given context is something that can only be decided on a case-by-case basis.

This then begs the question as to whether the concept of due diligence can be said to provide any additional clarity in relation to generalised positive obligations to act in order to protect, respect and fulfil the human rights of women. It may be that the same result can be achieved – namely, an evaluation of the different components of positive obligations to prevent and respond to violence

33 Report of the Special Rapporteur on violence against women, UN Doc. E/CN.4/2006/61, 20 January 2006, paras. 34–37.

34 Report of the Special Rapporteur on violence against women, UN Doc. E/CN.4/2000/68, 29 February 2000, paras. 51–53.

against women – by simply requiring that states effectively implement their positive obligations in good faith.

Due Diligence and the Obligations of Non-State Actors

We are currently witnessing a paradigm shift in the attribution of responsibility for preventing and responding to human rights violations. As non-state actors, including international organisations, the private sector and armed groups increasingly exercise control over territory and financial markets to an extent that often outstrips the power of states in this regard, it is clearly time to rethink the way in which international responsibility is conceived. This may mean that obligations to prevent and respond to human rights violations are no longer only applied through the 'back door' of state responsibility but that they also become directly applicable to non-state actors themselves.

Indeed, to a large extent the transformation from an international legal order within which states are regarded as having the principal (if not the sole) responsibility for ensuring that human rights obligations are met to one which admits that non-state actors have obligations in their own right has already occurred.[35] The development of individual criminal responsibility for international crimes, the growth of international commercial law and the expansion of international organisations have all contributed to a shift in thinking with regards to international responsibility for the promotion and protection of human rights. Initiatives aimed at the direct application of obligations of due diligence to non-state actors such as the Norms on the Responsibilities of Transnational Corporations and Other Business Enterprises with Regard to Human Rights[36] and the Office of the High Commissioner for Human Rights (OHCHR) Recommended Principles and Guidelines on Human Rights and Human Trafficking bear witness to this change.[37]

These developments in the international legal, political and economic landscape obviously have an important impact on the way in which the question of responsibility for violence against women is addressed. One important benefit of going beyond the traditional, state-centred approach to international human rights obligations is that by bringing non-state actors into the 'public' sphere of

35 Clapham (2006), see note 13 above.

36 UN Sub-Commission on the Promotion and Protection of Human Rights, *Commentary to the Norms on the Responsibilities of Transnational Corporations and Other Business Enterprises with Regard to Human Rights*, UN Doc. E/CN.4/Sub.2/2003/38/Rev.2, Article 1 (b).

37 Office of the High Commissioner for Human Rights, *Recommended Principles and Guidelines on Human Rights and Human Trafficking*, UN ECOSOC, UN Doc. E/2002/68 Add.1.

international law and holding them directly accountable for human rights violations, we contribute to eroding the so-called public/private dichotomy.[38]

While many commentators have expressed concern at the prospect of a restriction in state accountability for acts of violence against women if the possibility of direct responsibility of non-state actors is admitted, this fear will not necessarily be realised. The persuasive argument put forward by Andrew Clapham as a solution to this problem is that:

> 'With a multiplicity of jurisdictions for human rights claims, we have to accept that human rights obligations may attach to non-state actors in some jurisdictions and not in others. These different jurisdictional appreciations of the nature of human rights need not be contradictory. They can be considered complementary.'[39]

Obviously, the scope and content of due diligence obligations will differ depending upon the actor and the jurisdiction concerned but, as discussed previously, this kind of case-by-case analysis is already required in order to ascertain the responsibility of states for acts of private violence. If we use an approach that takes the complementarity of jurisdictions as its starting point, there is no reason to think that holding non-state actors directly responsible for failures to prevent or respond to violence against women will necessarily preclude action at the level of the state as well. In fact, if we wish to redefine the boundaries of international human rights law then it becomes not merely desirable but also necessary to move the analytical focus from one that is purely state-centred to one that fully encompasses the diverse and intersecting forms of power that operate at all levels from the international to the local.

Where Do We Go from Here: Challenges and Change

In recent years a number of feminist scholars have criticised the women's movement for its focus on the 'victim subject' and on the issue of violence against women, almost to the exclusion of other standpoints that could provide real alternatives to prevailing normative assumptions surrounding gender, sexuality and culture.[40] These commentators have argued that it is not effective to attempt to frame women's claims to freedom from violence within the familiar liberal, rights-based model that has thus far been used. As Ratna Kapur maintains:

> 'The VAW campaign continues to fall back on an uncomplicated position on rights, despite the critique of rights, and offers mitigation rather than transformation as a solution. The challenge lies in exposing the normative aspects of human rights discourse as

38 Report of the Special Rapporteur on violence against women, E/CN.4/2006/61, 20 January 2006, paras. 59–63.

39 Clapham (2006), see note 13 above, 57.

40 See for example, Sally Engle Merry, *Human Rights & Gender Violence* (Chicago: University of Chicago Press, 2006), 230.

> it applies to gender, culture and sexuality, rather than merely consolidating the regulatory effect of these rights. This requires a revisiting of the women's rights strategies and claims, and bringing a normative challenge to human rights discourse.'[41]

Under this vision, work on entrenching the notion of due diligence within the existing human rights framework serves as a distraction from the main game, which should be the development of a paradigm that goes beyond the current confines of our thinking on rights.

The arguments of post-colonial feminists are certainly compelling and provide an important critical perspective on efforts to challenge dominant norms on culture, sexuality and gender. The burning question that remains is: what would a new 'transformative' approach to human rights entail for women and how do we get there?

Several feminist writers have proposed the development of a framework that recognises differences and specificities among women while simultaneously developing a common language of equity and justice that can be effectively applied in different contexts.[42] The basis of this transformation would be an acceptance of the fact that human rights are a cultural practice in and of themselves.[43] This implies the need for those working in human rights to go beyond the simple application of purportedly objective and universal norms and to examine the ways in which rights discourses could potentially challenge the very ideologies on which they have historically been built.

Conclusion

Whether we call it due diligence, the implementation of positive obligations or something else entirely, it is established that states and certain non-state actors have responsibilities to ensure that violence against women is effectively prevented and responded to in accordance with international human rights law. Despite the fact that these obligations are frequently not complied with in practice, there is a growing recognition that states should ensure a minimum level of diligence in preventing, protecting, investigating, prosecuting, punishing and providing redress for acts of violence against women. The assessment of whether these obligations have been met may be made in the context of judicial or quasi-judicial proceedings in relation to the situation of individual women or it might occur within the framework of a more general inquiry. Either way, what is important are the systems and programmes that governments and certain non-state actors

41 Ratna Kapur, *Erotic Justice: Law and the New Politics of Postcolonialism* (Delhi: Permanent Black, 2005), 136.

42 Dianne Otto, 'A Post-Beijing Reflection on the Limitations and Potential of Human Rights Discourse for Women', in *Women and International Human Rights Law*, ed. Kelly D. Askin and Dorean M. Koenig, I, 115–135 (Ardsley/New York: Transnational Publishers, 1999).

43 Engle Merry (2006), see note 40 above.

have developed to prevent and respond to violence against women, including its root causes, and the manner in which these are implemented.

While it is clear that the primary responsibility for ensuring compliance with human rights obligations does and should continue to reside with the state, it must be recognised that non-state actors also have obligations under international law to respect, protect and fulfil human rights. It would be both ineffective and incongruous to ignore the fact that non-state actors such as international organisations, multinational corporations and armed groups often have the power to violate, or conversely to ensure, the full implementation of women's human rights in ways that go beyond the capacities of states.

The standard of due diligence serves an important purpose as a rallying point for focusing the attention of governments and relevant non-state actors on the concrete measures that must be taken in order to prevent violence against women, to protect women from it and to remedy its consequences. The standard is therefore a useful instrument in the toolbox of all those who advocate for women's human rights. That being said, the due diligence standard forms but one piece of a much larger puzzle within which changes in the nature of international relations and in feminist approaches to women's rights must be accommodated. It remains to be seen whether the due diligence standard is flexible enough to incorporate the new demands that are being placed on it by these multiple challenges to the classical framework of international responsibility for the promotion and protection of human rights.

Preventing Violence against Women: The Due Diligence Standard with Respect to the Obligation to Banish Gender Stereotypes on the Grounds of Article 5 (a) of the CEDAW Convention

Rikki Holtmaat

Introduction

Initially, in the context of international law, violence against women was mainly seen as a private matter, a matter of unwanted behaviour of some men and/or a matter of some backward or primitive cultures. It took a long time before it was accepted as part of the structure of the universal patriarchal culture that has been central to supporting the subordination of women in both the public and private spheres. It is now recognised that violence against women is widely pervasive and structural, in the sense that the principal causes of this phenomenon lie in social, economic and cultural/religious practices and institutions in which men and women are perceived of as being inherently *unequal* or in which women are being pictured as *inferior* to men.[1] Often, these practices reflect culturally dominant gender stereotypes, which contain strong ideological messages about the (different or unequal) values of men and women, about their respective roles in life, or about 'proper behaviour' between men and women.[2] Such stereotyped ideas fill the content of what is being perceived of as 'true' masculinity and femininity. In many traditional, patriarchal ideologies, part of those messages is that a man should dominate his wife and children (if necessary with physical force);

1 There are many empirical studies that prove the root causes of gender-based violence lie in patriarchal and unequal power relations between men and women. As far as the Western Balkans are concerned, a recent overview of empirical studies that clarify this background can be found in: Vesna Nicolić-Ristanović and Mirjana Dokmanović, *International Standards on Domestic Violence and Their Implementation in the Western Balkans* (Utrecht: Humanistisch Overleg Mensenrechten [HOM], 2006).

2 See also Yakın Ertürk, Report of the UN Special Rapporteur on violence against women, its causes and consequences, *The Due Diligence Standard as a Tool for the Elimination of Violence against Women*, UN Doc. E/CN.4/2006/61, 20 January 2006.

C. Benninger-Budel ed., Due Diligence and Its Application to Protect Women from Violence
 ISBN 978 90 04 16293 8. pp. 63-89

otherwise, he is not 'truly male' or he will lose his honour. Women, on the other hand, are often led to believe that violent behaviour of their partner or father is an expression of their 'true love'. Banishing gender stereotypes, therefore, is one of the main, general mechanisms to prevent[3] violence against women or gender-based violence.[4]

Article 5 (a) of the Convention on the Elimination of All Forms of Discrimination against Women (hereafter CEDAW Convention) is specifically directed at this goal.[5] This chapter sets out to examine what obligations for states parties to this Convention can be derived from this provision. In the context of this volume special attention is given to the question of what the *due diligence* standard means in the case of general prevention of violence against women by means of combating gender stereotypes.[6] This topic is related to another, more general issue concerning how to (best) combat violence against women. Focusing on the due diligence standard, in my view, means moving the focus of attention from protection of individual victims and the connected *welfare/humanitarian* approach to violence against women, to prevention in the sense of attacking the root causes of violence against women. In other words, it involves a move to a *human rights-based* approach to violence against women. In the framework of such an approach, in my view, we first and foremost need to identify which relevant rights already exist in international law. Next, we must analyse the content of these rights and indicate how these rights can be made instrumental in the fight

3 A distinction can be made between specific prevention or protection (e.g., barring the perpetrator from the vicinity or the home of his victims by locking him up in prison or by a restraint order that prevents him getting near them) and general prevention (e.g., criminalising violence against women or taking away the cultural or economic causes of violence). In this chapter I will concentrate on general prevention.

4 Since there is such a strong connection between violence against women and gender (in the sense of a social, economic and cultural construction of different sex roles and sex identities), I use the terms 'violence against women' and 'gender-based violence' as synonyms in this chapter. This is in accordance with the internationally accepted definition of violence against women in Article 1 of the Declaration on the Elimination of Violence against Women (DEVAW), UN Doc. A/Res/48/104, 20 December 1993.

5 Similar provisions can be found in Article 8 (b) of the Inter-American Convention on the Prevention, Punishment and Eradication of Violence against Women of 1994 (Convention of Belém do Pará) and in Article 4 of the 2003 Protocol to the African Charter on Human and People's Rights on the Rights of Women. See also Article 4 (j) of DEVAW and General Recommendation no. 19, Violence against Women (eleventh session, 1992), UN Doc. A/47/38, para. 11, of the Committee on the Elimination of Discrimination against Women.

6 This standard seems to become more and more prominent in international law concerning violence against women. See, e.g., Committee on the Elimination of Discrimination against Women, General Recommendation no. 19, ibid., para. 9; DEVAW, see note 4 above, Article 4 (c); Convention of Belém do Pará, Article 7 (b).

against this specific form of human rights violation. As far as Article 5 (a) of the CEDAW Convention is concerned, this is precisely what this chapter is about.[7]

The chapter proceeds as follows: first, it examines the place and role of Article 5 (a) within the CEDAW Convention. Next, it briefly summarises the findings of research that I have conducted into the meaning and scope of this provision.[8] A distinction is made between two different types of obligations of the states parties to the CEDAW Convention: (1) obligations with respect to the way women and men are portrayed or represented in social and cultural life (e.g., in TV commercials) and in educational materials and (2) obligations with respect to eliminating gender stereotypes in law and public policies. The next part moves on to examine these two obligations in relation to combating violence against women. In relation to this issue, some specific problems of the implementation of this provision are also discussed. The chapter ends with a somewhat critical question: Is due diligence the proper concept as far as combating gender stereotypes is concerned? In other words: does this concept offer us enough strongholds as to the accountability of states insofar as the prevention of violence against women is concerned?

The Place and Role of Article 5 (a) in the CEDAW Convention

It must be recognised that, contrary to some other provisions in the Convention, Article 5 (a) has as yet not attracted much attention from feminist legal scholars.[9]

---

7 This chapter focuses on Article 5 (a) of the CEDAW Convention, but most of what is said in that context can also be applied to the other international norms that have been mentioned in footnote 5.

8 See Rikki Holtmaat, *Towards Different Law and Public Policy: The Significance of Article 5 (a) CEDAW for the Elimination of Structural Gender Discrimination*, Research undertaken on behalf of the Ministry of Social Affairs and Employment, the Netherlands (Doetinchem: Reed Business Information, 2004).

9 See, e.g., Margareta Wadstein, 'Implementation of the UN Convention on the Elimination of All Forms of Discrimination against Women', *Human Rights Quarterly* (1988): 5–21; Noreen Burrows, 'The 1979 Convention on the Elimination of All Forms of Discrimination against Women', *Netherlands International Law Review* (1985): 419–460; Hillary Charlesworth, 'Feminist Methods in International Law', *The American Journal of International Law* (1999): 379–394; Hillary Charlesworth and Christine Chinkin, *The Boundaries of International Law: A Feminist Analysis* (Manchester: Juris Publishing/Manchester University Press, 2000); Hillary Charlesworth, Christine Chinkin and Shelley Wright, 'Feminist Approaches to International Law', *The American Journal of International Law* (1991): 613–645, who neglect this provision. On the other hand we have publications like those of Rebecca J. Cook, 'State Accountability Under the Convention on the Elimination of All Forms of Discrimination against Women', in *Human Rights of Women: National and International Perspectives*, ed. Rebecca J. Cook, 228–256 (Philadelphia: University of Pennsylvania Press, 1994), hereafter referred to as Cook (1994 (b)); Rikki Holtmaat, 'European Women and the CEDAW-Convention. The Way Forward', in *L'égalité entre femmes et hommes et la vie profesionnelle. Le point sur les développements actuels en Europe,*

Therefore, before turning our attention to the question of what obligations follow from Article 5 (a) of the CEDAW Convention its member states, I will first describe the place and role of this particular provision in the Convention.

The Place of Article 5 (a) in the Convention

In order to understand the significance of Article 5 (a) of the CEDAW Convention in the context of combating violence against women, it is necessary to keep in mind that the CEDAW Convention prohibits *discrimination* against women. In Article 1, this concept is defined as:

> 'any distinction, exclusion or restriction made on the basis of sex which has the effect or purpose of impairing or nullifying the recognition, enjoyment or exercise by women, irrespective of their marital status, on a basis of equality of men and women, of human rights and fundamental freedoms in the political, economic, social, cultural, civil or any other field'.

In addition, in its General Recommendation no. 19 on Violence against Women, the Committee on the Elimination of Discrimination against Women (hereafter CEDAW Committee) has clearly stated that violence against women is a form of discrimination under this Convention.[10]

Article 5 (a) of the CEDAW Convention provides that states parties to this Convention 'shall take all appropriate measures' to modify the social and cultural patterns of conduct of men and women, with a view to achieving 'the elimination of prejudices and customary and all other practices which are based on the idea of the inferiority or the superiority of either of the sexes or on stereotyped roles for men and women'. This provision is connected to Consideration 14 of the Preamble of the CEDAW Convention, in which the drafters of the Convention express their awareness that 'a change in the traditional role of men as well as the role of women in society and in the family is needed to achieve full equality between men and women'. Article 10 (c) of the Convention deals with the elimination of stereotypes in the context of education and educational materials. The latter provision can be seen as a *lex specialis* of the duty laid down in Article 5 (a).

Article 5 (a) is directly followed by Article 5 (b), which deals with the patterns of expectations with respect to the roles of men and women in the context of par-

153–174 (Paris: Edition Dalloz, 2003), hereafter referred to as Holtmaat (2003 (a)); Klaartje Wentholt, 'Over de potentie van rechtsbeginselen. Het discriminatieverbod en artikel 5 VN-vrouwenverdrag dwingen tot het rekening houden met zorgtaken', *Nemesis* (1997): 200–203.

10 Committee on the Elimination of Discrimination against Women, General Recommendation no. 19, Violence against Women (eleventh session, 1992), UN Doc. A/47/38.

enthood.[11] Monster, Cremers and Willems characterise the difference between Articles 5 (a) and 5 (b) as follows:

> 'The drafters of the Convention on the one hand wanted to recognise the important role of women in the reproduction of mankind, but on the other hand wanted to prevent that women are solely being seen as mothers. Parenthood involves responsibilities that rest both on men and women and creates obligations for the society as a whole....Article 5 CEDAW aims at disentangling the conceptual fusion of woman and motherhood by clearly separating between "culture" (the social and cultural roles on ground of sex in part a) and "nature" (the reproductive function of women in part b).'[12]

On the ground of this difference in meaning between the two parts of Article 5, I will concentrate solely on the analysis of Article 5 (a) of the CEDAW Convention.

Article 5 (a) in relation to the threefold purposes of the Convention

Article 5 (a) of the CEDAW Convention forms part of a group of general provisions in the Convention (Articles 1–5 and 24). Together with the Preamble, these Articles clarify the main object and purpose of the Convention, which – in very general terms – is *to eliminate all forms of discrimination against women.*[13] In its General Recommendation no. 25 on Temporary Special Measures on the ground

11 State parties should take all appropriate measures '(b) To ensure that family education includes a proper understanding of maternity as a social function and the recognition of the common responsibility of men and women in the upbringing and development of their children, it being understood that the interest of the children is the primordial consideration in all cases.'

12 W.C. Monster, E. Cremers and L. Willems, *Vrouwenverdrag, moederschap, ouderschap en arbeid* (Den Haag: Ministerie van Sociale Zaken en Werkgelegenheid, 1998), 50.

13 A thorough study of scope and purpose of the Convention, including the present analysis of the Convention's goals, can be found in the first National Report on the CEDAW Convention to the Dutch Parliament. See L.S. Groenman, C.E. van Vleuten, R. Holtmaat, T.E. van Dijk and J.H.J. de Wildt (Commission of Experts on the implementation of CEDAW in the Netherlands), *Het vrouwenverdrag in Nederland anno 1997* (Den Haag: Ministerie van Sociale Zaken en Werkgelegenheid/VUGA, 1997). I was part of this commission of independent experts assigned by the Dutch government to write this report. An English translation of parts of this report can be found as an appendix to Holtmaat (2004), see note 8 above. The CEDAW Committee for the first time endorsed this analysis of the Groenman Report in the Concluding Comments concerning the situation in the Netherlands, issued after the Committee's 25th session in July 2001; see Concluding Comments UN Doc. A/56/38, CEDAW/C/SR. 512 and 513, para. 196.

of Article 4 (1), adopted in January 2004[14], the CEDAW Committee clarifies that the object and purpose of the Convention is threefold, i.e.:

1. to achieve full equality of women before the law and in public administration,
2. to improve the *de facto* position of women, and
3. to address the prevailing gender relations and the persistence of gender-based stereotypes.

The Committee stresses that these aims cannot be separated from each other or ranked. All of them need to be fulfilled. Article 2 of the CEDAW Convention can be seen as the main expression of the first aim.[15] Article 3, in conjunction with Articles 4 and 24, expresses the second aim.[16] General Recommendation no. 25 links Article 5 (a) of the CEDAW Convention to the third objective:

> 'Thirdly, states parties' obligation is to address prevailing gender relations and the persistence of gender-based stereotypes that affect women not only through individual acts by individuals but also in law, and legal and societal structures and institutions.'[17]

The general provisions of the CEDAW Convention are followed by a group of provisions (Articles 6–16) in which the specific areas in which the Convention is applicable are described (such as trafficking in women, political and public life, nationality rights, education, paid labour and social security and health). In these Articles, states parties are provided with detailed instructions about what to do to put an end to discrimination of women. Finally there are a number of provisions on the implementation of the Convention's norms and supervision by the CEDAW Committee (Articles 17–30).

---

14 Committee on the Elimination of Discrimination against Women, General Recommendation no. 25 on Article 4, para. 1, of the Convention on the Elimination of All Forms of Discrimination against Women, on Temporary Special Measures (thirteenth session, 2004), paras. 6 and 7, www.un.org/womenwatch/daw/cedaw/recommendations/Generalrecommendation. See also Rikki Holtmaat, 'Building Blocks for a General Recommendation on Article 4 (1) of the CEDAW Convention. Report of the Expert Meeting in Maastricht 10–12 October 2002', in *Temporary Special Measures: Accelerating De Facto Equality of Women under Article 4 (1) UN Convention on the Elimination of All Forms of Discrimination against Women*, ed. I. Boerefijn, F. Coomans, J. Goldschmidt, R. Holtmaat and R. Wolleswinkel, 213–230 (Antwerp/Oxford/New York: Intersentia, 2003).

15 With legal equality the Committee not only means formal equality, but also substantive equality. See General Recommendation no. 25, ibid., paras. 8 and 9.

16 This means that a wide range of permanent and temporary measures are necessary that make it possible for women to fully participate on all levels and in all spheres of society. See General Recommendation no. 25, see note 14 above, paras. 10 and 11.

17 General Recommendation no. 25, see note 14 above, para. 7.

The Role of Article 5 (a) of the CEDAW Convention

Article 5 (a) of the CEDAW Convention can be used to lay the legal basis for a new, more sophisticated and progressive approach to the concepts of women's equality and not discriminating against women. In order to explain and ground this assertion, I need to clarify how these concepts have been understood thus far and what is special about the CEDAW Convention in that respect.[18]

The *fundamental* human rights principles[19] of equality between men and women and non-discrimination have predominantly been implemented in international, transnational and national legal systems by means of formal legal prohibitions of discrimination on the ground of sex or by means of so-called equal treatment legislation. Some of the most striking features of such legislation, which have been critiqued heavily by feminists,[20] are that they often:

- grant only formal equal treatment rights instead of also substantive rights (equality of outcomes);
- define discrimination restrictively as inequality of treatment in/before the law;
- do not specify what kind of treatment is necessary (as long as it is equal), so therefore levelling down standards to equally bad treatment fulfils the requirement of equal treatment;
- are oriented to protecting the rights of individuals instead of improving the situation of whole groups that are discriminated against or in a disadvantaged position;
- are symmetric instead of asymmetric, meaning that men as well as women are equally protected against discrimination under such legislation, which in fact often is to the benefit of men;
- are purely reactive (when harm has been done) instead of proactive (to prevent harm from happening);

---

18 For a more extensive discussion of the special character of the CEDAW Convention (as compared to European Union sex equality law), see Rikki Holtmaat and Christa Tobler, 'CEDAW and the European Union's Policy in the Field of Combating Gender Discrimination', *Maastricht Journal of European and Comparative Law* 12, no. 4 (2005): 399–425; Rikki Holtmaat (2003 (a)), see note 9 above, 153–174; and Holtmaat (2004), see note 8 above, chapter 4.

19 The fact that equality and non-discrimination are fundamental principles of international human rights law can be derived from the fact that these norms have a central place in many legal documents, from the Universal Declaration of Human Rights, the core Universal Human Rights Treaties (International Covenant on Civil and Political Rights, International Covenant on Economic, Social and Cultural Rights, Convention on the Elimination of Racial Discrimination and the CEDAW Convention), Regional Human Rights Treaties (e.g., European Convention on Human Rights and the Inter-American Belém Convention), in transnational documents (e.g., the European Union Treaty) and in virtually all national constitutions of democratic states.

20 See Holtmaat and Tobler (2005), note 18 above, for an overview of some of the most outstanding contributions from feminist legal scholars.

- impose only negative duties (to refrain from…) instead of also positive duties (to enhance…);
- require a comparison of cases (women/men are better/worse off) and tend to assimilation of excluded or discriminated-against groups to the (uncontested) dominant norms in society;
- require special (difficult to meet) justifications for programmes aimed at improving the position of disadvantaged or excluded groups in society;
- do not tackle the root causes of discrimination.

It should be no surprise that the effects of such legislation are not very positive. In a report, published in 1991, the Organisation for Economic Cooperation and Development (OECD) points out that: 'Although a necessary condition for achieving gender equality, the limited impact of anti-discrimination and equal opportunity measures points to the systemic nature of gender-based inequalities, and the need for a systemic solution.' Equal treatment, in the sense of prohibition of direct or indirect discrimination on the ground of sex, according to the OECD, is in itself insufficient to put an end to this type of systemic discrimination. In order to make real progress in terms of equality of men and women, this international organisation deems it necessary to strive for 'institutional change': 'That solution lies in applying an integrated approach to institutional change aimed at addressing the contradictions and tensions generated at the interface between the household, the community and employment structures.'[21]

In the case of violence against women, this critique becomes even more pregnant. It is apparent that instances of violence against women can hardly be captured under such equal treatment or non-discrimination legislation. Violence is not a matter of *inequality* of treatment, but a human rights violation in itself. In other words, for violence to be considered abject and to be condemned, it is not relevant that women are victims and that men are not![22] It is also apparent that especially with respect to violence against women legal norms prohibiting such behaviour are not enough, but that structural measures, aimed at the root causes thereof, are absolutely necessary.

It is significant that the CEDAW Convention, as compared to many other international standards, entails a far more sophisticated definition of discrimination and that violence against women is captured under this Convention as an

21 Organisation for Economic Cooperation and Development (OECD), *Shaping Structural Change: The Role of Women* (Paris: OECD, 1991), 8.

22 To bring violence against women under equal treatment legislation sometimes leads to absurd legal constructions. An example is the so-called 'I am a real bastard defense' in UK Equal Treatment case law in which an employer who is accused of harassment argues that he thereby makes no distinction on the ground of sex or race since he harasses all of his employees in the same way. See *Zafar v Glasgow City Council,* House of Lords, 13 October 1997, I.C.R. 1998, 120–126.

instance of discrimination against women.[23] Moreover, the Convention entails a substantive approach to equality, is asymmetric in nature (only aiming at elimination of discrimination against *women*), is proactive, includes positive duties, does not require a comparison of the situation of women and men (in the sense that women only have equal rights insofar men already have such rights), has a positive attitude towards 'temporary special measures' (or positive/affirmative action schemes) and – last but not least – does, in Article 5 (a), include the obligation to tackle the root causes of discrimination against women.

Three strategies to enhance equality and to eliminate discrimination

Based on the feminist critique of existing legal non-discrimination and equal treatment norms, and based on the above described threefold purposes of the CEDAW Convention, I have developed a more elaborate and sophisticated approach to equality and non-discrimination.[24] In this approach, the right to equality and non-discrimination is understood both in a formal and substantive way. Moreover, the approach combines both the traditional strategy of granting individual rights to victims of human rights violations and new – group-oriented – social and structural strategies. Finally, the approach aims both at constructing negative norms and positive obligations and is reactive as well as proactive. In this fashion, it is expected that the new, encompassing approach to equality, non-discrimination and combating violence against women, aims at changing the paradigm from only focussing on individual victims to laying groundwork for structural solutions to structural problems. No longer is protection the only issue (or focus), but also general prevention.

In order to make fighting violence against women more effective, it is proposed to follow a combination of three strategies to enhance equality and to combat and eliminate discrimination in such a way that it contributes to the empowerment of women:

---

23 As mentioned above, see General Recommendation no. 19, note 5 above. The following is based on the above analysis of the threefold goals of the Convention and on General Recommendation no. 25, see note 14 above, in which the CEDAW Committee clearly specified its own interpretation of the Convention.

24 This construction of a threefold strategy was published in various conference papers and in articles in Dutch legal journals as well as (for the first time in English) in Rikki Holtmaat (2003 (a)), see note 9 above. The groundwork for this construction can be found in earlier publications, e.g., Rikki Holtmaat, 'The Power of Legal Concepts: The Development of a Feminist Theory of Law', *International Journal of the Sociology of Law*, no. 5 (1989): 481–502; Rikki Holtmaat, 'The Issue of Overtime Payments for Part-Time Workers in the *Helmig* Case: Some Thoughts on Equality and Gender', in *The Regulation of Working Time in the European Union: Gender Approach*, ed. Yota Kravaritou, 411–444 (Brussels: P.I.E. Peter Lang, 1999); Rikki Holtmaat, 'Gender: The Analytical Concept that Tackles the Hidden Structural Bias of Law', in *Recht Richtung Frauen. Beiträge zur feministischen Rechtswissenschaft*, 159–182 (Lachen/St. Gallen: Dike Verlag, 2001).

1. An Individual Rights Strategy (IRS)
2. A Strategy for Social Support to groups that are in a disadvantaged position or are victims of discrimination[25] (SSS)
3. A Strategy for Social and Cultural Change (SSCC)

The following examples will make this empowering approach more concrete. In terms of combating and eliminating violence against women, the IRS would mean: granting victims the right to stand up against perpetrators and giving them legal entitlements to compensation and protection, including procedural rights and free legal aid. An individual right to be protected against violence also means that perpetrators cannot shield themselves behind 'cultural or religious defences', e.g., in the case of honour killings. The first aim of the CEDAW Convention, in connection to the IRS, means that all inherently 'unequal' laws should be abolished and that effective measures should be taken in order for protective laws to be implemented in practice. The second strategy (SSS) could mean creating social systems that make it possible for women to leave abusive husbands (e.g., granting them independent housing rights), developing programs for economic support of victims or giving victims free access to social services or social aid. The third strategy (SSCC) aims at changing social and cultural patterns of behaviour, ideologies and institutional structures in society that sustain the dominance of men over women or that negate the fundamental right of women to be free from violence and from threat of violence. It could mean the abolishment of certain parts of family law that are based on gendered presuppositions, e.g., the presupposition that the man is the breadwinner or the formal head of the household or that the man has patrimonial power over his children (instead of both parents sharing powers in that respect).

The main role of Article 5 (a) of the CEDAW Convention is that it *provides the legal basis for the third strategy.* This means that combating dominant gender stereotypes by means of a SSCC not only should be seen as a *desirable goal* or a *good practice* that should be advocated for, but that it should be acknowledged that there is a *legal obligation* for states parties to the CEDAW Convention to develop such a strategy. What exactly this obligation entails will be discussed in the next paragraph of this chapter.

The Meaning and Scope of Article 5 (a) of the CEDAW Convention

In the Netherlands, a debate has been going on for some time about the exact meaning and scope of Article 5 (a) of the CEDAW Convention. This discussion started with some academic studies and official reports in the 1990s and was – to some extent – concluded with the in-depth research I conducted on this particu-

25 The term 'discrimination' here is to be understood in the way it is defined in the CEDAW Convention, ergo, including violence against women.

lar provision in 2004.[26] For that purpose, I analysed the history of the Convention and the *Traveaux Préparatoires*, the interpretation of this provision by the CEDAW Committee, the history of ratification legislation in the Netherlands and the discussions in national and international academic literature.[27] The findings of this research are briefly repeated here.[28]

The Content of the Obligation to Combat Gender Stereotypes

The central question for consideration is: what is precisely the *content* of Article 5 (a) of the CEDAW Convention? In other words, what must a state party to the Convention do in order to implement this provision loyally, with due diligence, in a timely fashion (without delay) and in good faith. What are the 'appropriate measures' that states parties should take? Two kinds of obligations have surfaced during the research: (1) a duty to ban stereotypes from public life and (2) a duty to ban them from law and public policy. Both types of obligations are reflected in the way in which the CEDAW Committee, in its recent General Recommendation no. 25, interprets Article 5 (a). As mentioned above, the Committee connects this provision to the third objective of the Convention 'to address prevailing gender relations and the persistence of gender-based stereotypes that affect women not only through individual acts by individuals but also in law, and legal and societal structures and institutions'.[29]

The duty to banish negative gender stereotypes from social and cultural life

Based on Article 5 (a) of the CEDAW Convention, states parties have a duty to intervene in those social relations and institutions in which negative and damaging stereotyped images and views about women are expressed and/or used. This would embrace (re)presentations (that is, the image and presence or non-presence) of men and women in the media and in commercial advertising, (re)presentations of female and male roles in pornography and negative images that inspire violence against women. The CEDAW Committee does not leave any

26 See E. Lijnzaad, 'Over rollenpatronen en de rol van het Verdrag', in *Het Vrouwenverdrag: een beeld van een verdrag...*, ed. A.W. Heringa, J. Hes and E. Lijnzaad, 43–57 (Antwerpen/Apeldoorn: Maklu, 1994); J.C. Hes and C.E. van Vleuten, *Het Vrouwenverdrag in de Nederlandse rechtsorde* (Den Haag: Ministerie van Sociale Zaken en Werkgelegenheid, 1996); N. Holtrust, A.C. Hendriks and D.M.J. Bauduin ed., *De betekenis van artikel 12 Vrouwenverdrag voor Nederland: gezondheid als recht* (Den Haag: Ministerie van Sociale Zaken en Werkgelegenheid, 1996); Monster et al. (1998), see note 12 above; Groenman et al. (1997), see note 13 above.

27 See Holtmaat (2004), note 8 above. An extensive description of the findings in these sources was included in chapters 6–10 of that publication. The findings were summarised in chapter 11. Where appropriate, parts of that publication have been used literally in this chapter.

28 In the next paragraph of this chapter I will discuss the meaning and scope of this provision in relation to combating violence against women.

29 General Recommendation no. 25, see note 14 above, para. 7.

room for discussion that states parties are indeed obliged to develop and implement active policies in this field. This also includes teaching materials.[30]

In a Concluding Comment[31] on Morocco, the CEDAW Committee gives directions as to how the state party should contribute to the elimination of gender stereotypes in society:

> 'The Committee recommended the establishment of specific machinery located at the highest policy level, with adequate financial and human resources, that would co-ordinate and guide action in favour of women, would be able to prevent the persistence of attitudes, prejudices and stereotypes that discriminate against women and would narrow the gap between *de jure* and *de facto* equality.'[32]

On a number of occasions the Committee has expressed its approval about informative activities of the states parties.[33] The Committee also regularly urges states parties to undertake more activities in this field, especially through the media and in schools. What this can mean is expressed in a Concluding Comment on the situation in Lithuania:

> 'The Committee urges the Government to design and implement comprehensive programmes in education and the mass media in order to promote roles and tasks of women and men in all sectors of society. It also recommends that the draft Code of Advertising Ethics be amended in order to cover not only the prohibition of the promotion of discrimination against women and men, or of the alleged superiority of one sex over the other, but also of the more subtle utilization of and support for traditional role stereotypes in the family, in employment and in society.'[34]

---

30 As mentioned above, discussions about the obligations with respect to change the cultural bias against women in teaching materials are often conducted under the heading of Article 10 of the Convention.

31 Concluding Comments are the documents drawn up after each session of the Committee in which it has examined the obligatory reports by the member states.

32 Concluding Comment on Morocco (1997), UN Docs A/52/38, CEDAW/C/SR. 312, 313 and 320, para. 72.

33 Concluding Comment on Cyprus (1996), UN Docs A/51/38, CEDAW/C/SR.287, para. 51.

34 Concluding Comment on Lithuania (2000), UN Docs A/55/38, CEDAW/C/SR. 472, 473 and 480, para. 139. See also, e.g., Concluding Comments on Romania (2000), UN Docs A/55/38, CEDAW/C/SR. 481 and 482, para. 303; Concluding Comments on Egypt (2001), UN Docs A/56/38, CEDAW/C/SR. 492 and 493, paras. 334, 335; Concluding Comments on Vietnam (2001), UN Docs A/56/38, CEDAW/C/SR. 518 and 519, para. 251; and Concluding Comments on Estonia (2002), UN Docs A/57/38, CEDAW/C/SR. 539, 540 and 548, paras. 25, 26.

However, the scope for a government to bring about real change at the level of individual gender identity and at the symbolic level[35] is limited.[36] This is a good enough reason to pay particular attention to the second level at which the construction of gender stereotypes takes place: the level of social structures and institutions.

The duty to ban gender stereotypes from law and public policy

In the second place, Article 5 (a) of the CEDAW Convention (in combination with Article 2 (f)) implies that states parties have the duty to take all appropriate measures to track down and eliminate gender stereotypes that are at the basis of law and public policy. It is maintained that such stereotyped ideas (e.g., about different roles of men and women in the family or about the suitability of women for certain types of work) are present in many laws (e.g., breadwinner provisions in social security) or public policies (e.g., social benefits or education policies) and thereby sustain certain, fixed, gender divisions in society. The government itself is possibly culpable in terms of breaching the Convention's norms, and it is the government itself that has the responsibility to put an end to this situation.

However, opinions differ widely about how far-reaching this duty is. At one side of the spectrum there are authors who, at present, derive no concrete obligation from Article 5 (a) of the CEDAW Convention.[37] At the other side, there is the view that this provision obliges states parties to take very rigorous measures, such as abolishing all breadwinner provisions in the social security system.[38] These latter measures, however, should be taken with regard to the second objective of the CEDAW Convention: the improvement of the *de facto* position of women. That is to say that any measure undertaken on the basis of Article 5 (a) of the CEDAW Convention should be tested against the criterion of whether they have a genuinely positive effect on the conditions of life and the human rights of women.

Moreover, there are arguments contending that this provision of the Convention not only contains a negative obligation to eliminate all instances of damaging gender stereotypes in practice and in law, but also a positive obligation to

35 Holtmaat (2004), see note 8 above, chapter 13, a distinction is being made between two levels on which the construction of gender relations takes place: on the level of individual gender identity and symbolic representations of maleness and femaleness and on the level of structures and institutions in society. This distinction goes back to the works of Joan Wallach Scott, 'Deconstructing Equality-Versus-Difference: Or, the Uses of Poststructuralist Theory for Feminism,' *Feminist Studies*, no. 1 (1988): 33–50 and 'Gender: A Useful Category of Historical Analysis,' in *Coming to Terms*, ed. Elizabeth Weed, 81–100 (London: Routledge, 1998). (Originally published in *American Historical Review* (1986): 1053–1075.) See also Holtmaat (2001), note 24 above.

36 Among others, on the grounds of civil liberties that are guaranteed by national constitutions and in International Human Rights Conventions. See below.

37 E.g., Lijnzaad (1994), see note 26 above; and L. Lijnzaad, 'Het kussen van een kikker,' *Nemesis* 13, no. 2 (1991): 5–15.

38 E.g., Monster et al. (1998), see note 12 above.

take measures to enable men and women to take on different (than traditional or stereotyped) roles. An example could be the design of a system of parental leave that encourages or even requires fathers to take on caring activities.[39] In relation to violence against women, one could think of measures like restructuring family law or social law in such a way that more diversity in gender roles will become possible.

The duty to ban gender stereotypes from law and public policies can be rephrased as the duty to ban systemic or structural gender discrimination. From the analysis of the Concluding Comments of the CEDAW Committee it becomes apparent that the Committee at this point in history does not yet have a very clear view of how far-reaching this obligation is. However, the statement that there exists *no* such obligation is untenable in the view of the many concrete directions issued by the Committee. In several Concluding Comments a connection is made between on the one hand the obligation to eliminate gender stereotypes and on the other hand the necessity of a profound revision of existing legislation and public policy that maintain these stereotypes. The Committee urges the states parties, in clear language that cannot be misunderstood, to change such laws and public policy. The most far-reaching remark in that respect can be found in a Concluding Comment about Ireland, where the Committee is of the opinion that the Irish Constitution reflects a stereotyped image of the roles of women 'in the home and as mothers' and urges the Parliamentary Committee that works on a revision of the Constitution to be 'fully aware of Ireland's obligations under the Convention, including article 5'.[40] In other words: the Committee makes a direct link between the continued existence of gender stereotypes and the existence of certain laws in which these stereotypes are reaffirmed.[41] Sometimes the Committee connects this problem with the obligation to (also) combat indirect discrimination in law and make lawyers sensitive to this type of discrimination:

> 'The Committee recommended that Italy expand its existing legislation and/or enact new legislation, where needed, in order to effectively deal with the phenomenon of indirect discrimination. To that end it emphasized the importance of measures to sensitize judges, lawyers and law enforcement personnel to indirect discrimination and to Italy's international obligations, in particular those outlined in the Convention.'[42]

39 See Concluding Comments on Norway (1995), UN Docs A/50/38, CEDAW/C/SR.277, para. 486. See also Concluding Comments on Finland (1995), UN Docs A/50/38, CEDAW/C/SR. 272, para. 388.

40 Concluding Comments on Ireland (1999), UN Docs A/54/38, CEDAW/C/S. 440 and 441, paras. 193, 194.

41 Concluding Comments on Venezuela (1997), UN Docs A/52/38, CEDAW/C/SR. 323 and 324, para. 223; Concluding Comments on Mexico (1998), UN Docs A/53/38, CEDAW/C/SR. 376 and 377, para. 398; and Concluding Comments on Thailand (1999), UN Docs A/54/38, CEDAW/C/SR. 417 and 418, paras. 244, 245.

42 Concluding Comments on Italy (1997), UN Docs A/52/38, CEDAW/C/SR. 346 and 347, para. 357.

In a Concluding Comment on the Fiji Islands, the Committee recommends working on '...changes in laws and administrative regulations to recognize women as heads of households, and the concept of shared economic contribution and household responsibilities'.[43] Finally, in a report about Croatia, a comment can be found as to how the government should eliminate gender stereotypes in law:

> 'The Committee recommends that the Government take advantage of existing bodies of knowledge relating to indirect and structural patterns of discrimination. It emphasizes that the Government, rather than women themselves, have primary responsibility for implementing strategies to eliminate these forms of discrimination'.[44]

From all this, it can be concluded that there certainly are concrete obligations for states to put an end to laws and policies based upon gender stereotypes which are detrimental to women. This can mean that it is necessary to withdraw or to change laws that have this effect. In order to establish whether this is indeed the case, in-depth studies of the basic assumptions about gender and gender roles lying at the basis of these laws need to take place.[45] As for new laws and policies, the already existing tools of gender impact assessments and gender mainstreaming can be used in order to avoid stereotypes continuing to be at the basis of legal and social structures.

Some Considerations about the Nature and Instrumental Value of Article 5 (a) of the CEDAW Convention

In this part I will discuss some specific issues concerning the nature and instrumental value of Article 5 (a) of the CEDAW Convention that came to the surface during the above-mentioned research.

A dynamic interpretation of Article 5 (a) of the CEDAW Convention

From the study it became apparent that the meaning of Article 5 (a) of the CEDAW Convention is not fixed but is changing quite markedly over time (as illustrated by a comparison between the *Traveaux Préparatoires* of the Convention and, e.g., the history of the Dutch Ratification Act and the General Recommendations and Concluding Comments of the CEDAW Committee). This observation accords with the general idea that the CEDAW Convention is a *living instrument*

43 Concluding Comments on Fiji Islands (2002), UN Docs A/57/38, CEDAW/C/SR. 530, 531 and 538, para. 32.

44 Concluding Comments on Croatia (1998), UN Docs A/53/38, CEDAW/C/SR. 363, 364 and 368, para. 113.

45 The framework of this chapter does not allow me to expand on the ways in which these mechanisms and tools could become operational in the context of the implementation of Article 5 (a) of the CEDAW Convention. See Holtmaat (2004), note 8 above, chapter 15, where methodological directions and starting points for the eradication of structural gender discrimination are discussed in great detail.

that requires dynamic interpretation and implementation.[46] Below an impression is given of the changes in meaning and scope of this provision.

From awareness raising to structural change

The original meaning of Article 5 (a) of the CEDAW Convention mainly appears to aim at information campaigns and education, and the influencing or correcting of the media and advertising. Over the course of time, the CEDAW Committee developed a sense of the structural effects of the (continued) existence of negative and damaging images and ideas about women. The Committee has connected this 'evil' to almost all forms of structural subordination of women, especially in connection with paid labour, health and healthcare, family law and violence against women. The Committee not only considers that education, information and a change of mentality are important, but increasingly has moved to urge states parties to tackle the problem at a *structural level*, i.e., to do something about unequal payment of women, segregation in the labour market, the lack of scope for women to work full time and be economically independent, the disadvantaged position of women in family law, and so on.

From equality as sameness to equality as transformation

The shift from focussing on stereotypes as *a problem of mentality* to stereotypes as *a source of structural discrimination*[47] is especially evident in the legal literature and in-depth studies carried out in the Netherlands on the meaning and scope of the CEDAW Convention.[48] It seems that from early in the implementation history of the Convention in this country, Article 5 (a) of the CEDAW Convention has been interpreted to (also) imply a pressure for 'cultural change'. In Dutch legal literature the conclusion is that Article 5 (a) adds something special to the current interpretation of the non-discrimination principle.[49] Since this provision has such an important place in the Convention, it is assumed that the prohibition of discrimination in the CEDAW Convention not only seeks to offer individual women legal protection against discrimination, but also demands that attention be paid

46 Rebecca Cook states that the Committee can give autonomous interpretations of the meaning of the Convention's provisions: Cook (1994 (b)), see note 9 above, 234. See also Groenman et al. (1997), note 13 above, 9 and 31.

47 In the study the term structural or systemic discrimination is used in addition to the concepts of direct and indirect discrimination. See Holtmaat (2004), note 8 above, 18–19 and chapter 13, para. 2.

48 It should be noted that in the same period there was a lot of attention to *beeldvorming* (the construction of gender-stereotyped images) in Dutch emancipation policy and in feminist studies, and that the instrument of Gender Impact Assessment was developed. These texts undoubtedly have influenced the legal discussions about the meaning of Article 5 (a) of the CEDAW Convention. A description and analysis of this policy and these studies can be found in chapter 14 of Holtmaat (2004), see note 8 above.

49 See, e.g., Hes and Van Vleuten (1996), note 26 above; and Wentholt (1997), note 9 above.

to the structural causes of discrimination. In English-language legal literature this idea can be found in the work of Rebecca Cook, who grounds this obligation on a combined reading of Articles 2 (f) and 5 (a) of the CEDAW Convention.[50] It can also be found in the work of Sandra Fredman, who sees this Article as the expression of the (acknowledged) need for a transformation of society so that structural barriers which stand in the way of 'real' equality are overcome.[51]

In my opinion, Article 5 (a) of the CEDAW Convention not only expresses the principle of equality, but also the principle of diversity or freedom. That is, the possibility for individuals to make their own choices about what it means to be a man or a woman without being confined by social institutions or organisation to a traditional understanding of masculinity or femininity. The significance of Article 5 (a) of the CEDAW Convention can be summarised very briefly in the proposition that it is an expression of *equality as transformation*.[52] This means that the principle of equality and non-discrimination, as it has been laid down in the Convention, not only requires the *same* or *identical* rights for women but also the development of *different* law and public policy.

The instrumental value of Article 5 (a) of the CEDAW Convention

As with all law, in human rights theory the process of how to get from law in the books to law in action is one of the key issues. We can discern two principal ways in which this specific type of legal standards can become *law in action*. Internationally agreed human rights standards can be used:

1. as a legal basis for (new) policies and legislation (advocacy strategy)
2. as a basis for individual and group litigation (litigation strategy)

Traditionally, in human rights discourse, the second strategy has gained far more attention than the first. Human rights, thus understood, give individuals entitlements to stand up in court against human rights violations (especially by the state). However, I am of the opinion that the first strategy is most important and most fruitful in the case of this specific obligation in the CEDAW Convention. Therefore, some words need to be spent on what this strategy entails.

Human rights can (and should) serve as a legitimate basis for enacting certain legislation, for taking certain policy measures or for spending money on some social problems (and consequently not on others). For example, a government can enact a law in which women and girls get the right to bring a court action for an injunction against the perpetrator of domestic violence, based on international human rights standards in this respect (e.g., based on Article 24 sub (f) of

50 Cook (1994 (b)), see note 9 above; and Rebecca Cook, 'Obligations to Adopt Temporary Special Measures under CEDAW', in Boerefijn et al. (2003), see note 14 above, 119–141.

51 Sandra Fredman, 'Beyond the Dichotomy of Formal and Substantive Equality: Towards New Definitions of Equal Rights', in Boerefijn et al. (2003), see note 14 above, 111–118.

52 This term comes from Fredman (2003), ibid.

General Recommendation no. 19 on Violence against Women.) This means that human right standards can play an *argumentative* role in the political process and in processes of policymaking or the construction of development programs. Secondly, human rights provisions can form the *constitutive basis* of such legislation, policy measures or budget decisions. An example would be to base the decision to spend a considerable amount of money on shelters for battered women on the Commission on Human Rights Resolution 2003/45 on the Elimination of Violence against Women. Human rights can only play this role when there is a strongly developed sense that they contain specific, concrete obligations for states to meet certain human rights standards or to maintain these standards. In connection to this basic function, human rights can become a *tool for analysis* (scrutinising whether the national situation is sufficiently in conformity with international standards) and for *advocacy* (advocating for a correct implementation in national legislation and policies).[53]

The legal literature contains a great deal of discussion about the nature of the obligations arising under the CEDAW Convention in general. It can often be read that the Convention only contains so-called 'instruction norms' which cannot provide any enforceable legal rights available to women in individual litigation. Although in general it is *not* the case that this Convention does not entail any such rights,[54] it seems that Article 5 (a) is indeed phrased in such a way that it is hard to assume that (at this point in history) it could have direct effect in the sense that an individual woman could rely on it in legal proceedings. The wording of the Article is not sufficiently clear and precise to have this direct effect. This means the provision has to be primarily considered as an instruction norm, directed at the states parties.[55] What it instructs them to do is discussed below.

However, this provision can be of central importance in the first implementation strategy, as described above. In the context of legislation and policymaking Article 5 (a) of the CEDAW Convention can (and should, as we have seen above) be used as a yardstick against which to gauge whether laws and policies are free of stereotyped views about gender relations.[56] In addition, Article 5 (a) of the CEDAW Convention can also be used as a 'hat peg provision', that is, an interpretative framework on the basis of which the scope of the Convention might

53 For an example of how this can be done in the case of domestic violence, see Nicolić-Ristanović and Dokmanović (2006), note 1 above.

54 Heringa et al. (1994), see note 26 above.

55 However, this should not be taken to mean that Article 5 (a) of the CEDAW Convention cannot play any role at all in individual sex discrimination cases. The prohibition of gender stereotypes is an important norm when assessing whether there is a case of 'equal or comparable situations' or whether there is 'unequal treatment'. In the report on the study it is argued that Article 5 (a) could play an important supporting role as an interpretative framework to be applied in all sex discrimination cases. The use of this norm could help prevent the assimilating effect of equal treatment legislation as it exists now.

56 Wentholt (1997), see note 9 above.

be extended, as has been the case with violence against women, which was not included in the original Convention.[57] In the future other issues might be considered as discrimination in the same manner, based on such an extensive reading of the CEDAW Convention. Article 5 (a) therefore plays an important role in a dynamic interpretation of the Convention and helps render it a living instrument. Finally and perhaps most important, the instrumental value of this provision lies in the fact that it can serve as *a legitimate ground* for action by governments to combat negative and damaging stereotypes that are expressed in or distributed across society.[58]

The Scope of the Obligations under Article 5 (a) of the CEDAW Convention

On the basis of the legal literature and the General Recommendations issued by the CEDAW Committee, it is clear that the Convention in general can have an impact both on the relationships between government and citizens (vertical relationships) as well as between citizens themselves (horizontal relationships). In the latter case, relationships between citizens in the public sphere (when engaging with others, for example in paid labour, healthcare, education or banking) are distinguished from relationships in the intimate, private sphere of the home. Should the government – on the basis of the CEDAW Convention – issue legislation that affects this intimate or private sphere, it runs the risk of breaching the human right of privacy of the home or of family life. Although, under certain conditions, it seems to be acceptable that a state party takes measures based on this Convention that interfere in the intimate, private sphere,[59] this does not seem to be possible when the state takes such measures on the ground of Article 5 (a)

57 See Lijnzaad (1994), note 26 above. The fact that Article 5 (a) of the CEDAW Convention is not only a norm that stands on its own, but also serves as a provision that helps to fill in the content of other Articles in the Convention, can be inferred from the way in which the CEDAW Committee regularly refers to the obligation to eliminate sex stereotypes in other General Recommendations. This is very clear in the two General Recommendations (numbers 12 and 19) that the Committee has issued about violence against women. This subject is not explicitly regulated under the Convention. The Committee uses (among others) Article 5 (a) as a peg on which it can hang this subject under the overall scope of the Convention. This is done by making a direct link between negative stereotyping of women and violence against women.

58 Lijnzaad (1994), see note 26 above.

59 This certainly is the case as far as specific protective measures against violence against women are at stake. States are under a duty to protect women against violence as far as possible, no matter where this violence takes place, and cannot hide behind a divide between public and private spheres to avoid responsibility. The argument here concerns the obligation of the state to take general preventive measures. In that case, a different weighing of interests takes place: the general interest to eradicate stereotypes that lie at the basis of violence against women must be balanced against the specific interest to be free from state interference in the sphere of private intimate relationships.

of the CEDAW Convention. From the words 'to modify the *social and cultural patterns of conduct* [emphasis added]' it appears that this provision is directed in the first instance at the sphere of (open or covert) expressions of negative and damaging stereotypes about the roles of men and women in public, both in vertical and horizontal relationships. Expressions of gender stereotypes that take place in the private, intimate sphere do not seem to be covered by Article 5 (a) of the CEDAW Convention. Indirectly, measures undertaken by government or employers, healthcare institutions or schools[60] to combat such expressions can (and hopefully will) have an impact on the private or intimate relationships between people.

The Obligations of Article 5 (a) in Relation to Combating Violence against Women

This section discusses findings with respect to the meaning of Article 5 (a) in the context of combating gender-based violence. In addition, some remarks will be made about possible conflicts between obligations that stem from this Article and other human rights obligations of the state, e.g., to respect and protect the freedom of expression or the freedom of religion. And, what room is left for cultural or religious identities of certain (minority) groups?

Some Findings about the Meaning of Article 5 (a) of the CEDAW Convention in Relation to Combating Violence against Women

During the above-mentioned research, it appeared that at various places in the sources analysed, there were references to the importance of Article 5 (a) of the CEDAW Convention to combating violence against women or gender-based violence. These discussions mainly concerned the first type of obligations of the state under this provision, namely to banish negative gender stereotypes from social and cultural life.

In the first place, Article 5 (a) of the CEDAW Convention has been used as the legal basis for the extensive interpretation of the concept of discrimination in the Convention to (also) include a prohibition of violence against women. In connection to this, the norm entailed in Article 5 (a) of the CEDAW Convention is elaborated in Article 24, paragraphs d to f of General Recommendation no. 19 on Violence against Women adopted by the CEDAW Committee, in which the states parties are enjoined to take effective measures to ensure 'that media respect and promote respect for women', that in their Country Reports they should 'identify the nature and extent of attitudes, customs and practices that perpetuate violence

60 These organisations and institutions can take such measures on their own accord or they can be instigated by the government on the basis of the CEDAW Convention.

against women' and that they 'should take effective measures to overcome these attitudes and practices'.[61]

In the second place, Article 5 (a) of the Convention is discussed in detail in the Instructions that the CEDAW Committee has made available to the states parties on how they should report on their implementation of the Convention and progress in this respect.[62] In this document the Committee underlines the significance of this provision, shows that it is important for various subjects that fall under the scope of the Convention and presents a long list of questions that need to be answered in relation to this Article. On the specific issue of violence against women, and its relationship to Article 5 (a) of the CEDAW Convention, the Committee warns that prejudices and traditional practices cannot serve as a justification for gender-based violence. The list of questions proposed by the Committee clearly indicates that it is not only interested in how traditional customs and practices determine religious and cultural life, but also how these are reflected in law and public policy. For example, the Committee wants to know who is considered to be the 'head of the household', according to national law, and whether women are banned from practicing certain occupations.[63]

Thirdly, the Concluding Comments of the CEDAW Committee contain many references to Article 5 (a) in relation to the topic of violence against women. The CEDAW Committee frequently makes a link between violence against women, trafficking and prostitution and the failure to implement this Article.[64] An example of how the Committee sees the relationship between this issue and women's economic dependence can be read in a report of the constructive dialogue with Zambia, in which the representative of the Zambian government summarises this problem in the following way:

> 'Violence against women was widespread and even traditionally accepted as a way of disciplining a wife... Since most women were economically dependent on their husbands and afraid to lose their matrimonial home, they were very reluctant to prosecute

61 In the latter consideration an explicit reference is made to General Recommendation no. 3 about Article 5 (a) of the CEDAW Convention.

62 UN Division on the Advancement of Women, *Assessing the Status of Women: A Guide to Reporting Under the Convention on the Elimination of All Forms of Discrimination against Women* (New York: United Nations, 2000).

63 *UN Manual on Human Rights Reporting under Six Major International Human Rights Instruments* (Geneva: United Nations, 1997), 322–324.

64 Exploitation, prostitution and trafficking in women is prohibited in Article 6 of the CEDAW Convention. Since there is no provision prohibiting (sexual) violence against women in the Convention, the reporting and discussing of the issue of violence often takes place under the heading of Article 5. E.g., Concluding Comments on Uganda (1995), UN Doc. A/50/38, CEDAW/C/SR. 270 and 273, para. 332. The topic is also discussed in relation to General Recommendations no. 12 and no. 19.

their aggressors. Some women did not admit that they had been abused and considered battering as a sign of man's affection.'[65]

The Committee also often links the existence of gender stereotypes with the problem of sexual harassment in the workplace.[66] The issue of pornography is raised only a few times in the context of the discussion of Article 5 (a), at the same time stressing that legislation needs to be enacted that limits this phenomenon.[67] A review of the Concluding Comments reveals that the Committee does not always discuss Article 5 (a) of the CEDAW Convention as a freestanding obligation, but is increasingly making a connection between this provision and specific obligations under the Convention in relation to labour, health, political participation, violence against women and other relevant issues.

One further visible development is that over the years the Committee has placed less and less emphasis on information campaigns and education and has instead increasingly argued for concrete action to be taken (for example, with regards to violence against women based on gender stereotypes or unequal pay and labour market segregation). Finally, it is noteworthy that the Committee repeatedly stresses that formal equal treatment in law and public policymaking is not sufficient, and that there should be a critical review as to whether law and policy remains based on stereotyped role models and traditional ideas of masculinity and femininity.

Also in the Dutch sources, I have found evidence of the relevance of Article 5 (a) of the CEDAW Convention for the topic of violence against women. During the ratification procedure the Dutch government expressly conceded that there is a connection between gender stereotypes and violence against women, and that the Convention entails an obligation to put an end to this violence.[68] One of the in-depth studies that were carried out in the Netherlands about the content and scope of the CEDAW Convention and about necessary national legal and policy implementation measures puts great emphasis on the relationship between Article 5 (a) and the topic of violence against women.[69] Also, in international legal

65 Concluding Comments on Zambia (1994), UN Docs A/49/38, CEDAW/C/SR. 241 and 246, para. 330.

66 E.g., Concluding Comments on Japan (1994), UN Docs A/49/38, CEDAW/C/SR. 248 and 249, para. 570.

67 E.g., Concluding Comments on New Zealand (1994), UN Docs A/49/38, CEDAW/C/SR. 243, para. 641.

68 Documents of parliament: TK 1984–1985, 18 950 (R 1281), VV, nr. 4, 14 and TK 1986–1987, 18 950 (R1281), MvA, no. 6, 28.

69 Ineke Boerefijn, Mignon van der Liet-Senders and Titia Loenen, *Het voorkomen en bestrijden van geweld tegen vrouwen. Een verdiepend onderzoek naar het Nederlandse beleid in het licht van de verplichtingen die voortvloeien uit het Vrouwenverdrag* (Den Haag: Ministerie van Sociale Zaken en Werkgelegenheid, 2000). A summary of this report in English has been published as an appendix to the third periodic report of the Netherlands (UN Doc. CEDAW C/net/3, 25th session) of the Netherlands to the

literature Article 5 (a) is sometimes connected to the issue of violence against women. An example is the work of Rebecca Cook, who asserts that the Articles 2 (f) and 5 (a) of the CEDAW Convention play an important role in preventing and combating violence against women.[70]

Some Remarks about the Possible Conflicts between Article 5 (a) of the CEDAW Convention and Other Human Rights Obligations and about the Danger of Cultural Hegemony

The possible conflict with other human rights

At various points in the sources that were analysed for the in-depth study on the meaning and scope of Article 5 (a) of the CEDAW Convention, it appeared that the first duty of the state parties (banishing negative stereotypes from social and cultural life) is especially sometimes seen as problematic. Here, I briefly present some of these discussions.

Above, I have discussed the distinction between the public sphere (both in vertical and horizontal relations) and the private, intimate sphere of the home. There I held that Article 5 (a) cannot (or at least not yet) serve as a legal ground for taking measures that directly intervene in the private, intimate sphere. Even if a state party, in taking all appropriate measures to eliminate gender stereotypes, limits itself to the public sphere, the question may arise as to how far other constitutionally guaranteed human rights or civil rights (such as freedom of expression or freedom of religion) may be curtailed. Although many commentators discuss this issue and urge caution, these discussions would not warrant the proposition that such freedoms could prevent the application or implementation of Article 5 (a) of the CEDAW Convention altogether. As the Ethiopian Member of the Preparatory Committee stated, 'freedoms are not unlimited'.[71] In theory and practice they can be limited by other rights, such as not to be discriminated against on grounds of sex.[72] This opinion was also expressed by the authors of the Dutch 'Report on the impact of the CEDAW Convention on policy and legislation dealing with violence against women.' For them, a key consideration is the extent to which Article 5 (a) of the CEDAW Convention is weighed against other constitutional rights such as freedom of expression and freedom of religion. However, if it can be established that there is a causal relationship between negative gender stereotypes and sex-based violence, the rights to freedom of expression and freedom of religion should be afforded less protection on the ground of the principle of propor-

CEDAW Committee. The authors point at some reports of the Dutch Emancipation Council (*Emancipatieraad*) and to some UN documents, like the *Beijing Platform for Action*, in which this connection is also made.

70 Cook (1994 (b)), see note 9 above, 239–240.

71 Lars Adam Rehof, *Guide to the Traveaux préparatoires of the United Nations Convention on the Elimination of All Forms of Discrimination against Women* (Dordrecht/Boston/London: Martin Nijhoff Publishers, 1993), 80.

72 Cook (1994 (b)), see note 9 above, 241.

tionality.[73] The authors conclude that the Dutch government is too cautious not to interfere with the right to freedom of expression and that more should be done to combat the negative effects of gender stereotypes.[74]

The fact that the rights to freedom of expression and religion are not absolute means that a government that wants to put an end to gender-based violence and takes measures to that effect can cite Article 5 (a) of the CEDAW Convention as a legal basis for such measures. That is to say, if certain measures are contested as representing an encroachment on certain civil rights, it could be argued that this is justifiable on the grounds that Article 5 (a) of the CEDAW Convention requires such measures to be taken.[75] States parties are under all circumstances required to implement the Convention's obligations loyally, with due diligence, in a timely fashion and in good faith.[76] This is also the case with this provision.

The danger of cultural hegemony

In the previous section it has been made clear that in the possible clash between the right not to be subjected to gender-based violence and other civil rights, the first right will outweigh the latter. This is not only the case when specific protective measures are at stake, but also – to some extent[77] – when general preventive measures on the basis of Article 5 (a) of the CEDAW Convention are being taken. The following should be read with this standpoint in mind.[78]

The central aim of Article 5 (a) of the CEDAW Convention is to eliminate or abolish all traditional customs and practices that are damaging for the fulfilment of all the human rights of women, including those laid down in law or religious injunctions. This so-called 'abolitionist' method has been severely criticised in some human rights literature. The non-discrimination norms included in international law are held by some as to be too one-sided and unsuitable for the abolition of all forms of discrimination against women. In addition, this approach is said to deny the fact that women may have rights which are important for them as a result of some cultural and customary practices. As Celestine I. Nyamu wrote:

---

73 Boerefijn et al. (2000), see note 69 above, 39.

74 Boerefijn et al. (2000), see note 69 above, e.g., 106, 209 and 266.

75 Provided that they are proportional to this aim and appropriate and necessary to reach that aim.

76 Cook (1994 (b)), see note 9 above.

77 That has been argued only to the extent that these measures concern the public sphere, be it in horizontal or in vertical relations. Expressions of stereotypes in the private, intimate sphere are not considered to be covered by Article 5 (a) of the CEDAW Convention.

78 Therefore, it should not be concluded from the following that I take a 'cultural relativist' stance. Traditional culture and religion, in my view, can never be used as an excuse for the violation of basic human rights of women. See for an extensive discussion of this topic Frances Raday, 'Culture, Religion and Gender', *ICON* 1, no. 4 (2003): 663–715.

> 'Some critics have pointed out that these abolitionist responses create the impression that women's rights do not exist in custom or local practice, and that the solution therefore lies in substituting custom and local practice with alternatives offered by national legislation or the international human rights regime. Furthermore, the abolitionist approach does not encourage a holistic understanding of the context in which these practices are embedded, and as a result, prevents comprehensive solutions. The abolitionist approach has also suffered counter-accusations of cultural imperialism from interested Third World states.'[79]

I fully acknowledge that this danger does indeed exist and therefore subscribe to the importance of the alternative method of so-called cross-cultural dialogue.[80] This means that, for the purpose of guaranteeing all human rights of women, it cannot be assumed that the non-discrimination (or equal treatment) standards enshrined in national or international legal instruments are better or more suitable than norms that can be found in a number of cultures and customs. It is important to remember that the CEDAW Convention not only demands that formal equality be established and that gender negative and damaging gender stereotypes be banished, but also demands that the position of women be improved.[81] This means that instead of simply applying an abstract and general equal treatment norm and the radical elimination of customs and traditions, much attention must be paid to the concrete daily circumstances in which women need to realise their human rights. What is necessary in that respect is expressed by Nyamu in the following passage of her important essay:

> 'The non-abolitionist approach, therefore, calls for a non-hegemonic human rights practice that incorporates the two simultaneous processes of internal discourse and cross-cultural dialogue, in order to find legitimacy for human rights principles within all cultures.'[82]

79 Celestine I. Nyamu, 'How Should Human Rights and Development Respond to Cultural Legitimization of Gender Hierarchy in Developing Countries?', *Harvard International Law Journal* (2000): 381–418.
At this place Nyamu refers to works of Thandabantu Nhlapo, Daniel A. Bell and Katha Pollit.

80 See also Rikki Holtmaat, 'De meerwaarde van het Vrouwenverdrag in de multiculturele samenleving', in *Eén Verdrag voor alle vrouwen. Verkenningen van de betekenis van het VN-Vrouwenverdrag voor de multiculturele samenleving*, ed. Rikki Holtmaat, 129–145 (Den Haag: E-Quality, 2002).

81 In particular, if the right to equal treatment of women is understood in a formal sense (of treating likes alike) there is certainly no guarantee that this will have a positive effect on the situation of women. In Western countries the application of such a formal right to equal treatment of men and women has often led to a worsening of the position of women.

82 Nyamu (2000), see note 79 above, 393, referring to the work of Abdullahi An-Na'im.

Conclusion: Some Final Notes about the Concept of Due Diligence in Relation to the Prevention of Violence against Women

In the introduction to this chapter I welcomed the move from a welfare/humanitarian approach to a human rights-based approach to preventing violence against women. Such an approach encompasses the internationally accepted due diligence norm. By way of conclusion to this chapter, I would like to discuss this norm a bit further.

The concept of due diligence appears to have become of increasing importance in the international human rights discourse on combating gender-based violence.[83] It has been held that this concept '...provides a yardstick to determine whether a state has met or failed to meet its obligations in combating violence against women.'[84] However, by following Ineke Boerefijn at this point, I think that this concept is rather vague and perhaps is not always the best standard in the fight against gender-based violence.[85] In many international documents legal obligations have been laid down about what states should do to combat and eliminate violence against women. These obligations often are much more precise and more far stretching than the general obligation 'to act with due diligence'. The concept seems to suggest that as long as the state argues that it has done *something* this is enough, no matter whether the internationally *agreed result* (i.e., the abolishment of gender stereotypes) has been achieved in due time or not. This means that there is a danger that concrete obligations of result are replaced with the due diligence obligation.[86] For breaching such legal obligations of result, the state can be held internationally *accountable*.[87] State accountability certainly exists when an act of violence against women is perpetrated by a state actor or actors (e.g., police forces) and when it concerns the obligation of states to remove

83 See note 6 above.

84 See Ertürk (2006), note 2 above, para. 14.

85 Ineke Boerefijn, *De blinddoek opzij, Een mensenrechtenbenadering van geweld tegen vrouwen*, Inaugural Speech, University of Maastricht 8 December 2006.

86 In human rights theory often a typology of two types of obligations is made: obligations to achieve a certain, specified result and obligations to do one's best to achieve some progress. Another argument against using the due diligence standard as the paramount standard is that, in my view, the obligation to act with due diligence is just one out of the four general requirements as to how states that are members to a treaty or convention should implement the obligations captured in it (specifying the even more general phrase of *Pacta sunt servanda*). States are also obliged to act loyally, in good faith and without delay. In addition it should be remarked that as yet it remains somewhat unclear how the duty to act with due diligence relates to the three types of obligations that are normally derived from international law: the duty to respect, to protect and to fulfil.

87 See, for a detailed discussion of the issue of state accountability under the Convention, Rebecca Cook, 'Women's International Human Rights Law: The Way Forward', in Cook (1994), see note 9 above, 3–36; and Cook (1994 (b)), note 9 above.

the structural causes of violence against women.[88] As for the first obligation: when the state fails to protect women against violence by state actors, this can be labelled as an *internationally wrongful act* for which a state is fully responsible.[89] As far as the obligation to remove the causes of discrimination is concerned, I have clarified in this chapter what the obligations of the states that are party to the CEDAW Convention are, so far as these causes lie in negative and damaging gender stereotypes. Article 5 (a) of the CEDAW Convention clearly obliges states to combat such gender stereotypes *with all appropriate means*. This norm contains two types of obligations (to combat stereotypes in social and cultural life and to eliminate gender stereotypes in law and public policies), both of which the state should fulfil *loyally, with due diligence, in good faith* and *without any delay*. When states fail to take action in that respect, the normal mechanisms of international supervision of this Convention must do their work in order to compel them to implement this norm.

It must be admitted that the obligations incumbent on states parties arising from Article 5 (a) of the CEDAW Convention are not easily enforceable. The CEDAW Committee's competence is quite limited, and in fact it is only a supervisory body.[90] It cannot impose sanctions even when there is an outright breach of the Convention's provisions. This means that only constant pressure on the part of human rights organisations and the women's movement will possibly have some impact in the long run. In that respect, the process of 'naming and shaming' – continuously revealing violations of the Convention's norms in the international arena – of states parties who fail to implement the Convention appropriately is extremely important. The effect of this process can be that states parties begin to change their behaviour in the sense that they start the process of actively combating gender-based violence, including those forms of violence embedded in national law and policy and in culture and customs.

88 At this point Ineke Boerefijn makes a distinction between acts of the state or of state representatives and the responsibility of states to protect women against violence in the private sphere. In the latter case, she admits, the concept of due diligence does have some meaning, since the state cannot be held accountable for all acts of private citizens, especially not when they take place in the intimate sphere of the home. Boerefijn (2006), see note 85 above, 16.

89 UN General Assembly, Resolution 56/83: Responsibility of States for Internationally Wrongful Acts.

90 Notwithstanding the fact that its powers have been extended on the ground of the Optional Protocol of October 6, 1999, which makes individual complaints possible. See UN Doc. A/RES/54/4, Optional Protocol to the Convention on the Elimination of All Forms of Discrimination against Women. The text of the Protocol is included in an Annex to this Resolution.

Emerging Human Rights Obligations for Non-State Actors

Ineke Boerefijn and Eva Naezer

Introduction

States are the main actors in the international law of human rights. They are the law-makers, in the sense that intergovernmental organisations adopt treaties that individual states can ratify, and non-binding instruments to which states have committed themselves. Further, they play an important role in the monitoring and enforcement of obligations under human rights instruments in the context of political organs such as the recently established UN Human Rights Council, successor of the UN Commission on Human Rights. States express their consent to be bound by international rules and have created monitoring mechanisms under a number of human rights treaties, thus advancing accountability. International organs composed of independent experts, such as the UN Committee on the Elimination of Discrimination against Women (CEDAW Committee), play a major role in making states' obligations more concrete and in enhancing compliance with the obligations they have undertaken. The establishment of monitoring mechanisms has thus contributed significantly to the strengthening of international human rights law.

States are, however, not the only actors that have an impact on human rights of individuals. Non-state actors, such as international organisations, transnational corporations and individuals, are also capable of infringing on human rights. The role of such actors at the domestic and international level has changed in the past decades. In many cases they play a role as important as states. The European Union, for example, is an important actor in the international arena, but it is – so far – not a party to any human rights treaty. The activities of other international organisations, such as the United Nations and its specialised agencies, also affect human rights. Organisations such as the World Bank and the International Monetary Fund (IMF) can take actions that facilitate the promotion of human rights, but also either directly violate human rights or indirectly by more or less forcing states into non-compliance with obligations under human rights treaties. For example, where the World Bank requires states to maintain or even increase fees

C. Benninger-Budel ed., Due Diligence and Its Application to Protect Women from Violence
 ISBN 978 90 04 16293 8. pp. 91-107

for primary education, instead of abolishing them as required under Article 13 of the International Covenant on Economic, Social and Cultural Rights (ICESCR), it contributes to the state's non-compliance with its obligations under international human rights law. Yet these organisations do not (and, at present, cannot) ratify human rights instruments and cannot be called on to submit periodic reports to the Committee on Economic, Social and Cultural Rights (ESC Committee) – although the latter may issue recommendations to specialised agencies under Article 22 ICESCR.[1] Thus, they are not held accountable before the international monitoring bodies. The extent of their obligations to respect and protect human rights is the subject of much debate.[2]

Transnational corporations can be more powerful than the government that hosts them. Also their activities can have a great influence on the enjoyment of human rights; for example, they can discriminate against women in remuneration or profit from forced labour. States may be unwilling or incapable of holding them accountable for their behaviour. As a consequence, infringements on human rights committed by enterprises often remain unaddressed. The same can be said about armed groups distinct from the armed forces of a state exercising control over a territory. They are often involved in human rights violations, including violations of women's human rights. Such groups exercise power over territory and individuals, yet they are not in a position to ratify international human rights instruments.

The situation is somewhat different for private individuals. Whereas actions of the above-mentioned non-state actors remain unaddressed by states because of their strong position *vis-à-vis* the state, impunity for human rights violations by private individuals is generally not so much the result of their powerful position, but of a failure of the state to exercise due diligence in preventing and combating violations.

Since states do not always take the necessary measures to prevent and combat violations by non-state actors, there are numerous instances in which non-state actors are not held accountable at the domestic level for their behaviour, and human rights violations are not remedied. Furthermore, non-state actors cannot be held accountable under procedures established under international human rights instruments. Only states ratify such instruments and accept the competence of organs monitoring the implementation of standards. Hence, in case of an infringement of human rights by a non-state actor, states can be held accountable at the international level if, for example, they failed to act with due diligence to prevent or respond to the infringement. There is thus a gap in the protection of

1 Committee on Economic, Social and Cultural Rights, General Comment no. 2, International Technical Assistance Measures, 2 February 1990, UN Doc. E/1990/23.

2 Mac Darrow, *Between Light and Shadow: The World Bank, the International Monetary Fund and International Human Rights Law* (Oxford: Hart, 2003); François Gianvitti, 'Economic, Social and Cultural Rights and the International Monetary Fund', in *Non-State Actors and Human Rights*, ed. Philip Alston, 113–138 (Oxford: Oxford University Press, 2005).

human rights. This has been recognised in the past decades and various initiatives have been taken to try to fill this gap.

This chapter will examine steps that have been taken and the extent to which non-state actors can be held accountable under international human rights law for their actions that affect the enjoyment of human rights. It will in particular deal with issues relating to the monitoring of the implementation of norms, as this is crucial for giving effect to their accountability.

The Current System

As was mentioned in the introduction, states are the main actors in international law; they create international law and can accept obligations under treaties. Human rights treaties constitute a special category of treaties in international law. Whereas most treaties regulate relations between states, human rights treaties primarily regulate relations between states and individuals. States parties to human rights treaties are under an obligation to take measures to prevent and combat violations of treaty obligations by its agents, such as police officials and civil servants. If the state party fails to do so, it is directly responsible for these violations, and can be held accountable under international law.[3]

Additionally, human rights treaties require states parties to take measures to ensure that individuals do not violate each others' rights. This implies, *inter alia,* that states must prohibit certain acts of individuals and other actors – under certain circumstances even criminalise behaviour – and ensure enforcement of such legislation. Article 2 of the Convention on the Elimination of All Forms of Discrimination against Women (CEDAW Convention) is quite elaborate on the different obligations of states. It requires states parties to guarantee equality and non-discrimination in the law, to ensure that public authorities and institutions do not discriminate (Article 2 (d)) and to take all appropriate measures to eliminate discrimination any person, organisation or enterprise (Article 2 (e)). As a consequence of the scope of the definition of discrimination in Article 1 of the CEDAW Convention, this obligation does not only extend to the public sphere, but also to the private sphere. The relevance of this can hardly be underestimated. Like other human rights instruments, the CEDAW Convention obliges states parties to take measures to eliminate discrimination by state organs and public organs in the public sphere. They are, for example, under an obligation to eliminate discrimination in employment. The CEDAW Convention goes much further than that by also requiring steps to eliminate discrimination in private life, both by state organs, public organs, private enterprises and persons. For example, under Article 16 of the CEDAW Convention, dealing with equality within marriage,

3 See International Law Commission, *Draft Articles on Responsibility of States for Internationally Wrongful Acts*. The General Assembly has taken note of the Draft Articles and invited governments to comment to them, see General Assembly Resolution 56/83, adopted on 12 December 2001; the Annex to the resolution contains the text of the Draft Articles.

states parties are under an obligation, *inter alia,* to ensure 'the same rights to decide freely and responsibly on the number and spacing of their children'. According to the CEDAW Committee this implies that decisions to have children or not, 'while preferably made in consultation with spouse or partner, must not nevertheless be limited by spouse, parent, partner or Government'.[4]

The obligation to protect individuals from each other can be derived from states' general obligation to not only respect human rights, but also from the obligation to protect. In its general comment on the nature of obligations under the International Covenant on Civil and Political Rights (ICCPR), the Human Rights Committee stated that:

> 'the positive obligations on States Parties to ensure Covenant rights will only be fully discharged if individuals are protected by the State, not just against violations of Covenant rights by its agents, but also against acts committed by private persons or entities that would impair the enjoyment of Covenant rights in so far as they are amenable to application between private persons or entities. There may be circumstances in which a failure to ensure Covenant rights as required by Article 2 would give rise to violations by States Parties of those rights, as a result of States Parties' permitting or failing to take appropriate measures or to exercise due diligence to prevent, punish, investigate or redress the harm caused by such acts by private persons or entities.'[5]

Even though various human rights can be applied in horizontal relations – including the right not to be subjected to ill-treatment – this does not lead to accountability of private actors under international human rights law. In this context, the Human Rights Committee has pointed to the need for states parties to provide effective remedies under Article 2 (3) of the Covenant,[6] in order to ensure that individuals whose rights have been violated have access to a remedy at the domestic level.

Only in narrowly defined circumstances can individuals be brought before an international criminal court or tribunal for violations of international crimes such as war crimes or crimes against humanity that include sexual violence.[7] The codification of various sexual offences as international crimes reflects the consen-

4 Committee on the Elimination of Discrimination against Women, General Recommendation no. 21, Equality in Marriage and Family Relations, 1994, UN Doc. A/49/38, *Report of the Committee on the Elimination of Discrimination against Women, 13th session,* chapter I.A., para. 22.

5 Human Rights Committee, General Comment no. 31 (80), The Nature of the General Legal Obligation Imposed on States Parties to the Covenant, 29 March 2004, UN Doc. CCPR/C/21/Rev.1/Add.13, para. 8.

6 Ibid.

7 Articles 7 (1) (g), 8 (2) (a) (xxii) and 8 (2) (e) (vi), Rome Statute of the International Criminal Court. See also Anne-Marie de Brouwer, *Supranational Criminal Prosecution of Sexual Violence: The ICC and the Practice of the ICTY and the ICTR* (Antwerp: Intersentia, 2005).

sus reached at the international level on the seriousness of these crimes and the progress made in the recognition of such offences as a violation of women's right to physical integrity. It may contribute to combating impunity for these grave human rights violations, also at the national level. Various human rights treaty bodies have pointed to states parties' responsibilities under human rights instruments, which may have been inspired by developments in international criminal law. For example, recent concluding comments of the Committee against Torture (CAT Committee) display an interest of this human rights organ for sexual violence. For example, in the case of Burundi, the CAT Committee stated that it was 'alarmed at reports of large-scale sexual violence against women and children by state officials and members of armed groups, as well as at the systematic use of rape as a weapon of war, which constitutes a crime against humanity'. The CAT Committee expressed its deep concern at the apparent impunity enjoyed by the perpetrators of such acts, and the extrajudicial or amicable settlement of rape cases, including by the administrative authorities, when emphasis is placed on practices such as marriage between rapist and victim.[8] Until recently, the CAT Committee did not pay much attention to gender-based violence. Concluding Comments such as these thus constitute a step forward. First, because the CAT Committee specifically deals with gender-based violence, categorising the acts as a crime against humanity and rejecting impunity and practices apparently aimed at 'restoring the honour' of the rape victim is an improvement. Second, its dealing with acts committed by state officials as well as members of armed forces is another improvement. Since Article 1 of the Convention against Torture and Other Cruel, Inhuman or Degrading Treatment or Punishment limits the definition of torture to acts 'inflicted by or at the instigation of or with the consent or acquiescence of a public official or other person acting in an official capacity', the fact that the comments refer to members of armed groups under the heading of torture is significant.

In this context, it is noteworthy that developments are taking place towards the accountability of staff members of UN peace-keeping operations for sexual exploitation and abuse. A report of the UN Secretary-General, drawn up by his adviser His Royal Highness Prince Zeid Ra'ad Zeid Al-Hussein, contains various recommendations to ensure that peace-keeping personnel who commit acts of sexual exploitation and abuse are held individually accountable through appropriate disciplinary action, that they are held financially accountable for the harm they have done to victims and that they are held criminally accountable if the acts constitute crimes under applicable law.[9] The report points to the problems in cases where a functioning judicial system is absent in some peace-keeping locations. It is recommended that the Secretary-General establish a group of experts to study the issue and make recommendations to the General Assembly on whether

8 Committee against Torture, Concluding Comments on Burundi, 20 November 2006, UN Doc., CAT/C/BDI/CO/1, para. 11.

9 UN Doc. A/59/710, *A Comprehensive Strategy to Eliminate Future Sexual Exploitation and Abuse in United Nations Peacekeeping Operations*, para. 94.

an international convention or other means could be used to ensure that United Nations staff and experts on mission who commit defined crimes in peace-keeping areas are held criminally accountable for their actions.[10]

In spite of the fact that under human rights treaties, individuals and other non-state actors cannot be held accountable before international organs, states can be held responsible under certain circumstances for conduct of non-state actors. For example, individuals can submit complaints before an international organ about the failure of states parties to take the necessary measures to prevent and combat domestic violence.[11] The first case dealt with on the merits by the CEDAW Committee clearly illustrates this case in point. A Hungarian woman had been the victim of domestic violence. She had been severely beaten for a long time by her common-law husband. She could not find refuge in a shelter because there was no shelter available that could take her as well as her children, one of whom was disabled. The court did not impose a restraining order on her abusive partner, and the sentence ultimately imposed on him was very lenient. The CEDAW Committee concluded that Hungary had violated various provisions of the CEDAW Convention, *inter alia,* by not taking the necessary measures to end the violence to which the woman had been subjected, to protect her and to punish the perpetrator.[12]

This illustrates the current system. The state party is held accountable before the CEDAW Committee for the failure to act, not the perpetrator who is responsible for the domestic violence. In its recommendations, the state party was urged to take 'immediate and effective measures to guarantee the physical and mental integrity of A.T. and her family; and ensure that A.T. is given a safe home in which to live with her children, receives appropriate child support and legal assistance and that she receives reparation proportionate to the physical and mental harm undergone and to the gravity of the violations of her rights.'[13] The Committee can only issue a recommendation for the state party to remedy the violation suffered by the victim, not to impose a specific punishment on the perpetrator. In this respect, it must be noted that the Committee formulated recommendations to prevent similar violations in the future, including to bring offenders to justice.

The primary role of states in the promotion and protection of human rights may also be illustrated by the example of privatisation and the response thereto by international monitoring bodies. In various instances, states have privatised tasks that were traditionally mainly their responsibility, such as the management of prisons and the provision of health services. The privatisation of such services does not imply that states can evade their responsibility for the treatment of pris-

10 Ibid., para. 93.

11 See the contribution by Joanna Bourke Martignoni in this book.

12 Committee on the Elimination of Discrimination against Women, Communication no. 2/2004, *A.T. v Hungary,* View adopted on 26 January 2005, UN Doc. A/60/38 (Part I), Annex III.

13 Ibid., para. 9.6.

oners,[14] or for the accessibility of health care facilities. With respect to health, the ESC Committee has stated that:

> 'While only States are parties to the Covenant and thus ultimately accountable for compliance with it, all members of society – individuals, including health professionals, families, local communities, intergovernmental and non-governmental organizations, civil society organizations, as well as the private business sector – have responsibilities regarding the realization of the right to health. State parties should therefore provide an environment which facilitates the discharge of these responsibilities.'[15]

Enabling the private sector to provide services does not diminish the obligations of states under human rights instruments. They continue to have an obligation to monitor and regulate the conduct of non-state actors to ensure that they do not violate human rights.[16]

The above examples illustrate that much progress has been made in defining the responsibilities of states to protect individuals against human rights violations by non-state actors, and to hold states accountable at the international level for such acts. Since the 1970s, various initiatives have been taken in an attempt to formulate human rights obligations for non-state actors, especially transnational corporations. The following sections focus on such initiatives and will examine to what extent obligations under human rights law for non-state actors are emerging.

A preliminary question we need to ask ourselves is whether the changing role of the non-state actors that have a capacity to violate human rights implies that they should be involved in lawmaking. Clapham suggests to uphold as a starting point the principles and rules of international public international law with its origins in the lawmaking power of the state. We agree with this view as well as with his argument that at the same time some of the obligations that have traditionally only been applied to states, should also be applied to non-state actors.[17] New standards are not necessary.

14 See for example, Human Rights Committee, Concluding Observations on New Zealand (2002), UN Doc. CCPR/CO/75/NZL, para. 13; International Law Commission, *Draft Articles on Responsibility of States for Internationally Wrongful Acts,* Article 5.

15 Committee on Economic, Social and Cultural Rights, General Comment no. 14 (2000), The Right to the Highest Attainable Standard of Health, UN Doc. E/C.12/2000/4, para. 42.

16 Committee on Economic, Social and Cultural Rights, General Comment no. 16 (2005), Equal Right of Men and Women to the Enjoyment of All Economic, Social and Cultural Rights, UN Doc. E/C.12/2005/3, para. 20.

17 Andrew Clapham, *Human Rights Obligations of Non-State Actors* (Oxford: Oxford University Press, 2006), 28.

Transnational Corporations and Other Business Enterprises[18]

As a result of various widely publicised disastrous incidents, such as the execution of Ken Saro-Wiwa and eight other Ogonis that was connected to Shell's operations in Nigeria, the Bhopal disaster and the operation of UNOCAL in Myanmar, transnational corporations were called on to recognise that they do have obligations to respect human rights. Efforts have been made to persuade them to adopt their own rules, and voluntary codes of conduct have come into existence. However, these apply only for the corporation that has drafted them and consequently there are many different codes with different scopes of application. While some refer to human rights norms, others do not, or only in the most general terms. Additionally, many problems exist with respect to the monitoring of such codes, which is often not regulated at all, or not entrusted to an independent institution.[19] Another argument not to aim for these institutions to be lawmakers is that the problem is not so much in the formulation of the norms, but rather in their application by non-state actors. It would therefore be more pragmatic and appropriate to seek to apply existing standards.

At the international level various efforts have been made to regulate to some extent the activities of businesses. These include the OECD (Organisation for Economic Co-operation and Development) Guidelines for Multinational Enterprises[20] and the ILO (International Labour Organisation) Tripartite Declaration of Principles Concerning Multinational Enterprises and Social Policy.[21] Another interesting example of a voluntary initiative existing within the framework of the United Nations is the Global Compact. This has been initiated by the UN Secretary-General to enhance the awareness of businesses regarding their role in the field of human rights. Within the framework of the Global Compact, businesses commit themselves to advance ten universal principles in the areas of

18 Many scholarly publications exist on this issue. See, *inter alia,* Michael K. Addo ed., *Human Rights Standards and the Responsibility of Transnational Corporations* (The Hague: Kluwer, 1999); Philip Alston ed., *Non-State Actors and Human Rights* (Oxford: Oxford University Press, 2005); Nicola Jägers, *Corporate Human Rights Obligations: In Search of Accountability* (Antwerpen: Intersentia, 2002); Sarah Joseph, 'Taming the Leviathans: Multinational Enterprises and Human Rights', *Netherlands International Law Review* 46 (1999): 171–203; Menno T. Kamminga and Saman Zia-Zarifi ed., *Liability of Multinational Corporations Under International Law* (The Hague: Kluwer, 2000); David Weissbrodt and Muria Kruger, 'Norms on the Responsibilities of Transnational Corporations and Other Business Enterprises with Regard to Human Rights', *American Journal of International Law* 97 (2003): 901–922.

19 Nicola Jägers, *Corporate Human Rights Obligations: In Search of Accountability* (Antwerpen: Intersentia, 2002), 132–136.

20 OECD, *Guidelines for Multinational Enterprises,* as amended in 2000 (Paris: OECD, 2000).

21 ILO, *Tripartite Declaration of Principles Concerning Multinational Enterprises and Social Policy,* first adopted in 1977, 4th edition (Geneva: International Labour Office, 2006).

human rights, labour, the environment and anticorruption. The overall goal is to 'help realize the Secretary-General's vision: a more sustainable and inclusive global economy'.[22] The first two principles of the Global Compact deal with human rights; stating that businesses should 'support and respect the protection of internationally proclaimed human rights within their sphere of influence' and 'make sure they are not complicit in human rights abuses'.[23] As of the beginning of 2007, over 2,900 businesses in 100 countries around the world have joined this initiative.[24] It is relatively easy for businesses to join the Global Compact. They must send a letter to the UN Secretary-General expressing support for the Global Compact and its principles and set in motion changes to business operations so that the Global Compact and its principles become part of strategy, culture and day-to-day operations. The business is expected to publicly advocate the Global Compact and its principles via communications vehicles such as press releases and speeches. In terms of 'accountability', it need do no more than publish in its annual report a description of the ways in which it is supporting the Global Compact and its principles.[25] The Global Compact is entirely voluntary; there is no external monitoring or enforcement mechanism to establish whether or not the businesses that have committed themselves adhere in practice to the principles. Furthermore, there are no sanctions for businesses that do not comply with the principles, although there are some guidelines seeking to avoid abuse of the UN name and logo.[26]

An initiative of the UN Sub-Commission on the Promotion and Protection of Human Rights, a body composed of twenty-six independent experts, resulted in the Norms on the Responsibilities of Transnational Corporations and Other Business Enterprises with Regard to Human Rights in 2003.[27] These Norms aim to be significantly less voluntary, and to establish obligations for businesses. They do, however, recognise states' primary responsibility for the promotion and protection of human rights by stating:

> 'States have the primary responsibility to promote, secure the fulfilment of, respect, ensure respect of and protect human rights recognized in international as well as national law, including ensuring that transnational corporations and other business enterprises respect human rights. Within their respective spheres of activity and influence, transnational corporations and other business enterprises have the obligation to promote, secure the fulfilment of, respect, ensure respect of and protect human rights recognized

22 http://www.unglobalcompact.org/AboutTheGC/index.html (2 March 2007).

23 http://www.unglobalcompact.org/AboutTheGC/TheTenPrinciples/humanRights.html (2 March 2007).

24 http://www.unglobalcompact.org/ParticipantsAndStakeholders/index.html.

25 http://www.unglobalcompact.org/AboutTheGC/faq.html.

26 http://www.un.org/partners/business/otherpages/guide.htm.

27 Sub-Commission on the Promotion and Protection of Human Rights, *Norms on the Responsibilities of Transnational Corporations and Other Business Enterprises with Regard to Human Rights*, UN Doc. E/CN.4/Sub.2/2003/12/Rev.2 (2003).

> in international as well as national law, including the rights and interests of indigenous peoples and other vulnerable groups.'[28]

The Norms do not use the term 'accountability', but state that businesses have 'obligations' and 'responsibilities'. This is more or less in line with Article 29 (1) of the Universal Declaration of Human Rights, which provides that '[e]veryone has duties to the community in which alone the free and full development of his personality is possible.' This provision is crucial in the debate on the responsibilities of non-state actors. According to their preamble, the Norms aim to 'contribute to the making and development of international law as to those responsibilities and obligations'. The language used in the Norms is quite similar to language used in human rights instruments applying to states. The Norms do not explicitly address violence against women, but contain some provisions that may be relevant. For example, Article 2 provides that transnational corporations and other business enterprises 'shall ensure equality of opportunity and treatment'. Article 7 states that transnational corporations and other business enterprises 'shall provide a safe and healthy working environment', which includes, presumably, the obligation to prevent and punish sexual harassment at the workplace.

The Norms as they currently stand do not provide protection to many jobs in which women traditionally work. The Norms have defined a transnational corporation as 'an economic entity operating in more than one country or a cluster of economic entities operating in two or more countries, whatever their legal form, whether in their home country or country of activity, and whether taken individually or collectively', whereas 'other business enterprise' includes 'any business entity, regardless of the international or domestic nature of its activities, including a transnational corporation, contractor, subcontractor, supplier, licensee or distributor; the corporate, partnership, or other legal form used to establish the business entity; and the nature of the ownership of the entity'.[29] This implies that jobs such as waitressing, nursing, cooking and domestic work in private households do not fall within the scope of the Norms.

The Norms seek adherence from businesses. Under Article 15 they are encouraged to 'adopt, disseminate and implement internal rules of operation in compliance with the Norms' and to establish their own monitoring system. As to external monitoring, the Norms provide in Article 16 that businesses shall be:

> 'subject to periodic monitoring and verification by United Nations, other international and national mechanisms already in existence or yet to be created, regarding application of the Norms. This monitoring shall be transparent and independent and take into account input from stakeholders (including non-governmental organisations) and as a result of complaints of violations of these Norms. Further, transnational corporations and other business enterprises shall conduct periodic evaluations concerning the impact of their own activities on human rights under these Norms.'

28 Ibid., Article 1.

29 Ibid., Articles 20–21.

According to their principal drafter, David Weissbrodt, 'the many implementation provisions show that they amount to more than aspirational statements of desired conduct'.[30]

It is quite unlikely, however, that the Norms will be adopted by a political organ of the United Nations. After their adoption by the UN Sub-Commission in 2003, the Norms were submitted to the UN Commission on Human Rights. According to the Commission on Human Rights, the Norms contain 'useful elements and ideas for consideration by the Commission', but it also stated the Norms had 'not been requested by the Commission and, as a draft proposal, has no legal standing, and that the Sub-Commission should not perform any monitoring function in this regard'.[31] In 2005, the Commission on Human Rights decided to appoint a Special Representative on the issue of human rights and transnational corporations and other business enterprises, with the following mandate:

> '(a) To identify and clarify standards of corporate responsibility and accountability for transnational corporations and other business enterprises with regard to human rights;
> (b) To elaborate on the role of States in effectively regulating and adjudicating the role of transnational corporations and other business enterprises with regard to human rights, including through international cooperation;
> (c) To research and clarify the implications for transnational corporations and other business enterprises of concepts such as "complicity" and "sphere of influence";
> (d) To develop materials and methodologies for undertaking human rights impact assessments of the activities of transnational corporations and other business enterprises;
> (e) To compile a compendium of best practices of States and transnational corporations and other business enterprises.'[32]

The Commission on Human Rights, and its successor the Human Rights Council, organs composed of states, was clearly not prepared to adopt a document such as the Norms; in the resolution establishing the Special Representative's mandate the Norms are not even mentioned. The Special Representative, appointed by the Commission, John Ruggie, has made clear that he will not advocate the Norms, nor strive for their adoption. In his interim report he has expressed se-

30 David Weissbrodt and Muria Kruger, 'Norms on the Responsibilities of Transnational Corporations and Other Business Enterprises with Regard to Human Rights', *American Journal of International Law* 97 (2003): 913.

31 *Responsibilities of Transnational Corporations and Related Business Enterprises with Regard to Human Rights*, 22 April 2004, UN Doc. E/CN.4/DEC/2004/116.

32 Commission on Human Rights, Resolution 2005/69, para. 1. For the Special Representative's interim report see UN Doc. E/CN.4/2006/97, for his report on *Human Rights Impact Assessments – Resolving Key Methodological Questions*, see UN Doc. A/HRC/4/74.

vere criticism on the Norms. In his view, 'its exaggerated legal claims and conceptual ambiguities created confusion and doubt even among many mainstream international lawyers and other impartial observers'.[33] He argues that the claim 'that international law has been transformed to the point where it can be said that the broad array of international human rights attach direct legal obligations to corporations' finds no support in international law.[34] He also holds the view that the Norms inaccurately distribute human rights responsibilities to states and corporations.[35] The Norms will not constitute a basis for moving his mandate forward.[36]

This position taken by the Special Representative is regrettable and is a step backwards in the discussions on the responsibilities of transnational corporations and other businesses. While the Norms may be a step too far for many, they could have constituted a valuable basis for further deliberations.

International Organisations

The activities of organisations such as the World Bank and the IMF can have great impact on the enjoyment of human rights. The ESC Committee has acknowledged this problem on various occasions. For example, in its general comment on the right to work, it observed that:

> 'The strategies, programmes and policies adopted by States parties under structural adjustment programmes should not interfere with their core obligations in relation to the right to work and impact negatively on the right to work of women, young persons and the disadvantaged and marginalized individuals and groups'.[37]

The extent to which international financial institutions have an obligation to respect and protect human rights is a subject of debate. According to a recent study, the core minimum obligation incumbent directly on the Bank and Fund as specialised agencies of the UN system and subjects of international law is 'a duty of vigilance to ensure that their policies and programs do not facilitate breaches of their member states' human rights treaty obligations'.[38]

33 Interim report of the Special Representative of the Secretary-General on the issue of human rights and transnational corporations and other business enterprises, ibid., para. 59.

34 Ibid., para. 64.

35 Ibid., paras. 66 et seq.

36 Ibid., para. 69.

37 Committee on Economic, Social and Cultural Rights, General Comment no. 18 (2005), The Right to Work (Article 6 of the International Covenant on Economic, Social and Cultural Rights), UN Doc. E/C.12/GC/18, para. 30.

38 Darrow, see note 2 above, 295. Also: Sigrun I. Skogly, 'The Human Rights Obligations of the World Bank and the IMF', in *World Bank, IMF and Human Rights,* ed. Willem

In its general comments, the ESC Committee as a rule includes a section entitled 'Obligations of actors other than states parties'. For example, in its general comment on the right to health, the ESC Committee not only points to the technical assistance and cooperation that the World Health Organisation can offer in formulating and implementing their right to health national strategies,[39] it also states that the relevant specialised agencies 'should cooperate effectively with states parties, building on their respective expertise, in relation to the implementation of the right to health at the national level, with due respect to their individual mandates'.[40] It observes that the international financial institutions should pay greater attention to the protection of the right to health in their lending policies, credit agreements and structural adjustment programmes. The ESC Committee announces that in examining the reports of states parties and their ability to meet their obligations under Article 12, it will consider the effects of the assistance provided by all other actors, including the role of health professional associations and other non-governmental organisations in relation to the states' obligations under Article 12. It does not, however, specify how it intends to implement this. In its activities under the reporting procedure, we see that the ESC Committee also points to states parties' responsibilities as members of the financial institutions to use their influence to contribute to improving the human rights performance of these international organisations. Upon conclusion of the examination of the report of the United Kingdom, for example, the Committee encouraged the state party:

> 'as a member of international financial institutions, in particular the International Monetary Fund and the World Bank, to do all it can to ensure that the policies and decisions of those organizations are in conformity with the obligations of States parties under the Covenant, in particular with the obligations contained in articles 2.1, 11.2, 15.4 and 23 concerning international assistance and cooperation'.[41]

In its General Comment on Plans of Action for Primary Education, the ESC Committee called on international agencies to assist states parties to the greatest extent possible to meet their obligations on an urgent basis.[42] Also the Committee on the Rights of the Child addresses the specialised agencies. In its General

van Genugten, Paul Hunt and Susan Mathews, 45–78 (Nijmegen: Wolf Legal Publishers, 2003).

39 Committee on Economic, Social and Cultural Rights, General Comment no. 14 (2000), The Right to the Highest Attainable Standard of Health, UN Doc. E/C.12/2000/4, para. 63.

40 Ibid., para. 64.

41 Committee on Economic, Social and Cultural Rights, Concluding Comments on the United Kingdom of Great Britain and Northern Ireland, 16 May 2002, UN Doc. E/C.12/1/Add.79, para. 26.

42 Committee on Economic, Social and Cultural Rights, General Comment no. 11 (1999), Plans of Action for Primary Education, UN Doc. E/C.12/1999/4, para. 11.

Comment on General Measures of Implementation for the Convention on the Rights of the Child it stated:

> 'In their promotion of international cooperation and technical assistance, all UN and UN-related agencies should be guided by the Convention and should mainstream children's rights throughout their activities. They should seek to ensure within their influence that international cooperation is targeted at supporting States to fulfil their obligations under the Convention. Similarly the World Bank Group, International Monetary Fund and World Trade Organisation should ensure that their activities related to international cooperation and economic development give primary consideration to the best interests of children and promote full implementation of the Convention.'[43]

A group of experts developed the Tilburg Guiding Principles on World Bank, IMF and Human Rights on human rights obligations for international financial institutions. According to these principles, the World Bank and the IMF should integrate human rights considerations into all aspects of their operations and internal functioning. The prevention of violations should receive high priority, and if violations occur, measures for mitigating the impact thereof and mechanisms of accountability and redress should be put into place.[44] They are under an 'international legal obligation to take full responsibility for human rights respect in situations where the institutions' own projects, policies or programmes negatively impact or undermine the enjoyment of human rights'.[45] Under existing arrangements, however, such obligations are not practically enforceable.[46]

The World Bank recognises the relevance of human rights to its activities. It holds the view that 'creating the conditions for the attainment of human rights is a central and irreducible goal of development'.[47] The organisation is, however, very cautious in formulating any obligations or responsibilities. According to Senior Vice President and General Counsel of the World Bank Group, Ana Palacio, the World Bank's role is 'a facilitative one, in helping our members realise their human rights obligations'. She stated that 'human rights would not be the basis for an increase in Bank conditionalities, nor should they be seen as an agenda that could present an obstacle for disbursement or increase the cost of

43 Committee on the Rights of the Child, General Comment no. 5 (2003), General Measures of Implementation for the Convention on the Rights of the Child, UN Doc. CRC/GC/2003/5, para. 64.

44 *Tilburg Guiding Principles on World Bank, IMF and Human Rights*, in Van Genugten et al. (2003), see note 38 above, 249-257, para. 24.

45 Ibid., para. 5.

46 On this aspect see further Adam McBeth, 'Breaching the Vacuum: A Consideration of the Role of International Human Rights Law in the Operations of the International Financial Institutions', *International Journal of Human Rights* 10, no. 4 (2006): 385–404, at 401.

47 World Bank, *Development and Human Rights: The Role of the World Bank* (Washington, DC: World Bank, 1998).

doing business.'[48] She admitted that '[a]lthough the Bank's pronouncements on human rights have always been broadly supportive, they never affirmed in concrete terms that the Bank had a specific role to play in relation to human rights as legal principles, or as legal obligations.' Yet, she also stated that 'the Bank can and sometimes should take human rights into consideration as part of its decision-making process.'[49]

Also in considering the extent of responsibilities of international organisations, states continue to be primarily responsible: 'States cannot "delegate" human rights obligations to, for instance, international financial institutions and relieve themselves of these obligations.'[50] Nevertheless, it is recognised that organisations whose activities impact on human rights bear responsibilities of their own. Because of their position within the United Nations system, specialised agencies such as the World Bank and the IMF have certain obligations. Under traditional international law, the Bank is accountable to its member states; the member states are accountable to the people. Within the World Bank, the establishment of the Inspection Panel is a major step forward, allowing for direct access by affected people to the Bank, subject to certain conditions. As to subject matter:

> 'The affected party must demonstrate that its rights or interests have been or are likely to be directly affected by an action of omission of the Bank as a result of a failure of the Bank to follow its operational policies and procedures with respect to the design, appraisal and/or implementation of a project financed by the Bank (including situations where the Bank is alleged to have failed in its follow-up on the borrower's obligations under loan agreements with respect to such policies and procedures) provided in all cases that such failure has had, or threatens to have, a material adverse effect.'[51]

The Inspection Panel can test compliance of the Bank with its own policies, not whether the Bank has violated international (human rights) law. People can, however, argue that the harm they suffered consisted of human rights violations. The panel takes up human rights violations to the extent that they result from an infringement of Bank rules.[52] The procedure opens political space for the voices of marginalised communities; groups that both borrower and the Bank 'were happy to ignore' become visible.[53]

48 Ana Palacio, *The Way Forward: Human Rights and the World Bank,* 27 October 2006, available on the Bank's website, in the section 'Law and development'.

49 Ibid.

50 Van Genugten et al. (2003), see note 38 above, 249–257, para. 5.

51 International Bank for Reconstruction and Development, International Development Association, Resolution no. 93–10, Resolution no. IDA 93–6, *The World Bank Inspection Panel,* 22 September 1993, para. 12.

52 Koen de Feyter, *Human Rights: Social Justice in the Age of the Market* (London: Zed Books, 2005), 148.

53 Ibid., 221.

In this connection, it is worth mentioning that the International Law Commission is currently studying the issue of 'Responsibility of international organisations' as part of its long-term programme of work.[54] One of the provisionally adopted Articles provides that:

> 'There is an internationally wrongful act of an international organization when conduct consisting of an action or omission:
> (a) Is attributable to the international organization under international law; and
> (b) constitutes a breach of an international obligation of that international organization.'[55]

It will thus be crucial to establish what does, and what does not, constitute an 'obligation', an issue that is not solved by the Draft Articles.

We see some fundamental changes. While not accepting concrete obligations, or expressing a 'consent to be bound' to human rights treaties, at least the World Bank has accepted that it has responsibilities to respect human rights and to prevent violations. The mere establishment of the Inspection Panel is a step forward, and those submitting claims to it could phrase these in human rights terms where appropriate, and refer to instruments such as the Universal Declaration of Human Rights, thus inviting the Bank to respond.

A Special Case: UNMIK Before the Human Rights Committee

Particularly worth mentioning is a recent initiative of the Human Rights Committee. During consideration of the initial report of Serbia and Montenegro under the Covenant on Civil and Political Rights, the Human Rights Committee took note of the state party's explanation that it was unable to report on the discharge of its own responsibilities with regard to the human rights situation in Kosovo, and suggested that, owing to the fact that civil authority is exercised in Kosovo by the United Nations Interim Administration Mission in Kosovo (UNMIK), the Committee may invite UNMIK to submit to it a supplementary report on the human rights situation in Kosovo.

The Committee 'encouraged' UNMIK, in cooperation with the Provisional Institutions of Self-Government (PISG), 'to provide, without prejudice to the legal status of Kosovo, a report on the situation of human rights in Kosovo since June 1999'.[56] UNMIK complied with the request and submitted a report[57] that was con-

54 For an overview see: *Report of the International Law Commission*, UN Doc. A/61/10, chapter 7.

55 Responsibility of international organizations, Article 3, in UN Doc. A/61/10, ibid., para. 90.

56 Human Rights Committee, Concluding Comments on Serbia and Montenegro, 28 July 2004, UN Doc. CCPR/CO/81/SEMO, para. 3.

57 UN Doc. CCPR/C/UNK/1, *Report Submitted by the United Nations Interim Administration Mission in Kosovo to the Human Rights Committee on the Human Rights*

sidered by the Human Rights Committee in July 2006. In its report, UNMIK referred to the authority granted to it under Security Council Resolution 1244 (1999) by which it had been established, and the protection and promotion of which formulates as one of the main responsibilities the protection and promotion of human rights.[58] The Human Rights Committee considered the report in a way similar to reports submitted by states parties, in the presence of representatives of Serbia and UNMIK, adopted its concluding comments, and requested information on the follow-up to its recommendations.[59] So far, this example is unique, and the willingness of UNMIK to participate in this procedure was instrumental in making it a success.

Concluding Remarks

The above sketched some recent developments with regard to obligations of non-state actors, and the monitoring of their implementation. While full accountability in the sense of being called to account before an international organ may not be achieved for some time, clearly, the notion of responsibility has been accepted by international organisations and businesses. International criminal law has imposed accountability on individuals who have committed grave human rights violations for which they can be prosecuted before an international tribunal. Establishing accountability depends to a large extent on the willingness of powerful non-state actors such as international organisations and businesses to be held accountable. This willingness has been advanced by initiatives from non-governmental organisations and academics that have demonstrated that their powers and – in the case of international organisations – their place in the United Nations system entail responsibilities. The aim should be to seek their adherence to existing standards, and not to have them create their own norms, which undoubtedly would lead to confusion and possibly to watering down of standards.

International human rights law has made much progress in elaborating state accountability for the conduct of non-state actors. The elaboration of the due diligence principle in assessing state responsibility in concrete cases or situations has helped determining the existence and extent of this responsibility. Even if direct *accountability* of non-state actors cannot be established at present, it is useful to continue to pursue the development of instruments in the form of guidelines, principles and norms, spelling out their *responsibilities* in order to shed light on the extent of their obligations, as well as to assist states in developing domestic legislation and establishing monitoring mechanisms at the domestic level through which they can comply with their own obligations to protect the rights of individuals against infringements by non-state actors.

Situation in Kosovo since June 1999 (United Nations: February 2006).

58 UN Doc. CCPR/C/UNK/1, ibid., para. 1. See also Security Council Resolution 1244 (1999), para. 11 (j).

59 Human Rights Committee, Concluding Observations on Kosovo (Serbia), 27 July 2006, UN Doc. CCPR/C/UNK/KO/1, para. 24.

Due Diligence and the Power of Economic Players

Helen O'Connell

Introduction

The Preamble to the Universal Declaration of Human Rights (1948) calls on 'every individual and every organ of society' to play its part in securing universal observance of human rights. As Amnesty International has pointed out many times, companies and financial institutions are organs of society, and as such need to play their part too in securing universal observance of human rights. Here, of course, lies the major challenge. How are multinational companies and international bodies to be made more accountable? This chapter seeks to examine to what extent macro structures, such as economic globalisation, play a role in the implementation of due diligence. More specifically the chapter addresses the question: do economic players, such as multinational[1] companies, hold legal duties under international human rights law, and if so which measures do they have to fulfil? And do they have their own due diligence obligations. The chapter begins with a short overview of where women are in the global economy and the implications of globalisation for women and for states' responsibilities with regard to women's human rights. It traces the development of international codes on corporate social responsibility. The chapter then examines the role played by civil society in research, campaigning and advocacy on the power and responsibilities of economic players and concludes that a new politics and greater engagement by feminists in democratic processes are needed to build accountable governance.

1 I use the term multinational company (MNC) to include a corporation or enterprise which manages manufacturing production or delivers services in more than two countries. The term is interchangeable with 'transnational,' which I use only when it occurs in a document or publication title.

C. Benninger-Budel ed., Due Diligence and Its Application to Protect Women from Violence
 ISBN 978 90 04 16293 8. pp. 109-126

Where Are Women in the Global Economy?

Alongside the traditional sectors of women's economic activity: small scale farming, food processing and employment in the caring professions, globalisation has opened new opportunities for women in garment and electronic production, in agriculture and horticulture for export, in food and fish processing, particularly, but not exclusively, in Southern countries. New opportunities have also opened up in the service sector, in call centres for international banks, airlines and others. While some of these jobs offer women higher salaries than they could earn elsewhere and many offer women opportunities for greater liberation from family constraints, there is a downside too. The jobs offer few opportunities for learning new skills or promotion and are exploitative in terms of working hours and conditions.[2]

Many women are now working in other parts of the supply chains linked to production or agriculture for export: as home-based workers, as casual workers and in small production units which carry out work out-sourced or subcontracted by larger companies. The number of women migrant workers has also grown within the global economy, but here again, women are found in the least well paid jobs in the caring sector, as nurses, child-minders and domestic workers (often in jobs well below their educational or professional qualifications). The sex industry and trafficking have grown too under globalisation with all the attendant abuse of women's rights. The International Labour Organisation (ILO) launched in May 2005 A Global Alliance against Forced Labour. It estimates that worldwide over 12 million workers are in forced labour: women and girls make up 56 percent of forced labour in agriculture and other economic areas, and 98 percent in forced commercial sexual exploitation. The ILO estimates that children under 18 make up 40 to 50 percent of the overall total (of 12 million).[3]

Women's increased access to paid work around the world has coincided with a worsening of terms and conditions for many workers as governments are encouraged to deregulate their labour market, and multinational and national companies compete for higher profits, greater market share, and lower production costs through scanning the globe for cheaper overheads and labour. The informal sector has also burgeoned in recent decades as globalisation and trade liberalisation

2 The situation of women workers in garments and electronic production and in agriculture and horticulture has been documented and analysed by many authors since the 1980s. See for example, Diane Elson and Ruth Pearson, 'Nimble Fingers Make Cheap Workers: An Analysis of Women's Employment in Third World Export Manufacturing' *Feminist Review* 7 (1981); Swasti Mitter, *Common Fate, Common Bond: Women in the Global Economy* (London: Pluto Press, 1986); Women Working Worldwide, *Common Interests: Women Organising in Global Electronics* (London: Black Rose Press, 1991); Linda Shaw, 'The Labour Behind the Label: Clean Clothes Campaigns in Europe', in *No Sweat: Fashion, Free Trade, and the Rights of Garment Workers,* ed. Andrew Ross (New York/London: Verso, 1991); and www.women-ww.org.

3 International Labour Organisation, *Global Report 2005: A Global Alliance Against Forced Labour*, available at www.ilo.org.

have increased the informalisation of employment. This is not to deny that some women, particularly but not exclusively in the North, are enjoying unprecedented access to high-powered and high-waged jobs; of course, all too often women's ability to hold these positions is dependent on the poorly paid labour of women from other countries as child-carers and domestic workers.[4]

Many jobs for women in the global economy are characterised by economic exploitation, many by sexual exploitation, many by low-level but intensive harassment and the threat or actual experience of violence by male managers and co-workers, and few, if any, labour rights. Recent experience from Central America shows women factory workers experience violence from men, including young men, also on the way to and from work.[5]

The Implications of Privatisation and Internationalisation of Services

Privatisation is a key tenet of the neo-liberal economic agenda, alongside economic liberalisation and deregulation, and has critical implications for women's human rights. Since the early 1980s privatisation has been part of the structural adjustment package promoted to Southern countries with the result that spending on essential public services in health, education, water, sanitation, transport and so on has been cut and provision, already inadequate, is sharply reduced. The reduction, or in some cases removal, of public services has severe implications for women in particular: the denial of rights and access to essential services so critical to enable women to claim their rights; pressure on women to fit the gaps left in provision, such as caring for the ill and elderly; increased economic pressure to find resources to pay user fees, a burden which again falls disproportionately on women.

Another fundamental change is also taking place in service delivery: the General Agreement on Trade in Services (GATS) being negotiated at the World Trade Organisation (WTO) is extending trade liberalisation to basic services, which is likely to mean exclusion for the poorest in Southern countries. Services in the South, like other economic sectors, have been internationalised with the growing involvement in multinational companies in service provision, for example, water companies. Services, like other goods, are now commodities that are sold and have to be bought. Similar privatisation processes have taken place in the North, with fundamental challenges to the social contract and social welfare spending, but with far better basic provision and safety nets.

The neo-liberal economic policies dominant since the early 1980s have the objective of wealth accumulation and not distribution. Markets and macro-economic flows of capital and trade are regarded as gender-neutral – are not ana-

4 My thanks to Yakın Ertürk, UN Special Rapporteur on violence against women, its causes and consequences, for reminding me to add this point.

5 Marina Prieto-Carrón, 'Gender-Based Violence in the Lives of Nicaraguan Women', *CAWN* (Central America Women's Network) *Newsletter* 21 (2006): 4–6, available on www.cawn.org.

lysed from a gender or social perspective by governments or international institutions.

The New Political Environment

Our globalised world is a hostile terrain in which to negotiate women's human rights. The neo-liberal economic agenda which runs counter to progress towards economic and social justice – so essential for women to enjoy their rights – is now partnered by a new political environment which is challenging the multilateral frameworks within which human rights achievements were made in the 1990s, for example, at World Conferences in Vienna 1993, Cairo 1994, Copenhagen and Beijing 1995. The Beijing Declaration and Platform for Action adopted at the UN Fourth World Conference on Women covers 12 Critical Areas of Concern[6] including violence against women and women in the economy and reiterates the declaration made at the Vienna Conference that women's rights are human rights. The rise of neo-conservatisms of many different hues presents a fundamental attack on women's human rights. The well-established trends towards global economic integration, the militarisation of our societies, and the conservatism of our political leaders have entered a new phase since September 11, 2001. The so called 'war on terrorism,' heightened security concerns and on-going old and new wars add a new worrying dimension to globalisation, restricting freedom of expression and movement, and closing down democratic space.

The foreign policy of the G8[7] and other rich northern governments that shapes their interactions with other governments and peoples is driven to a large extent by a quite narrow interpretation of national interest, mainly commercial (access to oil, access to markets, selling arms) and of security. These aspects of foreign policy are another dimension of economic globalisation. Many countries are experiencing extreme conflict and insecurity fuelled by external or internal aggression, manipulated ethnic, social, economic and religious differences and the arms trade. It is worth remembering that globally spending on defence is around US$900 billion (spending on aid is around US$60 billion); the arms trade is a major part of the economies of the UK, France, Germany, Switzerland and the US.

This is the economic, political and military context in which we work for women's human rights. It is violent on so many levels: economic, social, political, and at each of these levels women's rights are abused. The neo-liberal economic model, in particular, is deepening inequality and insecurity – between women

6 Poverty, education and training, health, violence, armed conflict, the economy, power and decision-making, institutional mechanisms, human rights, media, environment, the girl-child.

7 The G8 Group is an unofficial forum of the heads of the leading industrialised countries (Russia, the US, Britain, France, Japan, Germany, Canada and Italy). The European Commission also participates fully. The member states account for 49 percent of global exports, 51 percent of industrial output, and 49 percent of assets in the International Monetary Fund.

and men, poor and rich, disadvantaged and advantaged, the global south and the global north.

Certain aspects of globalisation, like telecommunications, enable human rights activists and organisations to network internationally, to exchange information and ideas globally, to mobilise quickly and efficiently around human rights abuses. However, the realities and power structures of our globalised world present significant challenges to human rights work. The extent to which citizens in Southern developing countries can enjoy and exercise their full human rights is curtailed to a large degree by the decisions and actions of the governments of Northern, so called developed countries, their ministries of finance, trade, foreign affairs, and the international institutions they control: the WTO, the International Monetary Fund (IMF) and the World Bank, and more problematically by multinational companies which they do not control, but should regulate. As Mary Robinson wrote: 'In significant ways, power has shifted from the public to the private, from national governments to multinational corporations and international organisations. This has resulted in a gap in accountability for human rights protection and an absence of transparency and broad public participation in critical policy decisions.'[8] This is another wall between public and private which needs to be broken down, that is, the public sphere of accountability and scrutiny and the private sphere of economic enterprise.

Can States Honour Their Responsibilities in This Context?

The primary responsibility for promoting and protecting human rights rests and must rest with national governments. Their obligations are clearly spelled out in international treaties, agreements and customary law. The Beijing Declaration and Platform for Action establishes clearly the duty on states to ensure private actors respect human rights, and particularly women's human rights.[9] It is clear that governments could and should do more to promote, protect and fulfil human rights responsibilities. But, of course, many do not have the political will to make rights a priority, and are unlikely to adopt a more rigorous approach to rights without intense and persistent pressure from their own citizens and some positive international pressure. But why do governments not inspect and monitor what is happening in workplaces, for example? They are doubly guilty by not positively promoting, protecting, fulfilling human rights obligations or punishing abuses, and by doing nothing or too little being complicit in the neglect and abuse of rights.

There are also many governments that do have the will but do not have the economic resources necessary to meet the human rights of their poor and poorest citizens – rights to food, safe water, education, shelter, health care and to political

8 Mary Robinson, 'Introduction: Making Human Rights Work in a Globalising World,' *Human Rights Dialogue,* series 2, no. 9 (Spring 2003): 3.

9 The Beijing Declaration and Platform for Action, Fourth World Conference on Women, Beijing China, 4–15 September 1995.

participation. The debt crisis continues despite some important progress towards its resolution. There is an urgent need to strengthen the capacity of Southern developing country governments to protect human rights nationally but also to better defend in international fora the needs and interests of their citizens. Progressive donors can play a very useful role here in supporting human rights initiatives, training for para-legals, lawyers and the police, and transforming traditional mediation structures.

The Responsibilities and Obligations of International Actors

We cannot deny that much power lies in the hands of international institutions and multinational companies. Hence they must take responsibility too. They have a heavy obligation and responsibility to support a political, social and economic environment which is conducive to the promotion and respect of women's rights. There should be no power without obligation. The exercise of power at whatever level from village council to IMF or WTO has to be accompanied by an expectation of due diligence. International institutions and corporations must be made to face the challenge and obligation of integrating equality, justice and respect for human rights into their decision-making so that the promotion of human rights law, and particularly women's rights law, and the protection of rights, are their starting point, guiding principle and outcome. They are failing in their human rights obligations to women, men and children, particularly in Southern countries.

The predominant engagement in economic decision-making in Southern countries of external actors – aid donors, IMF, World Bank – precludes democratic decision-making. Donors and the international financial institutions have enormous influence, not only on national policy priorities but also on the budget process. Analysis of this influence by Foster and Fozzard[10] indicates that donor budget meetings and IMF negotiations in Southern countries take place very early in the budget cycle, before the budget is approved by Cabinet and presented to Parliament for 'discussion' and 'ratification' and therefore before it enters the public domain. Thus any meaningful civil society influence is impossible.

International Codes and Standards, Guidelines and Campaigns

Much more could be done to demand and expect greater accountability and due diligence. The national parliaments of the rich Northern governments, for example, are remiss in not demanding greater accountability from their representatives to the international financial institutions and to the WTO and from multinational companies headquartered in their country. The following sections examine some of the international codes and standards which have been devel-

10 Mick Foster and Adrian Fozzard, 'Aid and Public Expenditure: A Guide ODI Working Paper 141' (London: ODI, 2000), cited in Andy Norton and Diane Elson, *What's Behind the Budget – Politics, Rights and Accountability in the Budget Process* (London: ODI, 2002), 8.

oped by the ILO, the Organisation for Economic Co-operation and Development (OECD) and the European Union (EU) over the last three decades as well as the UN 2003 norms for multinational enterprises. The shortcomings in implementation of these codes and standards leads to an examination of the research, campaigning and advocacy roles of civil society organisations and conclusion that action in the political sphere is critical to guaranteeing women's human rights.

Multinational companies have long been expected to behave in a socially responsible manner. Some international standards already refer directly or by interpretation to companies such as the Preamble to the Universal Declaration of Human Rights as mentioned above. The ILO Tripartite Declaration of Principles Concerning Multinational Enterprises and Social Policy (1977) set out socially responsible standards of behaviour. In 1998, the ILO set out Core Labour Standards in its Declaration on Fundamental Principles and Rights at Work. It expressed commitment by governments, employers' and workers' organisations to uphold basic human values – values vital to social and economic life. The Declaration covers four areas:

- Freedom of association and the right to collective bargaining;
- The elimination of forced and compulsory labour;
- The abolition of child labour; and
- The elimination of discrimination in the workplace.

Implementation is slow and the ILO does not have the clout or range of sanctions in its mandate of other international bodies like the IMF or WTO. It is a sad indictment on the part of the international community and national governments that freedom of association is limited in very many countries and that forced labour, child labour and workplace discrimination are growing. Companies continue to operate in Southern countries largely in a climate of impunity; there is no expectation of compliance to international standards and obligations.

The ILO's mandate includes a commitment to promote equality between all women and men in the world of work. This mandate is grounded in several International Labour Conventions[11] and informed by Resolutions of the International Labour Conference.[12] As I mentioned earlier, the ILO adopted in May 2005 A Global Alliance against Forced Labour[13] and a Special Action Programme to offer advice on appropriate legislation, carry out research, surveys and awareness raising and advocacy for the application of national laws and regulations and tack-

11 The four key equality conventions are: Discrimination (Employment and Occupation) Convention, 1958 (no. 111), Equal Remuneration Convention, 1951 (no. 100), Workers with Family Responsibilities Convention, 1981 (no. 156) and the Maternity Protection Convention, 2000 (no. 183), available at www.ilo.org.

12 Resolutions of the International Labour Conference in 1975, 1985, 1991 and the June 2004 Resolution on Gender Equality, Pay Equity and Maternity Protection.

13 Declaration on Fundamental Principles and Rights at Work, ILO Director General's Message at the Launch of 'A Global Alliance against Forced Labour,' 11 May 2005, available at www.ilo.org.

ling under-lying causes. The ILO's initiative is to be welcomed and applauded. It brings visibility to a dark corner of the global economy.

The OECD Guidelines for Multinational Enterprises (1976) were revised and strengthened in June 2000.[14] The Guidelines, already adopted by all the OECD countries and others (over 34 countries), aim to promote corporate social responsibility throughout the supply chain. They state that multinational enterprises should 'respect the human rights of those affected by their activities consistent with the host government's international obligations and commitments'. They cover a range of areas, including employment and industrial relations. Each adhering country is obliged to set up a National Contact Point (NCP) responsible for promoting and enforcing the Guidelines. In non-adhering countries, complaints about abuses can be brought to the NCP where the multi-national is headquartered. All of these instruments are valuable but they are non-binding and place no legal duties on companies. There is much work to be done to publicise these guidelines and the existence of the NCP and complaints procedure and to strengthen the gender dimensions of the guidelines.

In 1999, the European Parliament adopted a set of proposals on the accountability of European based multinationals. The resolution A European Code of Conduct[15] aimed to establish a European Monitoring Platform to focus on multinational accountability on a wide range of issues, including labour rights, environmental protection, non-discrimination, indigenous peoples' rights, etc. This was a significant victory for Richard Howitt, a Member of the European Parliament, who championed the resolution through the labyrinth of the Parliament. The resolution encourages the adoption of voluntary codes but also calls for international rules and demands that businesses report annually on the impacts of their work and meet a set of common standards. The discussion on corporate social responsibility continues with the European institutions (with a European Commission Green Paper[16] in 2001 and a European Commission Communication[17] in 2001) but there has been little concrete action to promote responsible business. The European Commission has refused to date to bring forward draft legislation which would ensure greater multinational compliance with international norms and standards. In the opinion of Richard Howitt[18] the Commission

14 Organisation for Economic Co-operation and Development, *OECD Guidelines for Multinational Enterprises*, http://www.oecd.org/department/0,2688,en_2649_34889_1_1_1_1_1,00.html.

15 http://www.europarl.europa.eu/oeil/file.jsp?id=162792.

16 Promoting a European Framework for Corporate Social Responsibility, http://www.europarl.europa.eu/oeil/file.jsp?id=211972.

17 Modernising Company Law and Enhancing Corporate Governance in the European Union – A Plan to Move Forward, http://eur-lex.europa.eu/LexUriServ/site/en/com/2003/com2003_0284en01.doc.

18 Richard Howitt MEP, European Parliament, Committee on Employment and Social Affairs, *Report on Corporate Social Responsibility: A New Partnership*, 20 December 2006 (A6-0471/2006).

is unwilling to confront and find a resolution to the polarised positions held by European business and other stakeholders (including investors, consumers, local communities, environment and other interest groups). The former see corporate social responsibility (CSR) as a matter for business alone while the latter want to see CSR subjected to transparency requirements laid down through external verification and/or legislation with an explicit role for all stakeholders.

Since 2000 significant progress has been made towards sharpening and clarifying the human rights obligations of multinational companies. In August 2003 the UN Sub-Commission on the Promotion and Protection of Human Rights adopted the Norms on the Responsibilities of Transnational Corporations and Other Business Enterprises with Regard to Human Rights.[19] The Norms make it clear that states' responsibility to promote, secure the fulfilment of, respect, ensure respect of and protect human rights includes ensuring that multinational companies and other business enterprises respect human rights. This duty on states places also indirect obligations on companies. The Commentary on the Norms expands on this point and states that 'transnational and other business enterprises shall have the responsibility to use due diligence in ensuring that their activities do not contribute directly or indirectly to human abuses, and that they do not directly or indirectly benefit from abuses of which they were aware or ought to have been aware.' Referring to the right to equal opportunity and non-discriminatory treatment, the Commentary explains: 'No worker shall be subject to direct or indirect physical, sexual, racial, psychological, verbal, or any other discriminatory form of harassment or abuse.' It further goes on to say: 'Particular attention should be devoted to the consequences of business activities that may affect the rights of women and particularly in regard to conditions of work.' This is the strongest statement in the Commentary on women's rights. The Norms and Commentary also cover the rights of workers in situations of forced or compulsory labour, the economic exploitation of children, working environment issues and voluntary overtime.

Another step was taken by the UN in July 2005 which showed its determination to press forward on this agenda. The Secretary General of the UN appointed a Special Representative of the UN Secretary-General on human rights and transnational corporations and other business enterprises. The mandate is 'to identify and clarify standards of corporate responsibility and accountability of transnational corporations and other business enterprises with respect to human rights', 'to elaborate on the role of States in effectively regulating and adjudicating the role of transnational corporations and other business enterprises with respect to human rights', and to carry out research, develop materials and compile a compendium of best practice.[20] The Special Representative submitted his first

19 Sub-Commission on the Promotion and Protection of Human Rights, *Norms on the Responsibilities of Transnational Corporations and Other Business Enterprises with regard to Human Rights* (2003), UN Doc. E/CN.4/Sub.2/2003/12/Rev.2.

20 Mandate of the UN Special Representative on business and human rights, available at http://www.reports-and-materials.org/Mandate-UN-Special-Representative.htm.

report in February 2006.[21] This report sets out the context, strategy and planned programme of activities.

How standards, norms and responsibilities can be anchored in a legal framework is the focus of much debate. International human rights law places primary obligation on states with respect to human rights but it is clear that these rules should be extended to place direct obligations on companies in addition to existing indirect obligations mentioned already above. Direct legal obligations are hard to press: however, it is argued that legal obligations might be enforced internationally on companies when states are unable or unwilling to take action themselves.[22] As we have seen above, socially responsible standards of behaviour have been expected of multinational companies for many decades (the Universal Declaration of Human Rights, the ILO Tripartite Declaration, the OECD Guidelines and the Beijing Platform for Action).[23] In addition, multinational companies' adoption of corporate- and industry-based codes indicates their taking on of social responsibilities. In recent years there has been a proliferation of voluntary codes of conduct adopted by multinational and other companies. The Business and Human Rights Resource Centre[24] reports that to its knowledge 98 companies now have a human rights policy. Most of these policy statements refer to the ILO Tripartite Declaration, some to the Universal Declaration of Human Rights.

The FTSE4Good Index Series,[25] an initiative of FTSE,[26] was designed to measure the performance of companies that meet globally corporate responsible standards and to facilitate investment in those companies. Although primarily about socially responsible investment, it lists as one of its objectives: 'To contribute to the development of responsible business practice around the world.' In April 2003 the Index Series inclusion selection criteria were changed to include criteria related to upholding and supporting universal human rights. The new criteria for companies cover policy and management which include, for example: having a public human rights policy; locating the strategic responsibility for the human rights policy with one or more board members or senior managers; adopting a statement of commitment to ILO core labour standards or the OECD Guidelines and of support of the Universal Declaration of Human Rights; monitoring the implementation of the policy and training for employees globally in the

21 Interim Report of the Special Representative of the Secretary-General, *The Issue of Human Rights and Transnational Corporations and Other Business Enterprises*, 22 February 2006, UN Doc. E/CN.4/2006/97.

22 International Council on Human Rights, *Beyond Voluntarism: Human Rights and the Developing International Legal Obligations of Companies* (Geneva: ICHR, 2002).

23 This elaborates actions to be taken by the private sector, including multinational and national corporations, for example, with regard to measures to prevent and eliminate violence against women.

24 http://www.business-humanrights.org/.

25 http://www.ftse.com/Indices/FTSE4Good_Index_Series/index.jsp.

26 FTSE is an independent company owned by The Financial Times and the London Stock Exchange.

human rights policy. Companies in the global resource sector (oil, gas, mining) are identified as having the highest human rights impact but the plan is to extend the criteria to other sectors, such as textiles and apparels, pharmaceuticals, chemicals, agriculture, banking and finance. The human rights criteria for companies which have a significant involvement in 'not free'[27] countries are set at an intermediate level. Social and stakeholder criteria, in existence since the beginning of the FTSE4Good, include having an equal opportunity policy and having more than 10 percent of managers be women or the proportion of managers who are women or from ethnic minorities exceed two-fifths of the representation of the workforce.

Whatever the shortcomings, and these are sometimes fundamental, we need to work to improve existing UN, OECD, ILO and EU instruments and use them to prise open space for action on women's human rights. We need to explore urgently how the concept of due diligence could be applied to economic players with respect to these various instruments and measures. The due diligence standard, drawn from international law doctrine, is designed to hold states accountable for their failure to take adequate steps to prevent rights' violations from occurring and/or their failure to provide adequate redress to victims for these violations. The due diligence principle requires that states have a full understanding of their rights' obligations and take all reasonable measures to ensure to prevent, investigate, prosecute and punish violations. While the due diligence standard to protect women from violence has been accepted its scope is vague. In the context of globalisation and the consequent shift in power between political and economic players, the principle of due diligence should, without question, also include economic players in its duty.

Peter T. Muchlinksi argues that there is a move towards a social dimension to the activities of multinational companies, one in which, he concludes, 'an active duty to observe fundamental human rights standards can be included.'[28] He proposes that positive legal duties to observe fundamental human rights can be introduced into international agreements that directly address multinational companies, but such legal duty has yet to be achieved in practice. Whatever progress is achieved in this area of international law, states should be held accountable for establishing effective regulation which ensures the promotion and protection of human rights.

27 Based on a range of sources, including reports from Human Rights Watch and Amnesty International. Companies with significant involvement (1,000-plus employees or £100m in turnover in the country) in countries with the greater human rights concern are identified as potentially having a significant impact. The double standard is rationalised by the level of development of human rights standards within the country.

28 Peter T. Muchlinksi, 'Human Rights and Multinationals: Is There a Problem?', *International Affairs* 77, no. 1 (2001): 31–48.

International Civil Society Campaigns

It is clear that the action by international bodies, government and companies requires organisation and advocacy on the part of trade unions and workers' organisations, political parties and other civil society organisations, including feminist organisations. Civil society and the media are playing key roles. They press for changes in national and international law where needed, for implementation of good laws and anti-discrimination measures and monitor practice. Civil society, in particular, continues to raise awareness of and publicise the human rights obligations of states and international institutions and companies, and the abuse of these obligations, and mobilise citizens to demand greater accountability.

The ILO now uses the concept of 'Decent Work' by which it means 'the promotion of opportunities for women and men to obtain decent and productive work in conditions of freedom, equity, security and human dignity'. This has been taken up by civil society organisations. For example, Solidar (an alliance of NGOs involved in social service provision, international co-operation, humanitarian aid and life-long learning, linked to the trade union movement) launched a 'Decent Life, Decent Work' campaign[29] to raise awareness of the rights of workers at the European and international level. Solidar also monitors and lobbies European institutions and international organisations (WTO, ILO, etc.) in order to promote the social dimension of globalisation and workers' rights. Thanks to the efforts of Solidar, the International Confederation of Free Trade Unions (ICFTU), the Global Progressive Forum and others, a Declaration called 'Decent Work: The Heart of a Fair Globalisation',[30] was agreed upon at the World Social Forum in Porte Alegre on 30 January 2005, which commits the participant organisations to take forward the debate and campaign for decent work.

The People's Health Movement,[31] started in 2000, is a growing coalition of grassroots organisations in around 80 countries dedicated to changing the prevailing health care delivery system. This system is considered to be failing to serve the deteriorating health of most of the poor worldwide. The goal is to re-establish health and equitable development as top priorities in local, national and international policy-making, with comprehensive primary health care as the strategy to achieve these priorities.

The International Gender and Trade Network (IGTN)[32] is articulating feminist alternatives to the current trade regime and analysing and questioning agreements, such as GATS and investment agreements, and demonstrating their impact on gender relations. They are putting forward feminist economic thinking which puts equality and security first. They are also demanding greater transparency and democracy within the WTO. The IGTN, Network Women in Develop-

29 http://www.solidar.org/doclist.asp?SectionID=6.

30 http://www.solidar.org/English/pdf/english%20WSF%2005%2017%20March.

31 http://www.phmovement.org/.

32 http://www.igtn.org/.

ment Europe (WIDE)[33] and others organised globally in the run-up to the WTO summit in Hong Kong in December 2005. There is also very useful and interesting pressure building up around the women's rights implications of the Economic Partnership Agreements currently being negotiated by the European Union and the group of African, Caribbean and Pacific countries.

A not-for-profit organisation based in Geneva, Switzerland, 3D → Trade – Human Rights – Equitable Economy (3D)[34] is working to ensure that trade rules are developed and applied in ways that are consistent with human rights. They believe that mechanisms such as the CEDAW Convention can be used to advocate for trade rules which are consistent with states' human rights obligations. 3D prepared a submission to the Committee on the Elimination of Discrimination against Women (CEDAW Committee) which audits the impact of agricultural trade liberalisation on women's employment in Niger.[35] They argue that current economic and trade rules relating to agriculture run counter to commitments on the right to work, to health, to participate and to temporary special measures, as established in the CEDAW Convention. This is a very powerful advocacy activity which could usefully be replicated by others.

A new civil society campaign for a General Agreement on Public Services (GAPS)[36] was launched in Geneva on September 20, 2005 to work for an agreement which would set out rules and standards for public services based on human rights. At present a small coalition of organisations[37] are beginning this campaign but it is hoped it will take off and become part of the Global Call to Action on Poverty (GCAP). The campaign's premise is that trade and investment in services, especially water, education, health and sanitation but also energy and telecommunications, should be based on, promote and seek to further human rights, and be organised and managed in a democratic manner. The coalition regards access to affordable, appropriate and gender-sensitive services as a fundamental human right, as critical to the sustainability of societies everywhere, and therefore matters which cannot be left to the vagaries of the marketplace. At present there are great inequalities in access and quality. A GAPS would provide an internationally agreed framework which would set out new relationships and responsibilities for government and other service providers, including the private sector and NGOs, and the international institutions – a framework which would guarantee access to quality services. It is very early days in the campaign so the nature of this framework is open for discussion and comment.

33 http://www.eurosur.org/wide/home.htm.

34 http://www.3dthree.org/en/.

35 3D, *Niger: Agricultural Trade Liberalisation and Women's Rights* (Geneva: 3D, 2006).

36 http://www.publicworld.org/ourwork/gapsintro.htm.

37 Consumers International, One World Action, Public Services International and Public World.

Another example of innovative and successful work is Women Working Worldwide,[38] a UK-based organisation started in 1983 with the aim of promoting the rights of women workers through networking with women workers' organisations, building direct solidarity and exchanging information. It is currently running a number of initiatives including a project on the rights of women workers in international supply chains. The aim is to make sure that in the midst of enthusiasm about calls for implementation of universal labour standards through company codes of conduct, social clauses, and ILO core labour standards, that two issues are not forgotten: firstly, the complexity of international supply chains which operate against the implementation of any form of regulation; and secondly, the relationship between core labour standards and the demands of women workers. The project has a focus on two sectors: garments in Asia and horticulture in Africa. The case of the Kenyan Flower farm workers[39] is a valuable example of what can be achieved by international action and the challenges remaining. Kenya's flower farms supply 24 percent of the cut flowers sold in the EU and employ thousands of women workers. The Kenyan Women Workers Association launched a campaign in 2002 to highlight the exploitative and hazardous working conditions on the farms. For example, workers were expected to return to greenhouses immediately following the spraying of pesticides without any protective clothing. As the farm owners were reluctant to engage, Women Working Worldwide suggested that a report on working conditions be taken to the Ethical Trade Initiative (ETI),[40] a UK-based alliance of companies, NGOs and trade union organisations. British supermarkets that had signed up to the ETI responded by agreeing to meet the workers. The result was a Stakeholder Committee with representatives of the workers' association, the farm owner and the government that led to establishing a better system of monitoring working conditions. However, the purchasing practices of the supermarkets, the root of the problem, remained unchanged; they constantly push the prices down and simultaneously make demands on quality and the speed of delivery. Supermarkets blame consumers for fluctuating demands and bargain hunting. Women Working Worldwide and its network partners are engaged in on-going campaigning and advocacy to raise consumer awareness and pressure.

Gender analysis of budgets/public spending is a useful strategy. Gender budget initiatives are happening in around 50 countries worldwide.[41] But influencing budget preparation is not simple as budget processes in almost all countries are secretive. It requires very effective organisation and advocacy on the part of women's organisations and others to access information about the budgetary process and to open up some space for citizen engagement and scrutiny. Sex-disaggregated and reliable figures are rarely available. In addition, extending gender

38 http://www.women-ww.org.

39 http://www.women-ww.org/campaigns.html.

40 See www.ethicaltrade.org.

41 Helena Hofbauer Balmori, 'Gender and Budgets Overview Report', in *BRIDGE Cutting Edge Pack* (Brighton: BRIDGE, 2003).

budget analysis to the local level is also difficult due to poor data, lack of unified systems and categories, and variable levels of resources and discretion over their use.[42] Even where policy and political commitment to improving gender equity exists, local and national government officials and elected representatives often lack the capacity and tools to undertake gender budget analysis. While several bilateral and multilateral donors have supported gender budgets initiatives worldwide, to date there has been little gender analysis of donor contributions to country budgets. This is especially surprising in countries where donor funds make up a large proportion of government revenue[43] and is an area that One World Action is now examining with some of its partners in Southern Africa. Increased capacity to engage with budgets and budget-making processes would greatly strengthen civil society's ability to hold governments and donors to account and contribute to the discourse on good governance. Such initiatives need to be supported and encouraged. Only in this way can significant shifts in public spending be achieved towards spending priorities which meet the needs and interests of the poorest citizens and enable them, and all others, to enjoy and exercise their full human rights. Gender budget analysis within the framework of feminist economics can contribute to bringing about significant shifts in public spending. However, such shifts are unlikely to be sustainable without fundamental changes also in the political sphere.

A New Politics

New ways of doing politics are urgently needed in order to build a world based on respect for human rights. For me the new politics needs real democracy at every level – local, national, and international. This democracy would comprise a process of decision-making which is inclusive, open and transparent, active and participative, respectful and accountable, where decisions are taken at the level most appropriate by those most affected, where everyone has the right and access to the same information, and where the views of the most marginalised are as valid as those of others. This, in my view, would be sustainable democracy and would bring the good governance which is essential for gender justice.

Advocates for the human rights of women need to commit to and engage with democratic processes to build accountable governance that is sensitive to gender and other social differences. The current processes towards greater democratisation and accountable governance presents opportunities which women must seize; these are at the very heart of everything feminism is about. If women do not engage fully, the precious women's rights gains can easily be reversed. Over the last decade or so, there have been some dramatic increases in the number of women being elected to political structures, for example, the millions of women

42 Carole Rakodi, *Influence and Accountability – Citizen Voices, Responsiveness and Accountability in Service Delivery* (London: One World Action, 2002).

43 Debbie Budlender, *Review of Gender Budget Initiatives*, Assessment commissioned by the Commonwealth Secretariat in collaboration with UNIFEM and IDRC, 2001.

elected to the *panchayat* in India and the thousands elected at local level in Bangladesh, and the election of women to around 30 percent of seats in South Africa, Mozambique and elsewhere. Women are claiming the space to speak, and the power to decide and act. This is inspiring. But, of course, it is clear that numbers are not enough. What is necessary is a critical mass of women who will work to transform the political structures themselves, their ways and hours of working, their secrecy, sexist attitudes, corrupt practices and male domination. At the same time women need to work to transform the agenda and priorities of political structures. The trend towards decentralisation provides opportunities for greater democratisation, but is also fraught with challenges.[44]

With greater political power feminists could ensure that promises such as those made at Vienna, Cairo, Beijing or at G8 meetings are fulfilled, that economic power players are scrutinised and controlled, that debt is cancelled, and that trade, aid and investment have the goal of eliminating injustice and inequality and promoting respect for human rights.

In Conclusion

The neo-liberal dogma which drives the global economic agenda and undermines all efforts by women's pressure groups, NGOs and governments to make sustainable progress towards full human rights for all – women, men and children – should be challenged. There is a growing critique of the neo-liberal economic model which has not worked even on its own terms.[45] It is clear that cracks are appearing in the edifice of neo-liberalism, but it is far from crumbling. And it is also far from obvious what would replace it. In my view, it is not possible for anyone to enjoy and exercise their full human rights within the global economy as it is currently structured.

44 In the minds of some international agencies decentralisation is merely an opportunity to slim down central state structures. In the eyes of many central governments, decentralisation is merely an opportunity to off-load responsibility for basic service delivery and local economic development to local government without the necessary power, resources, and support. I believe that decentralisation has enormous potential. Local government can become a locus of real local democracy and an opportunity for many more women to become political leaders. Real and sustainable democracy at the local level means local government must have the power to act locally with the necessary finances – from central government and the right to raise revenue locally. It needs skilled staff with real capacity and commitment to perform for the local community, and the full and active engagement of local citizens to ensure accountability. This kind of local democracy can provide the foundation for democracy at national and international levels, and begin to build the kind of world in which we would all like to live.

45 For good discussion of this see, 'Liberalisation and Deregulation: The Route to Gender Equality?' in *Gender Equality: Striving for Justice in an Unequal World* (Geneva: UNRISD, 2005) chapter 2.

The primary responsibility for promoting and protecting women's rights under international human rights law rests with national governments. Their obligations are clearly articulated in international treaties, agreements and customary law; their failure to fulfil these is also clear. Action on women's rights is not a high priority for most governments. Northern governments have dual obligations: to women in their own country and, as powerful international players and donors, to women in other countries. It is easy to be cynical about the North's commitment to promoting respect for human rights, democracy and good governance: the North's own institutions are far from democratic and Northern governments are failing in their due diligence obligations by their continued willingness, in direct correlation to their own narrow political and economic interests, to close their eyes to non-democratic and authoritarian regimes. Furthermore, as mentioned above, Northern governments are failing to take concrete action within the OECD and the EU to insist on greater accountability from multinational companies headquartered in their country. It is time to reject fully the view that corporate social responsibility is bad for business because of loss of profit or competitiveness.

International economic players also have responsibilities and obligations: their indirect obligations are clearly enunciated as, for example, in the 2003 Norms on the Responsibilities of Transnational Corporations and Other Business Enterprises with Regard to Human Rights referred to earlier. More could be done to enforce direct legal obligations on companies in situations where states do not have the capacity or political will to take action themselves. In addition, there is a long-standing expectation that companies should operate in socially, and more recently in environmentally, responsible ways; a more active duty to observe fundamental human rights standards could be developed based on these ways. Although primary responsibility for guaranteeing the promotion of respect for human rights rests with the state, the time is overdue to address concretely how non-state actors can be held accountable for their actions directly through international human rights law and/or indirectly through due diligence.

States and international actors have due diligence obligations to work for demonstrable policy coherence across different policy areas: actions to promote peace, respect for human rights, gender equity and equality, environment protection or to reduce poverty should not be undermined by actions in other policy spheres such as, macro-economics, trade, foreign and security policy, agriculture, fisheries, environment, migration or by sanctions or war. The EU has adopted strong policy statements on coherence[46], but coherence in practice is very slow in coming. States must work for new foreign policy approaches, conducive to hu-

46 See for example, 'The European Consensus on Development', Joint Statement by the Council and the Representatives of the Governments of the Member States meeting within the Council, the European Parliament and the Commission, November 2005, published in the Office Journal of the European Union C 46/1, 24 February 2006.

man rights[47] and human security, which would face up to the challenge of dealing with governments who deny or abuse human rights on a massive scale or who routinely neglect or abuse the rights of women, men, children, workers and marginalised social groups. And urgent progress towards an international arms trade treaty is essential.

All interested in women's rights and gender justice need to mobilise and engage politically to build sustainable and accountable democracy. This is the only sure way that international human rights commitments and laws could be honoured, that the goal of social, economic and political transformation could be achieved, and personal, social, economic, environmental and political security genuinely linked.

This article is dedicated to the memory of Angela Hale, a founder member of Women Working Worldwide and a tireless campaigner for women workers' rights.

47 An interpretation of national interest conducive to respect for women's rights would integrate peace, environmental sustainability and equality globally. It would seek to find a balance between local and global interests and political, social and economic interests which did not put narrow national interests above global. For example, it would move away from decisions which put short-term economic interests, such as arms trade jobs and orders, before long-term global security concerns. It would analyse investment decisions, not exclusively from the perspective of short-term local gain such as investment in the arms industry, but for their contribution to long-term global sustainability, such as investment in socially useful production or social services. Integral to such a 'foreign policy' is the rigorous scrutiny and control of what Northern-based multinationals do in other countries and incentives used by Northern governments to promote exports, such as export credit guarantees (cheap finance).

Due Diligence and the Fight against Gender-Based Violence in the Inter-American System

*Elizabeth A.H. Abi-Mershed**

Introduction

The present chapter looks at what due diligence means in the context of efforts within the inter-American human rights system to prevent and respond to gender-based violence.[1] It looks briefly at what this concept has meant in the regional human rights system as a basis to examine what it can contribute to advancing the right of women to be free from violence.

The due diligence standard has served the system as a flexible way of understanding what state obligation and responsibility mean in theory, and more importantly, in practice. The adoption of the Inter-American Convention on the Prevention, Punishment and Eradication of Violence against Women (Convention of Belém do Pará),[2] which expressly incorporates the principle of due diligence, has provided the regional system a means to re-envision human rights law to better respond to violations with gender specific causes and consequences.

While a state is clearly responsible for the acts and omissions of its agents, in certain circumstances it may also have obligations to prevent and/or respond to the transgression of protected rights by individual non-state actors. This has be-

* The opinions presented in this chapter are those of the author, and do not necessarily reflect those of the Organization of American States (OAS) or the Inter-American Commission on Human Rights (IACHR).

1 The Inter-American Commission on Human Rights provides comprehensive information about its work online at www.cidh.org. The site includes the instruments of the system, as well as all published reports and a search mechanism, and includes all reports cited in the present chapter. The Inter-American Court of Human Rights provides information at www.corteidh.or.cr.

2 Inter-American instruments referred to in the present articles may be found in IACHR, *Basic Documents Pertaining to Human Rights in the Inter-American System* [updated to January 2007], OEA/Ser.L/V/I.4 rev. 12, 31 January 2007, available at www.cidh.org.

C. Benninger-Budel ed., Due Diligence and Its Application to Protect Women from Violence
 Printed in The Netherlands. ISBN 978 90 04 16293 8. pp. 127-137

come increasingly clear in the area of human rights protection. The principle of due diligence has proven crucial in delineating the conditions under which a state may be obliged to prevent or respond to acts or omissions of private actors.

More broadly, through the evolving law and practice on the concept of due diligence, international human rights law is exploring what the duties of prevention and response require of states. Whereas the early years of the inter-American system were focused primarily on fighting gross and systematic human rights violations, current work applying the concept of due diligence focuses on prevention on the one hand, and accountability on the other as a means of dissuading future violations – with both ideas ultimately seeking to enhance the efficacy of human rights commitments. As a standard that responds to different contexts with flexibility, due diligence provides a juridical bridge between precepts of international law focused on the relationship between the state, its agents and its subjects and the role the state may have with respect to the conduct of and relations between private individuals.

The Inter-American Commission on Human Rights and its Special Rapporteurship on the Rights of Women have placed special emphasis on the issues of gender-based discrimination[3] and violence.[4] The present chapter provides a brief examination of how the concept of due diligence has informed that work. While the concept is important to the Commission's work in general, this chapter focuses primarily on how the system has used the concept to delineate state responsibility for acts of private individuals, because in these instances the duty of the state to prevent and respond to violations is thrown into sharp relief.

3 See, e.g., IACHR, Report no. 4/01, Case 11.625, Merits, *María Eugenia Morales de Sierra* (Guatemala), 19 January 2001; 'Considerations Regarding the Compatibility of Affirmative Action Measures Designed to Promote the Political Participation of Women with the Principles of Equality and Non-discrimination', in *Annual Report of the IACHR* vol. 2 (1999), OEA/Ser.L/V/II.106, Doc. 3 rev., 13 April 2000, 1525; Report no. 33/02, Petition 12.046, Friendly Settlement, *Mónica Carabantes Galleguillos* (Chile), 12 March 2002.

4 See, e.g., IACHR, 'Violence Against Women and Children', in *Report on the Situation of Human Rights in Haiti*, OEA/Ser.L/V/II.88, doc. 10, rev, 1995; Report no. 5/96, Case 10.970, *Raquel Martín de Mejía* (Perú), 1 Mach 1996; Report no. 54/01, Case 12.051, *Maria da Penha Maia Fernandes* (Brazil) 16 April 2001; Report no. 53/01, Case 11.565, Merits, *Ana, Beatriz and Celia Gonzalez Perez* (Mexico) 4 April 2001; *Violence and Discrimination against Women in the Armed Conflict in Colombia*, OEA/Ser/L/V/II. 124/Doc.6, 18 October 2006; *Access to Justice for Women Victims of Violence in the Americas*, OEA/Ser.L/V/II. Doc. 68, 20 January 2007; Report no. 21/07, Petition 161-02, Friendly Settlement, *Paulina del Carmen Ramírez Jacinto* (Mexico), 9 March 2007. See also, I/A Court H.R, *Miguel Castro Castro Prison v Peru*, Series C no. 160, Judgment of 25 November 2006.

A Brief Look at the Roots of Due Diligence in the Inter-American System: From *Velásquez Rodríguez* to Belém do Pará

The due diligence principle has roots in diverse areas of international law.[5] Its application in the context of human rights draws on traditional principles of international law, but applies those in innovative ways and contexts. Precisely because the principle can be applied in different contexts and with flexibility,[6] it has special value in the area of human rights generally and women's rights specifically.

The *Velásquez Rodríguez* case decided by the Inter-American Court of Human Rights in 1988 serves as a key reference on the concept of due diligence in human rights law.[7] *Velásquez Rodríguez* was the first contentious case decided by the Inter-American Court, and through it the Court made explicit what were and continue to be guiding principles and understandings of the system. One of those key principles has to do with the nature of state responsibility and the conduct that can give rise to it. As indicated in that judgment, the nature of state responsibility for acts carried out by a state's own agents or through the use of public authority is fairly clear. The Court went on to explain that there are other circumstances that can give rise to state responsibility:

> 'An illegal act which violates human rights and which is initially not imputable to a State (for example, because it is the act of a private person or because the person responsible has not been identified) can lead to the international responsibility of the State, not because of the act itself, but because of the lack of due diligence to prevent the violation or to respond to it as required by the Convention.'[8]

The organs of the system have continued to develop these obligations of prevention and response, as the system has continued to explore the extent to which states have obligations vis-à-vis the acts of private individuals. The *Velásquez Rodríguez* court articulated the basic standard for this inquiry:

> '...The violation can be established even if the identity of the individual perpetrator is unknown. What is decisive is whether a violation of the rights protected by the Convention has occurred with the support or acquiescence of the government, or whether the State has allowed the act to take place without taking measures to prevent it or to punish those responsible.'[9]

5 See Robert P. Barnidge, Jr., 'The Due Diligence Principle under International Law,' in *International Community Law Review* 8 (2006): 81–121 (tracing the development of the principle through different areas).

6 See generally, Barnidge (2006), ibid., 121.

7 I/A Court H.R., *Velásquez Rodríguez*, Series C no. 4, Judgment of 29 July 1988.

8 Ibid., para. 172.

9 Ibid., para. 173.

The evaluation of whether a state has taken sufficient measures of prevention or punishment does not rest on the existence of the particular violation, but rather on whether the state has taken reasonable steps of prevention, and has responded with seriousness to any violation.[10]

> 'The duty to investigate, like the duty to prevent, is not breached merely because the investigation does not produce a satisfactory result....[I]t must be undertaken in a serious manner and not as a mere formality preordained to be ineffective....Where the acts of private parties that violate the Convention are not seriously investigated, those parties are aided in a sense by the government, thereby making the State responsible on the international plane.'[11]

The Convention of Belém do Pará, adopted in 1994, drew from the evolution of these principles. Under this treaty, states parties expressly commit themselves to 'apply due diligence to prevent, investigate and impose penalties for violence against women'. This treaty was the result of a regional consensus on the need to take strong measures to combat the problem of gender-based violence and is the most widely ratified of all of the inter-American human rights treaties.[12] It may be noted that the reference to due diligence was not a given, but rather the result of an extensive drafting efforts.[13]

From the normative perspective, this Convention breaks new ground in a number of ways in terms of setting standards responsive to gender-based violence. To highlight a few key aspects, the Convention:

- Expressly recognises the link between gender violence and discrimination, indicating that such violence is a manifestation of the historically unequal power relations between women and men, and that the right to be free from

10 Ibid., para. 174.

11 Ibid., para. 177.

12 32 member states of the Organization of American States (OAS) are party to the Convention of Belém do Pará: Antigua and Barbuda, Argentina, Bahamas, Barbados, Belice, Bolivia, Brazil, Chile, Colombia, Costa Rica, Dominica, Dominican Republic, Ecuador, El Salvador, Grenada, Guatemala, Guyana, Haiti, Honduras, Jamaica, Mexico, Nicaragua, Panama, Paraguay, Peru, Saint Kitts and Nevis, Saint Vincent and the Grenadines, Saint Lucia, Suriname, Trinidad and Tobago, Uruguay and Venezuela.

13 Initial versions of the Article in question did not expressly refer to the due diligence standard. Compare, for example, Inter-American Commission of Women, 'Suggested Preliminary Draft for the Preparation of an Inter-American Convention on the Prevention, Punishment and Eradication of Violence against Women', OEA/Ser. L/II.7.5, CIM/RECOVI/doc.4/93, 10 March 1993, and Inter-American Commission of Women, 'Status of the Review Process Underway Concerning the Preliminary Draft Inter-American Convention on Women and Violence, Prepared by the Inter-American Commission of Women for Consultation with Member States', OEA/Ser. L/II.7.5/CIM/RECOVI/Doc.20/93 rev. 1 corr.1, 30 June 1993. It should also be noted that the vast majority of delegates and experts who participated in the decisive drafting meetings were women.

such violence includes the right to be free from discrimination and to be valued and educated free of stereotypes;[14]

- Recognises that such violence affects women in a multitude of ways, preventing them from exercising other fundamental rights, both civil and political, *and* economic, social and cultural rights;[15] and
- Bridges the so-called 'public–private sphere' divide, by defining violence against women as 'any act or conduct, based on gender, which causes death or physical, sexual or psychological harm or suffering to women, whether in the public or private sphere'.[16]

In sum, the Convention of Belém do Pará requires that states parties ensure that their agents refrain from acts of violence against women, and further requires that these states apply due diligence to prevent, investigate and punish such violence when perpetrated by non-state actors in the home, community or wherever it may occur. States parties undertake to ensure that these obligations are given practical effect and that women at risk for or subjected to violence have access to effective judicial protection and guarantees.[17]

The application of the concept of due diligence in the *Velásquez Rodríguez* case was influential in the formulation of the Convention of Belém do Pará, and has been cited numerous times as fundamental in understanding why international human rights law requires states to prevent and respond to violence against women by state and non-state actors.[18]

---

14 See Preamble, Articles 4 and 6.

15 See Preamble, Articles 4 and 5.

16 See Articles 1, 2 and 3.

17 See Article 7; see also Articles 8 and 9. The mechanisms for supervision of compliance include reports to the Commission of Women of the OAS (hereinafter CIM), and the processing of individual complaints alleging violations of the principal obligations through the petition system of the Inter-American Commission on Human Rights. See Articles 10–12. While the present chapter focuses on the concept of due diligence in the work of the Inter-American Commission on Human Rights, it may be noted that in 2005 the CIM created a mechanism to follow up on member state implementation of obligations under the treaty through a system of technical cooperation among states. Committee of Experts on Violence (CEVI), Follow-up Mechanism, Convention of Belém do Pará (MESECVI), Method for Evaluation of and Follow-up on the Implementation of the Provisions of the Convention of Belém do Pará, OEA/Ser.L/II.7.10, MESECVI/CEVI/doc.7/05 rev. 1, 24 August 2005, available at http://www.oas.org/cim/Documentos/MESECVI/MESECVI-CE-doc.7.ing.rev.1.DOC.

18 See, among many other sources, *Report of the Special Rapporteur on violence against women, its causes and consequences*, Radhika Coomaraswamy, submitted in accordance with Commission on Human Rights Resolution 1995/85, UN Doc. E/CN.4/1996/53, 5 February 1996, para. 36.

From Belém do Pará to *Maria da Penha*

The first case dealt with by the Inter-American Commission on Human Rights under the Convention of Belém do Pará concerned violence against a woman in the domestic sphere, the violence to which Maria da Penha Maia Fernandes had been subjected by her then-husband. That abuse, including attempts to kill her in 1983, left the victim permanently paralysed. The Commission applied both the American Convention on Human Rights and the Convention of Belém do Pará in establishing the nature of the state of Brazil's obligation to apply due diligence to investigate, prosecute and punish domestic violence.[19]

When the Commission decided the case, the criminal proceedings against the victim's husband had been pending for some 16 years. He had not been imprisoned, and appeals against an initial conviction had been left pending for years. In its findings, the Commission took into account the pattern and practice of violence against women in Brazil in establishing that the measures taken by the state to combat this problem were insufficient and had not had any effect in the particular case, in violation of Article 24 of the American Convention on Human Rights. The report emphasises that the pattern of impunity prevailing in domestic violence cases, and in this case in particular, stands in direct opposition to the state's duties under Article 7 of the Convention of Belém do Pará:

> 'The impunity that the ex-husband of Mrs. Fernandes has enjoyed and continues to enjoy is at odds with the international commitment voluntarily assumed by the State.... The failure to prosecute and convict the perpetrator under these circumstances is an indication that the State condones the violence suffered by Maria da Penha, and this failure by the Brazilian courts to take action is exacerbating the direct consequences of the aggression by her ex-husband. Furthermore, as has been demonstrated earlier, that tolerance by the State organs is not limited to this case; rather, it is a pattern. The condoning of this situation by the entire system only serves to perpetuate the psychological, social, and historical roots and factors that sustain and encourage violence against women.
>
> Given the fact that the violence suffered by Maria da Penha is part of a general pattern of negligence and lack of effective action by the State in prosecuting and convicting aggressors, it is the view of the Commission that this case involves not only failure to fulfill the obligation...to prosecute and convict, but also the obligation to prevent these degrading practices. That general and discriminatory judicial ineffectiveness also creates a climate that is conducive to domestic violence, since society sees no evidence of willingness by the State, as the representative of the society, to take effective action to sanction such acts.'[20]

---

19 Report no. 54/01, Case 12.051, *Maria da Penha Maia Fernandes* (Brazil), 16 April 2001.

20 Ibid., paras. 55–56.

This was the first case in the regional system to demonstrate what the state obligation to apply due diligence could require in a case of violence at the hands of a private individual. As indicated, one of the central themes running through the Commission's analysis is the need for states to take action to combat impunity, a requirement that continues to be a central issue for the Commission in cases concerning gender violence.

The Commission's report grew out of and was incorporated back into a larger strategy at the national level. The findings of the report helped to impel a number of changes at the local level, including that the perpetrator was finally brought before the judiciary, sentenced and imprisoned for a period.[21] More broadly, the case and report helped draw attention to deficiencies in both law and practice, and that attention led to the 2006 adoption of a new law on Domestic and Family Violence against Women known informally as the 'Maria da Penha law'. The new law includes measures to prevent harm to women, including better and more ample protective measures, as well as improved state responses for women who have been subjected to violence.[22]

From *Maria da Penha* to Ciudad Juárez

In 2002, the Rapporteurship on Women's Rights carried out its first thematic visit to Ciudad Juárez, Mexico, to examine the situation of violence against women. The resulting report *The Situation of the Rights of Women in Ciudad Juárez, Mexico: The Right to Be Free from Violence and Discrimination*, analyses the grave situation of violence faced by the women and girls of that city, including murder and disappearance, as well as sexual and domestic violence, and offers recommendations to assist the state in amplifying its efforts to respect and ensure those rights.[23] It is important to understand that the Inter-American Commission on Human Rights was petitioned by representatives of civil society to take action on the situation in Ciudad Juárez principally on the basis of a string of what were called 'serial' killings of young women. What the Commission found and detailed in its report, however, was a broader panorama of violence, of which the 'serial'

21 The state took action to implement a number of the recommendations issued by the Commission in that report, although several others remain pending. For a recent review of the status of compliance with the recommendations, see http://www.cidh.org/annualrep/2006eng/Chap.3L.htm#12.051.

22 See IACHR, Press Release no. 30/06, 'The IACHR Rapporteurship on the Rights of Women Celebrates the Adoption in Brazil of a Specific Law to Prevent and Eradicate Domestic and Family Violence' (recognising as well that the process to adopt the law had included substantive participation on the part of civil society), 11 August 2006; The law itself can be accessed in Portuguese at https://www.planalto.gov.br/ccivil_03/_Ato2004-2006/2006/Lei/L11340.htm.

23 IACHR, *The Situation of the Rights of Women in Ciudad Juárez, Mexico: The Right to Be Free from Violence and Discrimination*, OEA/Ser.L/V/II.117, Doc. 44, 7 March 2003.

killings were one manifestation. That pattern of violence was marked by a lack of measures of prevention or protection, and by a response that was deficient to the point of creating a climate of impunity for the perpetrators of the killings. The situation of violence was in turn inextricably linked with a larger situation of discrimination. That discrimination was particularly manifest in the way that complaints of violence against women were dealt with by the police and judiciary.

The recommendations issued by the Commission focus on ending the impunity that has characterised the vast majority of these crimes as a key means to punish past killings and prevent future killings. They consist of general recommendations, recommendations concerning the application of due diligence to investigate these crimes and prosecute and punish those responsible, and recommendations concerning the application of due diligence to prevent future such crimes.

What does the concept of due diligence require the state to do? Taking for example the recommendations concerning investigation and punishment, the Commission focuses on the need to: develop additional resources and technical capacities; provide independent oversight of investigating authorities; develop investigation plans that take into account the prevalence of violence against women as well as possible links between cases; the need to investigate 'cold' cases and correct past deficiencies; develop investigation plans seeking to cross-reference cases of disappearance with established deaths; provide enhanced training in technical aspects and in the causes and consequences of violence based on gender; and to establish mechanisms to hold officials who fail to discharge their responsibilities under the law accountable.

With respect to the situation in Ciudad Juárez, and with respect to this kind of violence more generally, states are obliged, pursuant to their treaty obligations, to use good faith to implement such recommendations and report back on the measures taken in that regard. The Commission's visit and report, along with important initiatives by civil society and other intergovernmental organisations, have impelled some changes in the situation in Ciudad Juárez. The Commission has carried out follow-up hearings in order to press for those and further changes. In connection with that visit and report, the Commission is processing a number of individual petitions,[24] and through its reports on the merits on these cases we will be able to analyse the requirements of due diligence in the context of concrete facts.

24 IACHR, Report no. 16/05, Petition 281–02, Admissibility, Claudia Ivette González, Mexico, 24 February, 2005; Report no. 17/05, Petition 282–02, Admissibility, Esmeralda Herrera Monreal, Mexico, 24 February, 2005; Report no. 18/05, Petition 283–02, Admissibility, Laura Berenice Ramos Monarrez, Mexico, 24 February, 2005; Report no. 32/06, Petition 1175–03, Admissibility, Paloma Angélica Escobar Ledezma et al., Mexico, 14 March, 2006; Report no. 31/06, Petition 1176–03, Admissibility, Silvia Arce et al., Mexico, 14 March 2006.

From Ciudad Juárez to Guatemala and Colombia

Following its work in Ciudad Juárez, the Rapporteurship then carried out a visit to Guatemala that had been requested by representatives of civil society as well as by the government, both concerned by the number of murders and the prevalence of other forms of violence against Guatemalan women.

The Commission's Rapporteur examined both the number of killings and the way the characteristics of those killings had been changing. The evidence presented showed that more bodies of women were being found with signs of torture and in certain cases, mutilation. The Rapporteur also gathered information about other forms of violence affecting women, such as family and domestic violence, rape, sexual harassment and abduction, amongst others, and indicated that, in the search for solutions to the murders, it was important to take into account the inter-relation between the different forms of violence. More specifically, many bodies showed signs of sexual violence and, in a significant number of the killings, the victim had been subject to violence within the family.

What does the concept of due diligence signify in the context of an examination of this nature? The initial conclusions from that visit centred on the obligation to use due diligence to investigate and punish crimes of violence against women.[25] In order to illustrate the existing deficiencies, the initial conclusions traced the route that women victims or their family members follow when trying to seek justice. Looking at the situation of a victim of domestic violence, for example, the first stop on that route might be a request for a protective order. The information gathered indicated that, even when such orders were obtained, there were no mechanisms in place to ensure their effective implementation. The Rapporteur received information during her visit about two women who, at the time they were murdered, were carrying their protective orders with them. The Rapporteur further detailed problems with lack of temporary shelters for victims of domestic violence, lack of resources generally for victims living in poverty and, in particular, lack of access to legal advice. As the Rapporteur indicated:

> 'One serious outcome of the cycle of violence against women is the impunity associated with those violations....During the week, the delegation followed the steps that must be taken by a victim in her search for justice. Our experience, after visits to the civil police, the Prosecutor's Office (Office for Crimes against Women, Office for Care of Victims), the morgue, and to the judiciary, was finally that the justice required is not found.... Representatives of the State and of civil society, as well as victims of violence or their families, confirmed that, of the cases reported, few get as far as the trial stage. As an example, of the cases of murder handled by the Office for Crimes against Women, only one has reached the trial stage.'[26]

25 IACHR, Press Release 20/04, 'The IACHR Special Rapporteur Evaluates the Effectiveness of the Right of Women in Guatemala to Live Free from Violence and Discrimination', 18 September 2004.

26 Ibid., paras. 17–18.

The Commission is presently processing certain individual petitions related to that visit.[27] The Rapporteurship conducted a follow-up visit in 2006, and is working on a report on the situation of violence against women in Guatemala with detailed recommendations.

More recently, the Commission issued a report prepared by its Special Rapporteurship on *Violence and Discrimination against Women in the Armed Conflict in Colombia*[28] which examines the obligations of the state with respect to state agents, members of the paramilitary forces and non-state actors. This report examines issues of violence and discrimination and how the situation of conflict can further exacerbate these human rights violations. It looks first at how the actors in the armed conflict employ different forms of physical, psychological and sexual violence to 'wound the enemy' by dehumanising the victim, injuring her family and/or spreading terror in her community, with the objective of widening their control of territory and resources. Second, it examines violence intended to forcibly displace women. It then analyses how sexual violence can be involved in the forced recruitment of women who are required to provide sexual services to members of guerrilla or paramilitary forces. Finally, it looks at violence intended to subject women to measures of social control imposed by illegal armed groups in communities or territories under their control. The report gives particular attention to the situation of indigenous women and Afro-Colombian women who suffer multiple forms of discrimination that leave them especially vulnerable to the infliction of different forms of violence.

Most recently, in January of 2007, the Commission issued the report prepared by its Special Rapporteurship on *Access to Justice for Women Victims of Violence in the Americas*.[29] The report places special emphasis on the fact that most acts of violence against women go unpunished, thereby sending the message that stopping this kind of violence is not a priority. The Commission reiterates that, in order to be in full compliance with the obligation to apply due diligence, states must do more to prosecute and punish acts of violence against women. The recommendations issued have three principal objectives: first, that states design comprehensive policies with proper resources to ensure that women victims of violence will have adequate access to justice and that acts of violence will be prevented, investigated, punished and adequately redressed; second, that states put in place the conditions necessary for women to have effective access to the justice system to remedy such acts of violence and so that public officials will treat victims respectfully when they seek protection; and third, that states adopt public measures to help undo the discriminatory socio-cultural patterns that stand in the way of women's full access to justice.

27 See IACHR, Report no. 92/06, Petition 95–04, Admissibility, *María Isabel Véliz Franco*, Guatemala, 21 October 2006.

28 IACHR, OEA/Ser.L/V/II., Doc. 67, 18 October 2006.

29 OEA/Ser.L/V/II., Doc. 68, 20 January 2007.

Conclusion

In the inter-American system, the concept of due diligence has evolved from the initial lines laid out by the *Velásquez Rodríguez* court, to the codification of the standard in the Convention of Belém do Pará, to its application in individual cases, and thematic and country reports. The utility of the concept is reflected in important advances in our understanding of the way in which states have obligations to prevent and respond to gender-based violence by both state actors and private individuals.

As indicated, due diligence has functioned as a key concept and standard in the inter-American system, particularly in taking on the challenge of violence against women. It has been applied in diverse contexts and with an important degree of flexibility. It is important to keep in mind, however, that it operates on the basis of certain parameters. Due diligence is a way of measuring state compliance with obligations under international law. It is, in principle, an obligation of means rather than results. In other words, it is not the existence of a particular violation that demonstrates the failure to apply due diligence, but rather a lack of reasonableness in measures of prevention, and/or a lack of seriousness in measures of response. Such an evaluation is generally made on a case by case basis, taking into account the particular circumstances of the situation in question.[30]

As the Commission and its Special Rapporteurship have emphasised, the legal framework, at both regional and national levels, now provides better responses to gender-based violence. The challenge is to bridge the gap between the formal commitments and the lived experience of the women of the region, and between what the law says and how it is applied in practice.

30 A recent case that further develops the basic principles laid out in the *Velásquez Rodríguez* case is the case of the *Massacre of Pueblo Bella,* I/A Court H.R. Judgment of 31 January, 2006. Series C no. 140. The sentence closely examines the state duty to prevent human rights violations at the hands of non-state actors. The Court specifies that a state is not automatically responsible in this context. Rather, the attribution of responsibility depends upon whether the state had knowledge of a real and present danger, and the possibility to take responsible steps to protect that danger. This examination is made on a case by case basis taking into account the circumstances and measures taken.

Applying the Due Diligence Principle in Asia Pacific

Lisa Pusey

Introduction

This chapter is drawn from the Report of the Asia Pacific NGO Consultation entitled *Realising Our Rights: Holding the State Accountable for Violence Against Women in the Asia Pacific*, with the UN Special Rapporteur on violence against women, Yakın Ertürk, on 5 and 6 October 2005.[1] The Consultation involved 30 women's NGOs from 16 countries around the region including: Australia, Burma, Cambodia, India, Indonesia, Japan, Kyrgyzstan, Malaysia, Mongolia, Nepal, Philippines, Pakistan, Republic of Korea (South Korea), Sri Lanka, Thailand and Tonga.

The Consultation was designed to facilitate the provision of input from these women's organisations into the 2006 thematic report of the Special Rapporteur on violence against women to the Commission on Human Rights on the due diligence standard.[2] The Consultation facilitated discussions on the critical issues in Asia Pacific surrounding states' failure to meet their due diligence obligations with respect to violence against women – to respect, protect, fulfil and promote women's rights – with an aim to proposing strategies to address these gaps. While the success of the international women's movement in challenging the public/private dichotomy and calling on states to exercise due diligence to prevent, investigate and punish acts of violence against women, whether such acts are committed by state or non-state actors, was a significant achievement in broadening state responsibility and protection for violence against women, there continues to

1 This report was authored by Lisa Pusey, Programme Officer for Violence against Women and Women's Human Rights Programmes at Asia Pacific Forum on Women, Law and Development (APWLD) and Mary B., volunteer with APWLD from July–November 2005.

2 Report of the Special Rapporteur on violence against women, its causes and consequences, Yakın Ertürk, *The Due Diligence Standard as a Tool for the Elimination of Violence against Women*, UN Doc. E/CN.4/2006/6, 20 January 2006.

C. Benninger-Budel ed., Due Diligence and Its Application to Protect Women from Violence
 Printed in The Netherlands. ISBN 978 90 04 16293 8. pp. 139-155

remain difficulties in ensuring state's compliance with obligations under the due diligence principle.

This chapter highlights the key points from these discussions, providing an overview of the effectiveness of state responses under their due diligence obligations in the region. It starts with explaining the context in which violence against women occurs in the Asia Pacific region. It examines some of the factors which have a determinative impact on the manifestations of violence against women: neo-liberalism, militarism and fundamentalism. The chapter then examines the intersectionality of women's different identities and how this reality requires particular address in applying the due diligence principle. The next part moves on to examine the common areas where states are failing the due diligence obligation and looks both at addressing violence where it occurs and prevention. The following part provides an insight into the particular challenges and obstacles the region is facing in the implementation of international human rights standards. In light of the gaps and challenges recognised, the conclusion identifies some strategies to address the failure and gaps of effective response to violence against women.

The Context: Violence against Women in Asia Pacific

The last decade has seen some important developments at the international level in the struggle to free women's lives of violence, including: the creation of international standards and mechanisms to address violence against women perpetrated by both state and non-state actors; the recognition of violence against women as a form of discrimination; and the recognition of the multiple forms of violence. Despite this, violence against women continues with impunity in many parts of the Asia Pacific region and continues to be one of the most visible manifestations of the unequal and unjust power relations between men and women in our societies.

While there remains no regional human rights mechanism in the Asia Pacific, at a national level measures have been taken to address violence against women. In her last report as UN Special Rapporteur on violence against women in 2003, Radhika Coomaraswamy undertook a survey of countries around the world and found that in nearly all countries at least some efforts had been made by governments to enact laws to address violence against women since the creation of her mandate in 1994.[3] Yet, violence against women has not decreased, but is in fact emerging in new and dangerous forms in the Asia Pacific. This occurs as globalisation and transnationalism result in the globalising of some harmful cultural practices and the increase of other practices such as trafficking and vulnerability to violence of migrant and displaced women. Thus, while a legal framework is useful in establishing normative standards, it is of little value if they are not implemented effectively, if mechanisms are not created for enforcing rights and re-

3 Report of the Special Rapporteur on violence against women, its causes and consequences, Radhika Coomaraswamy, UN Doc. E/CN.4/2003/75, 6 January 2003.

dressing violations, and if the environment in which they operate does not enable women to access their rights. For example, gender neutrality in law, state policy and programmes on the implementation of human rights standards may result in or perpetuate past discrimination against women including violence against women, and may produce inadequate and ineffective redress mechanisms (such as police, judiciary and medical services). The biological as well as socially and culturally constructed distinct characteristics of women require specifically targeted responses.

Any work on violence against women has to be placed in the context of the cultures and systems of patriarchy, inherent to which is the fundamental lack of respect and recognition of women as human beings to be treated equally. Patriarchal norms continue to perpetuate social, cultural, economic and political systems that are male-dominated and that perpetuate discrimination against women. Furthermore, as will be explained in detail hereunder, women are subjected to acts of gender-based violence as a manifestation of discrimination not only on the basis of their sex but as a result of the intersection with other factors such as class, caste, ethnicity, age, sexual orientation, disability, etc.

While globalisation has brought new reflections and dimensions into the women's movement and has transformed the arenas of our struggles, it has also had many deleterious impacts for women across the Asia Pacific region. These include new forms and trends of violence against women as mentioned above and elaborated below. Three main forces interact with the process of globalisation in the Asia Pacific today: *neo-liberalism*, *militarism* and *fundamentalisms*. These forces, particularly the interplay of these forces, have a direct impact on the form, the circumstances and the consequence of violence against women as well as the availability of and accessibility of reparation and redress to the women subjected to violence. These forces and their impact on the Asia Pacific Region will be discussed below in more detail.

Neo-Liberalism

The spread of neo-liberalisms through globalisation has contributed to the creation of a social, cultural, political and economic environment that increases the vulnerabilities of women and girls to violence. Over the past two decades, neoliberal doctrines and practices, characterised by trade liberalisation, privatisation and deregulation aimed at rapid economic growth, have spread quickly in Asia Pacific. A cycle of poverty, exploitation and violence define the experience of globalisation for many women across Asia Pacific.

While men and women are both affected by globalisation, their experiences are distinct because of their differing gender roles and inequality. The loss of livelihood as a result of the rampant privatisation and destruction of natural resources for profit and the largely unchecked power of corporate entities (including transnational corporations (TNCs) and multinational corporations (MNCs)) have increased poverty and the gap between the rich and the poor. This impacts most acutely on women, particularly rural women, as poverty and marginalisation fuel violence against women. Poverty has been an increasing factor in forcing women to enter new exploitative labour markets where they face new risks of violence (such as low-wage, unprotected industries like garment making throughout South-East Asia; moving from rural to urban areas or from countries with depressed economies to wealthier economies to work as either documented or undocumented migrant workers in poorly paid and unprotected industries and workplaces) and it increases women's vulnerability to trafficking and subsequent risk of violence. Increased poverty and marginalisation as well as a feeling of emasculation as women become wage earners have led to increased levels of violence towards women by men in their communities. The links between the erosion of women's economic, social and cultural rights and violence against women are clear.

Militarism

Increasingly, globalisation is adversely affecting democracy, thereby resulting in the erosion of state power over domestic affairs and an ascendancy of militarism and armed conflict in the region. The many conflicts which have taken place over the last years – such as in Aceh, Burma, India, Nepal, East Timor, Pakistan, Afghanistan, Iraq, Sri Lanka, South Thailand, Fiji, Solomon Islands, Bougainville and Papua New Guinea – have played witness to the increase in situations of armed conflict in the region. Armed conflict increases women's vulnerability to violence by both opposing forces and within their own community. A key characteristic of militarisation today is the increased powers given to the military to search, question, arrest and kill under the guise of national security. Women are particularly vulnerable to violence, particularly sexual violence, under these laws. Furthermore, increased state militarisation of certain areas due to conflicts over natural resources has led to an increase of violence against women perpetrated by the state (for example, in Aceh, the Philippines, and Thailand), implicating governments as the perpetrators of human rights violations. Furthermore, as will be discussed in further detail hereunder, conflict situations increase women's vulnerability to violence and trafficking as internally displaced persons, migrants and asylum seekers.

Fundamentalisms

Deeply tied to globalisation and the forces of militarisms and neo-liberalisms is the growth of cultural and religious fundamentalisms. There has been an expansion in Asia Pacific of extremist movements, founded on the basis of cultural or national fundamentalism and religious fundamentalism, such as Christian, Muslim, Hindu, and ethnic politics which discriminate against women. Conflict, poverty and marginalisation and the uncertainty left by the erosion of old paradigms by globalisation gives rise to fundamentalism. Fundamentalist values are selectively imposed on those spheres where structural and legal resistance can be overcome, most notably, in the private domain where the control of women is singled out as a bastion for the application of religious tenets and traditional notions of purity in the face of corrupting outside influences and threats from 'other' groups. Most often, this entails an imposition of patriarchal interpretations of religion or nationalism on women that is used to control and restrict their behaviour and to redefine their roles and prerogatives. Women's lives are made to exemplify the ideals to which fundamentalism aspire. Women who have challenged these religious interpretations and practices (including women religious leaders) have often met with even more violence, curtailment of women's rights, and death. Examples of correlating violence against women under fundamentalisms include: public shaming such as cutting the hair of women not wearing veils in Aceh-Indonesia; enforcing religious punishments for adultery in Malaysia; and the Gujarat massacre in India in 2002. A disturbing pattern in the region is the codification of fundamentalist values into the formal legal system as well as the revival of traditional justice mechanisms that frequently discriminate against women, thereby increasing women's vulnerability to violence and limiting their access to justice.

Throughout the region, culture and cultural norms are used to legitimise violence against women and create barriers to women accessing justice. While international law is clear that states cannot 'invoke custom, tradition, or religious considerations to avoid their obligations with respect to the elimination of discrimination against women' (Article 4 of the Declaration on the Elimination of Violence against Women),[4] in reality, culture, tradition and religion are politicised in many parts of Asia Pacific and are used by individuals, communities and governments alike to condone violence against women and to justify inaction in bringing perpetrators to justice and providing appropriate remedies for violence against women survivors. In the name of culture, women's human rights are undermined. The forces of globalisation are escalating the contraction of culture into a monolithic unchanging force. Women's rights are pitted against cultural rights and values and in this battle, women's human rights lose out. Furthermore, women are denied their right to interpret and influence culture as the bearers of cultural rights.

In the light of these developments, there is diminishing enforceability of women's human rights and diminishing opportunity for women to access justice as they are further marginalised at all levels of decision-making. Furthermore, there is a revival in strength of informal justice systems operating in the region, often with state endorsement. Combined with pressures on democracy caused by the interplay of globalisation, fundamentalisms and militarism, women's ability to access justice for violence against women is further eroded.

Intersectionality

In using the due diligence principle to address violence against women, it is necessary to consider the intersectionality of women's multiple identities with male

4 UN Doc. A/48/49 (1993), GA Res. 48/104.

dominance, as this has an enormous impact on how women with different identities experience discrimination and violence. Women are subjected to acts of gender-based violence as a manifestation of discrimination not only based on their sex and gender but also as a result of the intersection with other factors including class, caste, ethnicity, age, sexual orientation, disability etc. The intersection of different identities can in fact hide gender-based violence and make the underlying causes harder to differentiate.

The discussions during the Consultation focused on the importance of recognising that although an individual woman may have many different identities according to frameworks of race, culture, ethnicity, religion and caste, these intersectional identities all form part of the same system of patriarchal oppression. While the characteristics and practices of these collective identities may be viewed or represented as 'traditional' and 'customary', they are often shaped by power-holders to further their own agendas and maintain their privileged position within societal structures.

In order to address this system of oppression, women's groups need to demystify cultural discourse to ascertain the underlying power relations. Collective identities on the basis of religion, ethnic background and so on, are important, but women should not become victims of these identities. We are all part of culture and need to recognise that culture is an active construction, rather than a sacred taboo. Women too are the bearers of cultural rights and can shape culture.

By adopting an intersectional approach, and rejecting fragmentation according to differing identities, the women's movement can work together to address the overall structure of oppression. When women divide themselves as virgin, married, indigenous, migrant, etc., it dilutes their identity as women and impedes their ability to fight the overall system of patriarchal oppression. For example, privileged women often view the problems of women living in poverty as an issue separate from themselves, when instead it is a manifestation of the same system that oppresses them. In addition, participants noted the need to be conscious of 'exoticising' the issues of women belonging to minority groups, for example, the publicity surrounding 'fatwa'[5] cases in Pakistan, as this reinforces perceived differences between women with different identities and disguises problems in the majority group that are based on the same fundamental system of oppression.

Within this approach, it is also necessary to acknowledge that individual contexts play a significant role in determining how a particular woman experiences discrimination and oppression. While the overall system oppresses all women, some women will be much more vulnerable to violence due to discrimination and oppression under multiple identities.

Certain women, especially those in oppressed minority groups (such as Dalits, different ethnic groups in Burma, and many indigenous peoples), may not have the freedom to 'choose' which identity frames their existence, or to choose 'being a woman' as their dominant identity. For example, in the Shan State, and

5 'Fatwa' is a pronouncement made by a scholar of Islamic law on a specific issue. A fatwa is only binding on those that accept the authority of the scholar.

other states in Burma, women consistently experience rape and other forms of sexual violence as a war weapon to control the community. While they experience sexual violence as a result of their gender, the overt motive is to oppress them as a member of their ethnic community. In such situations women are not able to choose which identity is imposed upon them. In other situations, women belonging to minority groups may feel obliged to stay silent about issues such as violence in the home so as not to cause further problems for their community. For these women, strong identification with their caste or ethnic group rather than with gender may be necessary to be able to survive within the framework of a particular identity. The impact of multiple systems of oppression on the needs and rights of these women requires particular attention by the state in meeting their due diligence obligations. The difficulties of living with a particular identity need to be acknowledged and addressed, so that recognition of the same overall structure of oppression does not sideline the layers of oppression experienced by these women.

Applying the Due Diligence Standard

The principle of due diligence has the potential to be applied to ensure state accountability for addressing violence against women within the wider concern for women's human rights and discrimination. This means that states are required to both enact and implement comprehensive legal frameworks that address acts of violence against women when it occurs. It also imposes on states the responsibility to address the underlying causes of violence against women. Such a holistic approach is essential to effectively work towards the eradication of violence against women. In reality, however, there are clearly still many shortfalls in states' implementation of their obligations evidenced by the prevalence of violence against women committed with impunity by both state and non-state actors in the region. Outlined below are some of the common gaps where states are failing to meet their obligations in the region.

Enactment and Implementation of Laws

States have a positive obligation under the due diligence principle to investigate, prosecute and adequately punish perpetrators of violence against women. States must ensure that violence against women is not met with impunity, but rather that survivors are able to access 'justice' for the crime, and that redress is sought and obtained by and through the state. There are problems with both the adequacy of existing laws and the effectiveness of their implementation throughout the Asia Pacific region. In many countries in this region, laws dealing with particular kinds of violence against women are non-existent or inadequate. For example, in Thailand, the law addressing sexual assault prohibits forced sexual intercourse with any woman, except one's wife (Criminal Code, Article 276), effectively condoning marital rape. In addition, while the law is useful in establishing ground rules for the protection of women, it is of little value in preventing violence if the laws are not implemented and enforced effectively. Even though most of the countries in the Asia Pacific region have at least basic legislation and mechanisms to address violence against women, the lack of adequate implementation often allows violations to continue with impunity. Complaints of domestic violence and sexual assault are often not investigated, or inadequately investigated, by police and state authorities across the region. In Pakistan, for example, the murders of women in the name of 'honour' (termed 'honour crimes'), are often not investigated and the mass rapes of women in Gujarat, India in 2002 were not adequately investigated. The failure to investigate (or in many cases even respond to the complaints of women) often stems from prejudiced beliefs held by state agents that the violence is justified, that it is the male prerogative, or that what happens within the home is 'private'. Indeed, there is a disturbing pattern throughout the Asia Pacific where police treat domestic violence cases as a 'family matter' and encourage women not to press charges and to instead reconcile with their husbands. In other instances, such as in Pakistan, rape victims have been locked up in police custody for their own 'protection' while the perpetrator is allowed to go free.[6] Such situations violate women's human rights and put women at risk of further violence, both in the home and in police custody.

Judges are also failing to effectively implement laws in cases of violence against women. Judges have unduly questioned the credibility of female witnesses or allowed evidence regarding a woman's previous sexual history to be considered in sexual assault trials as 'evidence' of the woman's complicity in the offence. Sentences are reduced for irrelevant and discriminatory reasons and perpetrators are allowed to raise discriminatory defences. Sentences are, for instance, mitigated on the basis that the victim's 'socially unacceptable' behaviour encouraged the crime or 'justified' male violence (including behaviour such as wearing a short dress or talking to a man without a guardian). As these examples illustrate, the prejudicial beliefs of state actors that acts of violence against women are non-justiciable private or family matters, hinders the effective operation of existing laws. In many countries the legislated 'sentences' for crimes of violence against women are radically shorter than for other offences. For example, in Japan the sentence for sexual assault is less than for robbery, which clearly demonstrates the social acceptance of the male prerogative to inflict violence on women.

As mentioned above, gender discrimination often intersects with discrimination on other grounds such as class, caste or ethnicity, resulting in the discriminatory reduction of sentences or impunity for the crime. Such as in the case of the Gujarat massacres, religious/ethnic prejudices intersect with gender inequalities to foster acceptance of violence against women of certain religious or ethnic identities.[7] The intersection is also exemplified by a case in which a young

6 Lisa Pusey, *Talking About Taboos: Asia Pacific Women Reflect on Issues of Sexuality*, Report arising from the Consultation with the UN Special Rapporteur on violence against women, Yakın Ertürk, organised by APWLD, 25–28 July 2004.

7 Drawn from the intervention and input of Manisha Gupte, Masum, India, during discussions at the Asia Pacific NGO Consultation.

disabled woman in Kyrgyzstan was regularly sexually abused by her father. Her father denied the charges and the court dismissed the case on grounds which included that 'no one would want to have sex with a disabled woman'. Following the dismissal of the case, the woman was ostracised by her family and thrown out of the family home.[8] The NGO involved in the case helped her to find a house, but she has to earn her living begging on the street, as government welfare has been insufficient. This is a disturbing example of the intersection of gender discrimination with discrimination on the basis of disability, as well as the discriminatory implementation of laws that are intended to protect women.

Addressing the Underlying Causes of Violence against Women

As mentioned, the due diligence principle also requires states to effectively address the underlying causes of violence against women resting in the cultures and systems of patriarchy, inherent to which is the fundamental lack of respect and recognition of women as equal human beings. Patriarchal norms continue to perpetuate social, cultural, economic and political systems that are male-dominated and that perpetuate discrimination against women. Measures taken without addressing these underlying causes will be ineffective. Thus to eliminate violence against women these foundations, upon which gender hierarchies rest and violence against women are legitimised and perpetuated, must be addressed. While this obligation of prevention may be the most difficult to determine, it is also the most important in eliminating violence, enabling progress beyond just addressing violence when it occurs.

This most challenging obligation of the state under the due diligence principle is often further impeded by a lack of will on the part of the state to challenge cultural (and religious) norms which discriminate against women. In the context of increasing fundamentalisms in the Asia Pacific region and the contraction of culture into a monolithic force in the wake of policies adopted post-September 11, this objective is further from realisation.

Challenges to Applying the Due Diligence Principle in Asia Pacific

While violence against women is a human rights violation for which states can be held responsible, regardless of whether the perpetrator is a state or non-state actor, through the application of the due diligence standard, there are a number of challenges to applying this standard in the Asia Pacific region. The discussions during the Consultation highlighted a number of examples where states from the region have been particularly ineffective in addressing violence against women: a) the impact of dual justice systems; b) the reconstruction of minority cultural identity by the dominant group; c) the numerous conflict situations in the region;

8 Drawn from the presentation at the Asia Pacific NGO Consultation by Asipa Musaeva, Republican Independent Association of Disabled Women of Kyrgyzstan, Kyrgyzstan.

d) responsibility for certain non-state actors; e) migrant, trafficked, internally displaced women and refugees.

The Impact of Dual Justice Systems

Cultural, religious and traditional beliefs which are based on patriarchal gender hierarchies and inequalities frequently legitimise and perpetuate violence against women. In several countries and communities across the region, these beliefs are instilled and enforced through traditional authority or customary law which operate alongside the formal, statutory legal system. Village elders, religious courts, traditional chiefs or clan structures operate quasi-formal legal systems parallel to statutory law, sometimes informally but with social legitimacy and sometimes with powers formally granted to them by the state. These parallel judicial systems often emerged during the process of power-sharing during state-building, for example in post-armed conflict. By distributing power to other bodies such as religious leaders, the central authorities are able to reinforce their own position and power base by gaining the support of these other powerful and influential groups. These parallel legal regimes monitor and control community norms and practices, which often means reinforcing male power over women and permitting violence against women. When women depart from what the community holds to be 'appropriate' behaviour, they are often met with violent retribution – by their families, members of the community, or the state. These systems may also authorise violence against women by classifying acts of violence as acceptable under 'traditional' or 'religious' norms.

In Pakistan, traditional dispute resolution forums, such as the 'jirga' and 'punchiat',[9] significantly contribute to violence against women.[10] These forums apply and reinforce societal norms regarding appropriate roles and behaviour for women. They may authorise violence against women by classifying acts of violence as acceptable under 'traditional' or religious norms or by sentencing women to harsh punishments (for example, honour killings), for breaking societal norms or religious laws. In complaints regarding violations of women's rights, including violence against women, family honour is regarded as the primary consideration and is used as a mechanism to control female sexuality and ensure gender segregation. In addition, women are often treated like chattel in the resolution of disputes; for example, they may be forced into marriage or handed over to another tribe as compensation. State actors, such as the police, often help to enforce decisions.

9 'Jirgas' are tribunals/councils of elders; 'punchiat' are informal gatherings of a communities influential/family elders.

10 The following example from Pakistan is drawn from the presentation of Shahnaz Iqbal, Shirkat Gah: Women's Resource Centre, Pakistan, at the Asia Pacific NGO Consultation.

Dual legal systems also operate in Malaysia.[11] While the Constitution of Malaysia provides some rights to women, it also allows for shariah law to operate concurrently with the formal state legal system. This means some of the rights granted under the constitution are negated by the operation of shariah law for Muslim women in Malaysia. This overlapping of jurisdiction often impedes women's access to justice. For example, in one case involving a couple who were originally both Hindu, the husband divorced his wife after he had converted to Islam. As a non-Muslim, the woman had no recourse, as she couldn't access shariah courts, while Malaysian law provides that the state courts cannot intervene in shariah jurisdiction.

The strong influence of shariah law in Malaysia has also significantly impacted on women in other ways. For example, when women's groups in Malaysia were lobbying for the introduction of domestic violence legislation, Muslim authorities objected to the inclusion of Muslim women, arguing that some of the defined offences would not constitute violence under shariah law, and that the jurisdiction for Muslim family law should remain under shariah law. It required intensive campaigning by women's groups to ensure that the legislation was enacted and applied to everyone, including Muslims. In another example, despite strong efforts, women's groups in Malaysia still have not been able to successfully lobby for legislation criminalising marital rape, as Muslim leaders argue that it is against Islam and threatens the marriage institution. While there is now more discussion and critique regarding the operation of shariah law in Malaysia, Muslim authorities still tend to apply the most conservative interpretation of shariah law, with little opposition from civil authorities. In addition to these domestic restrictions, Muslim women are also denied rights at the international level, as Malaysia generally makes reservations to treaties on religious grounds.

Where women seek assistance from the formal justice system outside their community, frequently it does not have the power or will to intervene in a matter which has been dealt with under traditional law. If states sanction discriminatory decision-making by these alternate justice mechanisms, by either ignoring their existence or authorising their judgments, then this constitutes a breach of their international obligation to address violence against women with due diligence. Safeguards and procedures must be created within the informal processes to ensure that women's rights are not subordinated, that the informal processes are not used to control women and enforce discriminatory societal or religious norms, and that women have a full and free choice as to whether to have their complaint dealt with by either the formal or informal mechanism without fear of ostracism or threats of further violence.

11 The following example from Malaysia is drawn from the presentation of Hayati Kaprawi, Sisters in Islam, Malaysia at the Asia Pacific NGO Consultation.

Re-Construction of Minority Cultural Identity by the Dominant Group

The formal legal system may also discriminate against women from minority cultural identities by applying 'customary norms' on women from minority communities accessing the formal legal system in cases of violence against women. For example, in Australia there have been several cases where courts have applied contemporary Anglo-Saxon interpretations of indigenous culture to legitimise violence against women, particularly sexual assault perpetrated by an indigenous man against an indigenous woman.[12] In August 2005, a judge in Australia sentenced a 55-year-old man to just one month imprisonment for 'forcing' his 14-year-old 'promised bride' to have sex – he beat her with a boomerang[13], which constitutes assault with a weapon under Australian law, and anally raped her. In sentencing, the judge said he took into account that the man was a respected elder, and noted that he had 'great sympathy' for the man as he was living under a dual system and was unaware his actions were illegal under Anglo-Saxon law, since they were not illegal under his traditional law and customary practices (as represented by the man's lawyer).

While such decisions are framed as protecting minority rights and customs, they perpetuate oppressive structures against women in both indigenous societies and the wider Australian community. Judges in these decisions are applying re-constructed versions of 'traditional law' and 'customary practices,' as represented by the offenders or their legal representatives. Indigenous Australian women argue that they live under three different kinds of laws: 'White-Australian law' (formal legal system of Australia), 'Aboriginal Lore' (traditional law of Indigenous Australians) and 'Bullshit Law' (the term of contempt used by aboriginal women to describe the re-creation by male aboriginal elders of traditional law). These re-constructions of 'cultural rights' shield men in the community from accountability for violations of women's human rights. Frequently the white Australian legal system enforces 'Bullshit Law' upon indigenous women.

Negotiating cultural rights in the context of women's human rights frequently sees women's human rights lose out to cultural relativist arguments. Culture is fluid and constantly changing, and the above-mentioned example of imposing a monolithic interpretation of culture on women violates women's human rights and fails to recognise the role of women as agents of culture. States should ensure that the justice system does not impose discriminatory values upon women.

---

12 The following example is drawn from the presentation at the Asia Pacific NGO Consultation of Judy Atkinson, Southern Cross University, Lismore, Australia, citing Karen Michelmore, 'Traditional Law Role Queried,' *Australian Associated Press* (AAP), 17 August 2005.

13 A thick wooden stick used for hunting.

Conflict Situations

Women often experience significantly higher levels of violence in conflict situations than in peacetime from the military of both sides as well as within their own families and communities. In these situations, the difficulties in applying the due diligence obligation to prevent and address violence against women often results in impunity for violence against women perpetrated by both state and non-state actors.

Pre-existing gender inequalities and oppression within a woman's family and community generally become much more pronounced when a community is under threat. The burden of maintaining the routines of everyday life and the community's 'culture' and 'traditions' tends to fall on women, who are then required to conform more strictly to traditional gender stereotypes and face strong reprisals for any dissent or 'deviant' behaviour. Women often face increased levels of violence within their own communities as a result of intensified expressions of masculinity during situations of armed conflict. Conflict conceals violence within the private sphere. During times of armed conflict women absorb their men's frustrations and this violence is legitimised (frequently by women themselves) as insignificant in the face of the community's struggle. Thus, impunity prevails.

Where state agents are the violators, the justice apparatus frequently protects these agents from prosecution and denies women access to justice. Several examples from Nepal highlight this problem.[14] In one case, the wife of an insurgent from the Dalit community was sexually assaulted every night for many weeks by the 'unified command', demanding that she tell them the whereabouts of her husband. In another example, seven rapes of girls under 14 years occurred within three months in a community within five kilometres of an army barracks. One of these girls, who was 11 years old, complained of blood in her urine. She was examined by a doctor and interviewed by the police, who all concluded that she had not been raped. When she was later examined by a women's organisation, they found bleeding tears and a small stick still inserted in her vagina. Following pressure on the government by the women's organisation, a team was sent to investigate this matter. Although they found that the rape had been committed by several security personnel, no direct action was taken against the perpetrators. In addition, the provision of arms to untrained and inadequately monitored 'village defence forces' increases the risk of violence to women in the community.

Burma provides another striking example of the state committing acts of violence against women with impunity in a conflict situation, illustrating the ineffectiveness of the due diligence principle in these circumstances.[15] The military regime in Burma continues to use systematic sexual violence against women as a

14 Examples from Nepal drawn from the presentation at the Asia Pacific NGO Consultation of Renu Rajbhandari, Women's Rehabilitation Centre, Nepal.

15 Drawn from the intervention and input during discussions at the Asia Pacific NGO Consultation of Nang Lao Liang Won, Shan Women's Action Network/Women's League of Burma, Burma.

weapon of war, even though many countries have condemned the human rights record of the military regime, and a UN Special Rapporteur on Burma has been established. The military regime totally denies the violence, and it is not possible to adequately investigate the cases as the regime holds absolute power within Burma. While UN mechanisms have been able to highlight the issue and provide international attention, their ability to improve the situation for women in Burma has been limited.

Justice is equally as difficult to obtain where non-state actors such as insurgency groups are the perpetrators. This is generally due to dysfunctional state apparatus that prevents the state from effectively enforcing laws in these situations, as well as to fear of reprisal and power disparities between insurgents and civilians and the consequent risk to security. For example, in Nepal,[16] if a woman has been raped in certain areas controlled by the Maoists, the police will tell *her* to bring the perpetrator to the station as *they* are unable to enter the conflict area for security reasons. Even though Nepal has made international commitments to advance women's rights and has laws prohibiting discrimination against women, the state has claimed that it is unable to effectively implement these commitments due to the conflict.

Responsibility for Certain Non-State Actors

Discussions during the Consultation considered the difficulties in ensuring accountability for violence against women by certain groups of non-state actors, specifically foreign troops stationed under a long-term foreign military presence and MNCs and TNCs. Participants discussed the need to make state responsibility for these non-state actors more enforceable as well as the possibility of developing global accountability mechanisms to ensure more effective action against violations by non-state actors.

There is little discourse on the mechanisms of state responsibility for violence against women under long-term military presence in times of peace, even though these foreign troops can have a significant impact on local communities. For example, there have been many incidents of rape and other forms of violence against women committed by US military personnel while stationed at US military bases throughout Asia including Okinawa, Japan.[17] When crimes are committed by soldiers in a host country, they are often not investigated by local authorities because foreign military personnel generally have diplomatic immunity and the host country government often has only limited access to the foreign military bases. A desire to keep good diplomatic relations also plays a role in silencing these incidents. These impediments to obtaining accountability from the host government for violence committed by long-term foreign troops

16 Examples from Nepal drawn from the presentation at the Asia Pacific NGO Consultation of Renu Rajbhandari, Women's Rehabilitation Centre, Nepal.

17 Drawn from the presentation at the Asia Pacific NGO Consultation of Suzuyo Takazato, Okinawa Women Act Against Military Violence, Japan.

are exacerbated in Okinawa, Japan, by discrimination from mainland Japanese, including the central government.

Similarly, it can be very difficult to obtain justice for human rights violations committed by corporations, particularly MNCs or TNCs, or their agents. This is particularly problematic as MNCs and TNCs are the cause of many grave human rights violations in the Asia Pacific region, including violence against women. Examples from the region include corporations, such as with the Freeport copper and gold mine in Timika, West Papua, and the Newcrest copper mine in the Maluku Islands, Indonesia, employing oppressive and violent tactics to quash community resistance to their presence and activities, including the hiring of military or para-military groups to act as private security forces.[18] The actions of MNCs and TNCs are also indirectly the origin of increased violence against women in these communities, as men take out their frustration at the resulting poverty and displacement of their land and livelihoods on women.

States frequently ignore or fail to adequately address violations by MNCs and TNCs in order to maintain business relationships benefiting the government including large tax payments or shareholdings. Freeport, for example, is one of Indonesia's largest corporate taxpayers, and the government is also a shareholder.[19] In many cases states change domestic laws and policies to attract TNCs and MNCs to their countries by reducing regulatory requirements and environmental, labour and social responsibilities. By failing to provide adequate checks and balances to monitor the actions of TNCs and MNCs and protect citizens, states are complicit in the human rights violations resulting from the activities or presence of such corporations. On the other hand, global regulatory mechanisms to hold TNCs and MNCs directly accountable need to be further developed and strengthened.

Migrant, Trafficked and Internally Displaced Women and Refugees

Undocumented migrant workers, internally displaced women, refugees and trafficked women are all particularly vulnerable to violence and disadvantaged in accessing their right to justice. For example, in Thailand, Burmese undocumented migrant workers fear arrest and deportation to Burma if they make a complaint of violence to police. In addition, they often work in unregulated industries, increasing their vulnerability to sexual harassment and assault, as well as economic exploitation.[20] Migrant workers are at increased risk of exploitation, abuse and

18 Stephanie Fried and Titi Soentoro ed., *A Brief Overview of Export Credit Agencies in the Asia-Pacific Region, Indonesia: Environmental Defence and NADI*, presented at the World Social Forum, Mumbai, India, 2004. Unpublished paper, http://www.eng.walhi.or.id/kampanye/tambang/031031_freeport_rtinto_expose.

19 From the report of Freeport McMoran Copper and Gold Inc., *Riverine Tailings Transport* (June 2004), 2, http://www.fcx.com/envir/RiverineTransport.pdf.

20 Drawn from the intervention and input at the Asia Pacific NGO Consultation of Pranom Somwong, Map Foundation, Thailand, during discussions.

violence and at the same time are deprived of legal protection, health care, safe working conditions, job security and the right to organise.

Burmese women refugees living in camps along the Thai border also experience significant levels of violence, both from the military and from members of their family and community.[21] The increased violence in the home is due to a number of factors, including increased frustration and alcoholism among men as well as the close living quarters with limited privacy. Women who experience violence in these communities face many difficulties in obtaining justice or preventing further violence. For example, in regard to violence in the home, women are often reluctant to bring an action against their husband because if their husband is taken away and jailed, they face ostracism from the community and will not have anyone to protect them. In addition, women who have been raped are often stigmatised by the community.

Trafficked women are also particularly vulnerable to violence as a result of the illegal nature of the industry and the deceptive and often violent tactics used to ensnare women. Women who have been trafficked do not usually have passports or any legal papers, may be under threat of their lives, and generally have no legal rights in the country to which they are taken. When combined with language barriers, isolation and prejudice on the part of the authorities, accessing justice for trafficked women can be immensely difficult. In Japan, many migrant women married to Japanese men have escaped from trafficking and fled to the security of marriage where they then rely on their husbands for their security and well-being.[22] If their husband does not help them to obtain a visa and is violent, they are generally unable to access legal protection. In one example, a Filipino woman experiencing violence in the family requested assistance from the police in Kawasaki city, Kanagawa prefecture, located next to the Metro Tokyo, in 2004. Instead of protecting her, the police arrested her and detained her for four months for being undocumented. NGOs[23] are lobbying for greater recognition of the rights of trafficked women, as the police currently have no discretion under the law and are required to automatically arrest undocumented people, even if they are requesting protection from violence.

The specific vulnerability and risks of violence against women faced by these particular groups of women require states to implement their due diligence obligations with due regard to this. As illustrated above, these groups of women are often alienated from accessing their rights (for example as a result of the language barriers, lack of documentation, fear of deportation). The due diligence obligation must extend to ensuring an environment in which women can access their rights (i.e., substantive equality and justice). The inaction and complicity of states

21 Drawn from the intervention and input at the Asia Pacific NGO Consultation of Nang Lao Liang Won, Shan Women's Action Network/Women's League of Burma, Burma, during discussions.

22 Ibid.

23 Forming a national wide network coalition (Japan Network Against Trafficking in Persons [JNATIP]).

in failing to address the marginalisation of these groups of women, resulting in the violation of their human rights and right to access to justice, is a further example of states failing in their due diligence obligations.

Conclusion

To effectively end violence against women, the foundations upon which gender hierarchies are constructed and violence against women is justified and perpetuated must be challenged – patriarchy and the power imbalance between men and women. This requires not only state intervention and will to address harmful cultural norms and practices, but also an active and rights-driven civil society who will hold states true to their obligations. The women's movement needs to continue to develop a feminist critique of culture and its role in perpetuating and compounding discrimination against women which fosters a discourse which recognises women as the agents of culture rather than its victims. Civil society (the women's movement) plays an important role in pushing for state reform by utilising existing international mechanisms for the protection of rights, to push states to drop their reservations to Article 16 of the Convention on the Elimination of All Forms of Discrimination against Women and lobbying for the creation of new mechanisms such as a permanent regional human rights mechanism in Asia Pacific. At a national level too, both the state and civil society share a common obligation to work towards the eradication of violence against women to which end the implementation of legal and policy reforms and engendering change of attitudes must be worked towards.

Strengthening state accountability for violence against women is necessary to ensure effective prevention of violence against women and mechanisms to address violence against women. However, in the context of the combined forces of fundamentalism, militarism and neo-liberal economic policies in the Asia Pacific region, a multi-pronged approach aimed at different levels (including individual, community/civil society, state and transnational) is essential for us to effectively work towards the eradication of violence against women.

The importance of the due diligence principle for women lies in the fact it makes states equally accountable for both state and non-state actors as well as for addressing the root causes of violence against women. As the UN Special Rapporteur on violence against women, Yakın Ertürk, noted, furthering this interpretation of state obligation under international law is an important step in moving us towards a concept of human rights with the potential to transform society into a world without violence against women.[24] Ensuring states meet these human rights obligations is the next important component which requires common will, determination and pressure nationally and internationally.

24 Report of the Special Rapporteur on violence against women, its causes and consequences, Yakın Ertürk, see note 2 above.

Section II

Due Dilligence in Context

Domestic Violence

South Africa's Response to Domestic Violence

*Dee Smythe**

Introduction

In April 2005 – the week that Andrea Dworkin died – Katherine MacKinnon gave a lecture at Stanford Law School. In this lecture she contrasted the international response to the 'war on terror' with that against the 'war on women'. She pointed to the immense resources that had gone into fighting those nebulous enemies that had been defined as terrorists and she urged her own country and the international community to put as many diplomatic, financial and military resources into addressing gender-based violence (and the deaths of tens of thousands of women every year at the hands of intimate partners) as they had into fighting these other forms of terror. At its extreme, she suggested, this meant sending in the peacekeepers. Assuming that one followed through on MacKinnon's suggestion, the immediate question that came to mind was why our own country, South Africa, should not be the first to host the 'pink-helmets' or, perhaps more realistically, to be sanctioned in some way for failing to exercise due diligence towards its citizens.

To put this question into context, there are a number of important realities of violence against women in South Africa that are worth mentioning. South Africa has amongst the highest reported rates of rape in the world.[1] Between a third and half of these are multiple perpetrator rapes[2] and many are perpetrated at

* The author would like to thank Lillian Artz for her assistance and input in drafting this article.

1 In 2003–2004 the South African Police Service (SAPS) reported that 55,114 rape complaints were made to the police. This represents a prevalence rate of 118/100,000 of the population. See http://www.saps.gov.za/statistics/reports/crimestats/2005/_pdf/crimes/rape.pdf for detailed police statistics.

2 Lu-Anne Swart, Angela Gilchrist, Alexander Butchart, Mohamed Seedat and Lorna Martin, 'Rape Surveillance through District Surgeons Offices in Johannesburg, 1996–1998: Evaluation and Prevention Implications', *South African Journal of Psychology* 30 (2000): 2–10; Lorna Martin, 'Violence against Women: An Analysis of the

C. Benninger-Budel ed., Due Diligence and Its Application to Protect Women from Violence
 Printed in The Netherlands. ISBN 978 90 04 16293 8. pp. 161-171

the instigation or with the complicity of men with whom the victim was or had been in a domestic relationship. Rape is used in this context to punish women for their insubordination and to defile them, to put them back in their place and to diminish their chances of forming an intimate relationship with another man. It is estimated that one in six women in South Africa is regularly beaten by a male partner.[3] Four out of five rural women report being victims of ongoing violence within the home.[4] In over 40 percent of domestic violence cases surveyed by the Gender, Health & Justice Research Unit a gun or knife was used to threaten or injure the victim.[5] A recent national mortuary-based study concluded that in South Africa a woman is killed every six hours by an intimate partner.[6] And that figure does not account for the tens of thousands of women who will die every year from HIV/Aids, because the threat of violence or the reality thereof means that they are unable to negotiate safe sex with their intimate partners. When we look at the numbers the picture in South Africa is incredibly bleak. It seems that we are ripe for the introduction of peace-keepers.

Legal Framework

South Africa is, on the other hand, also perhaps the country in Africa (with only one or two possible exceptions) that has done the most to meet the international standards required of it in addressing domestic violence. At an international level, South Africa has acceded to the Convention on the Elimination of All Forms of Discrimination against Women (CEDAW Convention)[7] and its Optional Protocol[8] and is a state party to every other major human rights treaty. Regionally,

Epidemiology and Patterns of Injury in Rape Homicide in Cape Town and in Rape in Johannesburg' (Masters of Medicine forensic pathology thesis, University of Cape Town, 1999).

3 According to the Advice Desk for Abused Women one in six South African women is regularly assaulted by her partner and at least one in four women has been forced to flee a life-threatening situation in her home at some point in her life. See Human Rights Watch, *Violence against Women in South Africa: State Response to Domestic Violence and Rape* (Human Rights Watch, 1995).

4 Lillian Artz, *Access to Justice for Rural Women: Special Focus on Violence against Women* (Cape Town: Institute of Criminology and Black Sash, 1998).

5 Penny Parenzee, Lillian Artz and Kelley Moult, *Monitoring the Implementation of the Domestic Violence Act: First Report 2000–2001* (Cape Town: Institute of Criminology, University of Cape Town, 2001).

6 Shanaaz Mathews, Naeemah Abrahams, Lorna Martin, Lisa Vetten, Lize van der Merwe and Rachel Jewkes, *Every Six Hours a Woman is Killed by Her Intimate Partner: A National Study of Female Homicide in South Africa* (Medical Research Council Policy Brief no. 5, June 2004).

7 UN Doc. A/34/46 (1979).

8 UN Doc. A/RES/54/4 (1999).

South Africa has ratified the African Charter on Human and Peoples' Rights,[9] which obliges member states, through Article 18, to work towards the elimination of discrimination against women. In 2003 the African Union adopted an Optional Protocol on the Rights of Women in Africa, which was ratified by South Africa in 2004 and finally came into effect in November 2005 with the fifteenth ratification. Sub-regionally, the Southern African Development Community (SADC), of which South Africa and 12 other Southern African countries are members, issued a Declaration on Gender and Development in 1997. In 1998 SADC issued an Addendum on the Eradication of All Forms of Violence against Women, which places far-reaching obligations on member states. We are paper rich and policy prolific: a shining example of the complexity of applying international standards in a developing country context.

Domestically, South Africa's Constitution enshrines the right of all persons to be free from violence, whether from public or private sources.[10] In this it replicates the guarantees of the UN Declaration on the Elimination of Violence against Women.[11] The Bill of Rights, contained within the Constitution, also imposes specific positive duties on the state to protect the interests of the country's residents, including the rights to dignity[12] and privacy.[13] The positive nature of these state duties is described in section 7 (2) of the Constitution, which directs the state to 'respect, promote, protect and fulfil the rights in the Bill of Rights'. The equality provisions[14] of the Constitution are progressive and far reaching, protecting South Africans from both direct and indirect discrimination on the bases of race, gender, sex, pregnancy, marital status, ethnic or social origin, colour, sexual orientation, age, disability, religion, consciences, belief, culture, language and birth. In addition, the South African Constitution requires our courts to consider international law when interpreting the Bill of Rights[15] and empowers it to consider decisions from other countries, thereby ensuring decisions that are consonant with and draw on the experiences of other jurisdictions. Combrinck reminds us that the importance of this section lies not only in the fact that South African courts must consider international law, but that the court's inquiry is not limited to treaties to which South Africa is party or to rules of customary international law that have been accepted by the courts.[16] The combined force of the constitutional right to be free from all forms of violence and the constitutional requirement to consider international law as well as the obligations imposed by international human rights law has

9 OAU Doc. CAB/LEG/67/3 rev. 5, 21 I.L.M. 58 (1982).

10 Section 12 (1) (c) of the Constitution of South Africa (1996).

11 UN Doc. A/RES/48/104 (1993).

12 Section 10.

13 Section 14.

14 Sections 9 (1)–9 (5).

15 Section 39 (1) (b).

16 Helene Combrinck, 'Positive State Duties to Protect Women from Violence: Recent South African Developments', *Human Rights Quarterly* 20, no. 3 (1998): 666–690.

created enormous scope for the protection and development of women's rights to be free from violence in South Africa. Our Constitutional Court (in particular) has been using the language of rights to enforce state accountability for acts and omissions that cause gender-based harm. Acts for which the state has been held accountable by our courts include those where there has been direct harm (for example the rape of a woman by uniformed police officers) and indirect harms (including injuries suffered through failure by police and prosecution to retain a known sex-offender in custody while awaiting trial; and the failure to remove a firearm from a man who had previously pointed it at his wife and threatened to kill her). In reaching these decisions our courts have emphasised the need to comply with international standards relating to violence against women, although ultimately framing this imperative as a 'general norm of (state) accountability' to human rights and constitutional standards. Our courts have also begun to take account of a failure to fulfil these standards – and protect victims of intimate partner violence – in sentencing women convicted of killing abusive spouses, treating a history of violent victimisation as a mitigating factor.

Because our common law is based on precedent – lower courts are bound to follow the legal decisions of higher courts – and therefore very slow to change, the Bill of Rights requires that in coming to decisions and thereby developing the law our courts must promote the objects of the Bill of Rights. This has opened the way for a number of innovative gender-based legal challenges in which our Constitutional Court has signalled strongly to elements of the due diligence standard as it pertains to international law and to the Constitution. The first significant domestic violence case that came to the Constitutional Court was in the case of *S v Baloyi* in 2000, where the applicant challenged the constitutional validity of the enabling legislation under which a domestic violence interdict had been granted against him.[17] In dismissing his application the Court made a number of important pronouncements regarding the nature of domestic violence and the state's obligation to act against it. Judge Sachs points out that domestic violence undermines a number of core constitutional and human rights, saying that, '[t]o the extent that it is systemic, pervasive and overwhelmingly gender-specific, domestic violence both reflects and reinforces patriarchal domination, and does so in a particularly brutal form.' Within this context, and given the imperative to act in accordance with the state's international treaty obligations, it was therefore found to be appropriate and necessary for the state to pass legislation that protects women, in particular, from domestic violence.[18]

While *Baloyi* addresses the issue of domestic violence, it is the subsequent case of *Carmichele* that has been particularly notable in developing a due diligence approach to violence against women.[19] In this case the complainant was brutally

17 *S. v Baloyi* 2000 (1) SACR 81 (CC). The interdict was granted under the Prevention of Family Violence Act 1993, which was replaced by the Domestic Violence Act 1998.

18 Para. 13.

19 *Carmichele v Minister of Safety and Security* 2001 (4) SA 938 (CC); *Carmichele v Minister of Safety and Security* 2004 (2) BCLR 133 (SCA).

attacked by a man who had a previous conviction for indecent assault and a history of violent behaviour towards women. At the time of the attack he was awaiting trial on charges of attempted murder and rape. Despite this background the police officer investigating the case had recommended that he be released on warning pending trial, the prosecution had consequently not opposed bail, and the Court had released him on his own recognisance. The man took to loitering outside Carmichele's house and she approached the prosecutor and the police on a number of occasions to report that he was acting suspiciously. She was told that there was nothing that they could do. Following the attack on her, Carmichele brought a claim for damages against the state. The key to her claim lay in proving that these criminal justice agents were under a legal duty to protect her, that they had negligently breached this duty and that, as a result, she had suffered damages. Neither the High Court nor the Supreme Court of Appeal was prepared to acknowledge the existence of such a duty.[20] On appeal to the Constitutional Court, Carmichele argued that the police and prosecution owed her a duty to '...ensure that she enjoyed her constitutional rights of, inter alia, the right to life, the right to respect for and protection of her dignity, the right to freedom and security, the right to personal privacy and the right to freedom of movement.'[21]

Furthermore, it was argued that the Constitution placed a particular duty on the state to protect women from sexual violence.[22] The Constitutional Court found that the Constitution did indeed explicitly impose positive obligations on the police, and that although prosecutors were not targeted in the same way under the Constitution, these actors had always owed a duty to carry out their functions in the public interest.[23] Furthermore, per the Court:

> 'South Africa also has a duty under international law to prohibit all gender-based discrimination that has the effect or purpose of impairing the enjoyment by women of fundamental rights and freedoms and to take reasonable and appropriate measures to prevent the violation of those rights [footnote reference to CEDAW omitted]. The police is one of the primary agencies of the state responsible for the protection of the public in general and women and children in particular against the invasion of their fundamental rights by perpetrators of violent crime.'[24]

---

20 See *Carmichele v Minister of Safety and Security and Another* 2001(1) SA 489 (SCA).

21 Para. 27.

22 Para. 28.

23 At para. 72. The Court draws on the *United Nations Guidelines on the Role of Prosecutors* in explicating this function. The Guidelines were adopted by the 8th United Nations Congress on the Prevention of Crime and the Treatment of Offenders held in Havana, Cuba from 17 August–7 September 1990, and have been incorporated by reference into South African law through the National Prosecuting Authority Act 1998.

24 Para. 62.

The question that then arises is how one translates constitutional obligations 'placed on the state to respect, protect, promote and fulfil the rights in the Bill of Rights and, in particular, the right of women to have their safety and security protected'[25] into a duty to pay damages under the law of delict (or torts) in respect of individual violations. It seems that this must be done on a case by case basis, but there is, for example, no reason in principle why a prosecutor who negligently fails to put before the court information that an accused person has a history of violence and poses a potential threat to community members should not be held liable for damages resulting from that omission.[26]

On this basis, the Constitutional Court referred the matter back to the trial court, which heard evidence on the matter and subsequently found in Carmichele's favour.[27] This approach has been followed in a number of subsequent Supreme Court of Appeal judgments. In one of these[28] the court had to contend with the failure of the police to revoke the firearm license and remove the firearm of a man known to them to be violent. It was argued that, as a result of this failure the man, in a drunken rage, was able to shoot and kill his wife and daughter and to injure a neighbour who had come to their assistance. Holding the police liable, the Court confirmed that where the rights to life, liberty and security of a person are at stake '[t]he state, represented by its officials, has a constitutional duty to protect them'.[29] The principle of state accountability for negligent acts and omissions by state agents, which in turn enable violence against women, has been entrenched through these cases in South African law. They have clearly established that the courts will intervene to ensure that the state takes positive steps to protect women against violence, and will impose liability on the state for failure to do so. While the full ambit of state obligations to protect, investigate, punish and compensate victims of domestic violence has not been fully challenged in South African courts, these cases have provided a useful foundation upon which public interest litigation can be used to support state compliance with the duties imposed through international and domestic law.

Domestic Violence Legislation

The first piece of domestic violence legislation was passed in South Africa in 1993. The Prevention of Family Violence Act essentially focused on physical violence

25 Para. 57.

26 Para. 74.

27 In *Carmichele v Minister of Safety and Security and Another* 2002 (10) BCLR 1100 (C).

28 *Minister of Safety and Security v Van Duivenboden* 2002 AllSA 741 (SCA).

29 Para. 22. A similar finding was made in the case of *Van Eeden v Minister of Safety and Security* 2002 AllSA 346 (SCA), where the court found that the police had breached their legal duty towards the applicant, who was raped by a serial rapist who had escaped from police custody. In both cases the court placed substantial emphasis on the state's obligation to protect, promote, and enforce the right to freedom from violence.

occurring within a marital relationship. Notably, it outlawed marital rape. Although it came at a time when there was a strong international impetus towards addressing violence against women through legislative reform, it was also seen by many in South Africa as a cynical attempt by the apartheid government to secure women's votes in what would be our first democratic election in 1994. That said, South Africa's transition to democracy did create an important window of opportunity for progressive law reform. Because apartheid had been so effectively entrenched and institutionalised through a set of laws governing social relations, gender activists (and, indeed, other social activists) were naively optimistic about the ways in which law could now be used to replace that system of oppression with an idealised one that entrenched racial and gender equality. At the same time our readmission to the international community and the consequent ratification of various human rights treaties provided feminist activists with a powerful tool for holding the state accountable and motivating as to why – when we already had a family violence law, which was only three or four years old – we now needed to replace it with a more wide-ranging piece of legislation.

The Domestic Violence Act (DVA)[30] resulted from intensive lobbying by women's activists and is explicitly founded on South Africa's international commitments and obligations towards ending violence against women. The Act draws heavily on the model framework for domestic violence legislation[31] developed by the UN Special Rapporteur on violence against women, its causes and consequences, as well as on broad definitions of domestic violence that include psychological, emotional and economic abuse. It also seeks to protect parties within a range of domestic relationships, including customary and same-sex relationships. The DVA is particularly notable in that it places positive duties on the police, the state agency which had been identified by various studies to be the most recalcitrant institution when it came to dealing with domestic violence. Police members are required, in terms of the Act, to:

- Accompany the complainant to collect personal property
- Seize dangerous weapons from perpetrators
- Assist the complainant in obtaining medical treatment and shelter
- Inform the complainant of her rights under the Act
- Explain the contents of a notice which sets out what the complainant must do to enforce her rights under the Act
- Serve notices and protection orders on respondents
- Exercise powers of arrest without a warrant where the complainant is in danger of imminent harm
- Arrest perpetrators upon a breach of the protection order

Non-compliance with these duties exposes police members to disciplinary action. The explicit inclusion of specific obligations with which police officers must

30 No. 116 of 1998.

31 Submitted to the UN Commission on Human Rights on 2 February 1996, UN Doc. E/CN.4/1996/53/Add.2.

comply when attending to domestic violence matters has substantially improved the service provided to victims by these criminal justice agents.

The DVA also empowers the courts to order payment of rent or mortgages and emergency expenses, thus anticipating some of the negative economic impacts that may flow from a protection order and that typically keep women in abusive relationships. By providing for the abuser to be removed and restricted from entering the shared residence, the DVA seeks to ensure that victims of domestic violence are able to remain in their homes, thereby attempting to minimise the impact on victims and their families. Duties on various officials in the justice sector are further spelled out through sector-specific instructions and regulations formulated under the DVA, which spell out processes to be followed and duties to be fulfilled in more detail. Finally, at each police station the station commander is required to develop station orders that take into account the Act and instructions within a localised context.

Challenges for Implementing the Due Diligence Standard

Positive Duties Are Restricted to Criminal Justice Agencies

While South Africa's domestic violence legislation places positive duties on the police, and our courts have recognised that other criminal justice agents may be liable under due diligence standards at certain times, women's activists in South Africa continue to lobby for such duties to be placed on other key role-players and for the obligations of other sectors to be recognised. A critical element that is missing in South Africa is the health sector, which is one of the state agencies with which victims of domestic violence are most likely to come into contact. It is also the sector which is most substantially impacted and most able to respond to the inter-relation between domestic violence and HIV/Aids. Similarly we do not see obligations placed on the state to provide redress in the form of, for example, social welfare grants or preference in terms of accessing government-subsidised housing to victims of domestic violence. Legal assistance (beyond that provided by the police and courts) is generally provided by non-governmental organisations and mental health services are not part of the referral process by the state. Compensation for medical, legal, and social costs of violence is also not a feature of the system (apart from provision for emergency monetary relief, which covers the immediate costs of attending court to apply for a domestic violence protection order or receiving emergency medical care). In these instances international instruments such as the CEDAW Convention and the Declaration on the Elimination of Violence against Women are not adequately articulated within protective legislation or adjunct social policies.

Resources

Resources and competing demands for government spending remain a challenge. To some extent budgets are being allocated for the implementation of the DVA, but this has been slow to come, and the lack of access to personnel and to basic requirements such as stationery and photocopy facilities has been almost crippling in courts that experience large numbers of applications for protection orders. In some courts as many as 60–70 women a day are applying for protection orders, with only one court clerk and one magistrate attending to these applications. The state is, however, addressing these questions of under-resourcing and poor implementation by criminal justice personnel. Budgets have been allocated both for physical infrastructure, such as victim support rooms, and for training. The training developed by the police is thorough and aimed at not only providing knowledge of the legislation contents, but also an understanding of the social context in which domestic violence occurs.

Researchers from the Gender, Health & Justice Research Unit have systematically monitored the implementation of the DVA from the time that it came into operation. Most recently, during 2005, they were requested by the police to look at how the Act was being implemented at 29 designated police stations. Although there are many problems with the technical and procedural application of the legislation, changing attitudes and greater compliance with the legislation is encouraging. At the same time the number of domestic violence cases being reported to police stations and the courts appears to be increasing. It is an almost inevitable, but generally unexpected, outcome of improved service delivery on the part of the police: to the extent that women feel more comfortable reporting domestic violence to the police and to the extent that the police take these matters more seriously, it is likely that one will see an increase in reporting of these cases. This means that more spending is required. It also means that using police statistics and a decrease in reported cases as the basis on which to gauge state compliance is problematic and probably a fallacious measure of efficacy.

The South African government, while doing far more than most of its African counterparts, does not act proactively to protect women from domestic violence by providing them with access to exit opportunities – shelters, social welfare support, skills development, educational support for victims and their children – that may very well reduce the risk of harm for victims of abuse. In this we fall short of international and regional standards of protection. But the reality is that such interventions require resources. While it is certainly possible, and important, to make an argument for an increased portion of the budget to be committed to protecting women from domestic violence, it seems obvious that when we impose standards that are subject to 'available resources' we are positing that, in fact, different standards of protection apply to women from developed and developing countries. We need to ask ourselves therefore whether a global commitment to due diligence in domestic violence does not, of necessity, mean a commitment to some level of targeted donor-intervention into resource-constrained countries. To the extent that this has been happening in South Africa, the lesson learned is that focussing on the state as locus of responsibility may result in more bilateral funding and less money flowing directly to the women's NGOs that have taken up the challenge of providing legal services to victims of domestic violence, establishing victim support centres at police stations and courts, and running battered women's shelters. Getting countries to legislate against domestic violence is, in many respects, the easy part. Ensuring that they are adequately implemented and that services, shelters, and preventative mechanisms are put in place is what requires substantial resources, coupled with constant monitoring from civil society bodies.

Working with Traditional Leaders

One of the areas in which we see the most complex interaction between international norms regarding state responsibility, progressive legislation and effective implementation is in traditional societies. Commentators tend to set up the issue of traditional mechanisms for dealing with domestic violence (working, for example, through traditional or community leaders) as dichotomous to formal state-based dispute resolution occurring through the criminal justice system. That is, either women use the formal justice system or they use informal alternative dispute resolution mechanisms. We would argue that this is not the case. On a daily basis in some of our most rural provinces one hears women's rights activists speaking of the CEDAW Convention and they are well acquainted with the contents of the Domestic Violence Act. They bargain with the violent men in their communities and with their traditional leaders in the shadow of international instruments and municipal laws. It matters to them that the international community has condemned domestic violence and, by doing that, has used these instruments to finally 'name' their experience of domestic violence. In the majority of over 1,200 domestic violence dockets analysed by the Gender, Health, & Justice Research Unit this year in these largely rural contexts, women have repeatedly stated that they are bringing their case to the criminal justice system because, in their words, 'NO person has the right to hit me'. This speaks of a rights-consciousness. What is also apparent from these dockets is that women have obtained the permission of their traditional leaders to take the matter to the criminal justice system.

We see an escalation in the scale of intervention over time in South Africa's traditional communities: women may seek to sort out the matter within the family, requesting help from a trusted family member, then perhaps a community leader, then the chief, and – when these interventions fail – from the courts. Given that so many women are subject to customary law or living in traditional contexts, the pressing question is how we educate traditional leaders about domestic violence and how we hold these governance structures accountable to the standards enunciated in international and regional human rights instruments. Can the due diligence standard apply directly to these structures, or does the locus of responsibility remain with the state, which surely provides the ultimate imprimatur for traditional authorities and the entrenchment of customary law (along with the conditions under which it is entrenched)? To illustrate: although all SADC countries have constitutions that enshrine gender equality, only South Africa and Namibia make customary law subservient to their Bill of Rights. Women in customary marriages throughout most countries in Southern Africa are therefore legally regarded as perpetual minors absolutely subject to the marital power of their husbands. The state's failure to provide for gender equality is obviously problematic in this context. At the same time a recurrent refrain coming from proponents of customary law is that within traditional relationships and fulfilling traditional gender-roles is where women are best protected against domestic violence. This is not a novel argument, but it is one that unfortunately has yet to be adequately (and empirically) debunked in the South African context. It is in this delicate balancing act – between custom and 'formal' law – that international standards become difficult to apply.

Conclusion

In South Africa, the due diligence standard – although not necessarily part of the legal parlance of the courts – has been slowly evolving over the past decade. References to 'positive legal duties', 'fiduciary duties', and 'legal or statutory obligations' are evident in the development of protective legislation, such as the DVA, and in the jurisprudence of our courts relating to violence against women. The combined influence of international human rights law on state obligations to address violence against women and the South African Constitution have gone a long way in ensuring the inclusion of due diligence in post-apartheid law and policy reform as well as the development of progressive jurisprudence. In addition to progressive legislation the government has developed campaigns to 'end domestic violence' on National Women's Day and during the 16 Days of Activism, while the President has named ending violence against women and children a national priority.

That said, while campaigns may raise awareness and legislation provide some protection to victims, they do not provide remedies for the structural inequality and dependency that makes women particularly vulnerable to intimate abuse, enabling and perpetuating domestic violence. Perhaps most importantly therefore it is in the realm of protection that the South African government fails its citizens, in the lack of attention to women's lived experiences of poverty and class-based vulnerability, which means responding to domestic violence only once it has occurred. For the rest, we face the challenges of a multi-cultural developing country. South Africa has certainly made substantial efforts towards meeting our international obligations to exercise due diligence in dealing with domestic violence. Many challenges remain, but perhaps we can reasonably dissuade MacKinnon's peace-keepers from descending on us – for the moment.

Violence against Women by Non-State Actors, a Responsibility for the State under Human Rights Law: Amnesty International's Work on Domestic Violence

Lisa Gormley

Introduction

Amnesty International's research and campaigning experience on women's right not to suffer gender-based violence has received new impetus on the launch of its global campaign *Stop Violence against Women*, which began in March 2004. The expanse of Amnesty International's research and campaigning has shown without doubt that violence against women cannot be addressed as an isolated and independent human rights issue. Its causes, consequences, and solutions are intimately linked with achieving women's human rights in all their manifestations, across economic, social and cultural rights as well as civil and political rights.[1]

A significant part of Amnesty International's work on women's rights relates to states' obligations of due diligence to prevent, investigate, punish and provide reparation for acts of violence by non-state actors.[2] This legal concept was

1 See, for example the following Reports of Amnesty International, *Papua New Guinea: Violence Against Women – Not Inevitable, Never Acceptable!*, AI Index ASA 34/002/2006, 4 September 2006; *Sexual Violence Against Women and Girls in Jamaica: 'Just a Little Sex'*, AI Index AMR 38/002/06, 22 June 2006; *Sierra Leone: Women Face Human Rights Abuses in the Informal Legal Sector*, AI Index AFR 51/002/06, 17 May 2006; *Russian Federation: Nowhere to Turn to – Violence against Women in the Family*, AI Index EUR 46/056/2005, 14 December 2005; *Spain: More than Words – Making Protection and Justice a Reality for Women Who Suffer Gender-Based Violence in the Home*, AI Index EUR 41/005/05, 12 May 2005; *Gulf Cooperation Council (GCC) Countries: Women Deserve Dignity and Respect*, AI Index MDE 04/004/05, 11 May 2005.

2 Although this article will concentrate on women's right not to suffer gender-based violence, the concept of state responsibility to exercise due diligence for violations of rights by non-state actors should not be seen as confined to the rights of women alone; it is equally applicable to the interference in the enjoyment of human rights of men and children. Commonly it has been used when addressing women's rights, as their concerns have historically been viewed as belonging to the 'private sphere' to

C. Benninger-Budel ed., Due Diligence and Its Application to Protect Women from Violence
 ISBN 978 90 04 16293 8. pp. 173-184

highlighted in one of the first phases of the campaign on domestic violence, also known as intimate partner violence. The legal analysis on which the due diligence approach was based was developed for some years before the start of the *Stop Violence against Women campaign*,[3] and materials containing this analysis were published during the recent campaign against the use of torture.[4] This article seeks to explain the benefits and limits of the use of the due diligence approach, including areas of practical success, and challenges for future developments in law and practice to combat domestic violence.

Traditionally, international human rights law concerned itself mainly with the direct actions of states and their agents towards individuals, but over the last decades, more interest has been shown for the effect of actions by non-state actors on the rights of other private individuals, and the state's legal responsibility to address effectively such actions. The General Assembly in its Declaration on the Elimination of Violence against Women included a significant reference to the due diligence principle, which emphasises that the duty of due diligence – that states should take effective action to enforce human rights principles – applies to the actions of state actors and non-state actors alike where these affect women's right not to suffer violence.[5]

The basis of due diligence for states' responsibility to address the violence against women by state and non-state actors in international law is based on a number of inter-related principles:

- There is a general right to a remedy for violations of human rights;

---

address the perception women's rights are most frequently violated by non-state actors. The concept of due diligence has been taken up and explored by successive Special Rapporteurs on violence against women, its causes and consequences, as well as non-governmental organisations working on women's human rights. However, significant scholarship, primarily Professor Andrew Clapham, has explored the concept of the question of non-state actors and respective obligations of state and individuals across a variety of rights in *Human Rights in the Private Sphere* (Oxford: University Press, 1993), and in *Human Rights Obligations of Non-State Actors* (Oxford: University Press, 2006).

3 Amnesty International, *Respect, Protect, Fulfil – Women's Human Rights: State Responsibility for Abuses by 'Non-State Actors'*, AI Index IOR 50/001/2000, 1 September 2000.

4 Amnesty International, *Broken Bodies, Shattered Minds*, AI Index ACT 40/001/2001, 8 March 2001.

5 'States should pursue by all appropriate means and without delay a policy of eliminating violence against women and, to this end, should: (c) Exercise due diligence to prevent, investigate and, in accordance with national legislation, punish acts of violence against women, *whether those acts are perpetrated by the State or by private persons*', Article 4, Declaration on the Elimination of Violence against Women, General Assembly resolution 48/104 of 20 December 1993 [author's italics for emphasis].

- The customary international law principle of non-discrimination on the grounds of gender and sex has been universally accepted;[6]
- Gender-based violence has been identified as a form of discrimination by the Committee on the Elimination of Discrimination against Women (CEDAW Committee) under Article 1 of the Convention on the Elimination of All Forms of Discrimination against Women (CEDAW Convention);[7]
- Human rights treaties call for the eradication of discrimination, which must therefore logically include gender-based violence, whether by state or non-state actors.[8]

This constellation of human rights obligations gives Amnesty International the basis of its legal mandate to call states to account to eradicate violence against women, whether the perpetrators are agents of the state or non-state actors.[9]

As well as responding to the existing international human rights law framework, Amnesty International was responding to the demand for consistency and coherence in addressing human rights concerns caused by the same kind of assaults against women in various different contexts. Amnesty International had worked for many years on aspects of violence against women that when commit-

6 As well as the general principle of non-discrimination between men and women elaborated across a number of specific rights in the Convention on the Elimination of All Forms of Discrimination against Women, Articles 2 (1) and 3 of the International Covenant on Civil and Political Rights, and Articles 2 (2) and 3 of the International Covenant on Economic, Social and Cultural Rights all require substantive equality in the enjoyment of rights between men and women. A significant international legal authority, Professor Brownlie in *Principles of Public International Law* (Oxford: University Press, 2003), 546, has indicated that this is a binding principle of international law in itself, independent of treaty obligations. This is a position supported by an advisory opinion from the Inter-American Court of Human Rights (Juridical Condition and Rights of Undocumented Migrants, Advisory Opinion OC-18 of 18 September 2003).

7 Committee on the Elimination of Discrimination against Women, General Recommendation no. 19, Violence against women (eleventh session, 1992), UN Doc. A/47/38. For a specific reference to non-state actors, see Article 9 of the Recommendation: 'Under general international law and specific human rights covenants, States may also be responsible for private acts if they fail to act with due diligence to prevent violations of rights or to investigate and punish acts of violence, and for providing compensation.'

8 Article 2 of the CEDAW Convention contains the binding commitment that 'States Parties condemn discrimination against women in all its forms, agree to pursue by all appropriate means and without delay a policy of eliminating discrimination against women' and Article 2 (e) requires states '[t]o take all appropriate measures to eliminate discrimination against women by any person, organization or enterprise'.

9 See in general: Amnesty International, *Respect, Protect, Fulfil – Women's Human Rights: State Responsibility for Abuses by 'Non-State Actors',* AI Index IOR 50/001/2000, 1 September 2000, and *Making Rights a Reality: The Duty of States to Address Violence Against Women,* AI Index 77/049/2004, June 2004.

ted by state actors would constitute torture, notably rapes in armed conflict and in custody; it seemed inexcusable not to address the same acts in other legal contexts, notably violence against women committed within homes and families.

Amnesty International's work on domestic violence is very similar to much of the long-term work securing justice for victims of torture, extrajudicial execution and 'disappearance': campaigning for the establishment of fair and effective laws and procedures for ensuring prompt, effective, independent and impartial investigations and prosecuting alleged perpetrators. As in this work for survivors of torture and the relatives of victims of extrajudicial execution and 'disappearance', Amnesty International addresses the difficulties of survivors and families in seeking legal and other assistance in approaching the state for justice and seeking medical and other practical assistance. In this work, Amnesty International also identifies intangible yet nonetheless real barriers to justice and recovery such as discrimination on the part of the authorities against victims, including protection from scrutiny for perpetrators due to their relative power and influence in comparison with survivors.

Despite the long-standing public/private separation in international human rights law,[10] there is a significant link between the obligation of due diligence for the acts of non-state actors and direct state violations. In cases of public and private abuses alike, persistent failures to address basic administration of law and services violate the right to equality before the law, and the right not to suffer torture or cruel, inhuman, or degrading treatment. Frequently these discriminatory laws and practices remain in force due to the lack of political will or pandering to political demands of particular groups. The state is often clearly operating through apparently independent traditional or cultural adjudication systems. Whether through this kind of knowing negligence or active violation, states are failing to adhere to their legal obligations to respect and ensure women's human rights. Each state's case requires an appraisal of the level of complicity in order to provide appropriate recommendations to rectify the situation in each case, but the violation of human rights law remains the same.

The fact that women's rights are not fully implemented as required by international human rights law in the overwhelming majority of cases is not to say that each and every act of violence against women, regardless of the identity of the perpetrator, is the responsibility of the state. The basic requirement established in *Velásquez Rodríguez v Honduras* is that:

> 'If the State apparatus acts in such a way that the violation goes unpunished and the victim's full enjoyment of such rights is not restored as soon as possible, the State has

10 However, the strict existence of the public/private divide has been rightly contested, as often families are intensely regulated by the state, i.e., through marriage, divorce and child protection and custody laws.

> failed to comply with its duty to ensure the free and full exercise of those rights to the persons within its jurisdiction.'[11]

It is not unreasonable for the state to be required to establish the basic rule of law, not just for women, but for all; the concept of due diligence does not demand state omniscience or an unwarranted interference in individuals' lives in its efforts to prevent, investigate, and punish violence against women. This principle has been articulated compellingly:

> 'The human right to a private and family life is of special importance, but cannot be tolerated to condone private conduct within families in which one partner enforces dominance by violence over the other. The key human rights principle is that violence deliberately directed against any other person is never a purely private matter.'[12]

From the Principle of Law to Practical Implementation of Women's Right Not to Be Subjected to Domestic Violence

International law requires that states should exercise due diligence, but this requires in practice that a variety of public servants should act according to this principle. The state is multi-faceted, multi-sited, with competing aims and spheres of influence, all interdependent in how they work to ensure women's rights. Following women's journey from experiencing violence in the family, it is clear that a variety of state actors working directly with the public will be required to provide an effective and rights-respecting response to ensure women access to appropriate remedy: those working in housing, health, social services, and in the administration of justice at the very least. Real effective long-term prevention over the next generations will require a transformation of education, promoting equality between girls and boys from the earliest ages, and with all forms of media working towards this aim through promotion of women's true equality with men.

On a wider level, central government officials such as internal affairs ministries, ministries of justice and ministries for women may all have conflicting views and priorities on implementing policies to assist women living with domestic violence. In federal countries, the diversity of agents involved may be complicated by local officials being responsible for some functions. Given that normally the Ministry of Foreign Affairs takes the main role in engaging with international human rights procedures, the extent to which this discourse of human rights obligations is a real part of government policy across all ministries and government functions

11 Inter-American Court of Human Rights, *Velásquez Rodríguez v Honduras*, Judgment of 29 July 1988, Series C: Decisions and Judgments, no. 04, para. 176.

12 Rebecca J. Cook, Bernard M. Dickens, Mahmoud Fathalla, *Reproductive Health and Human Rights: Integrating Medicine, Ethics and Law* (Oxford: University Press, 2003), 390.

and approaches varies enormously. However, such complexities should not be an excuse for failing to implement human rights obligations.[13]

Despite the variation in human rights legal regimes which apply to violence against women in different contexts, in practice, the research and campaigning work that Amnesty International has undertaken on violations of women's rights by non-state actors concentrates more on the state's reaction and response and less on the physical details of the violence perpetrated by non-state actors because, even when dealing with non-state actors, international human rights law focuses on the responsibility of the state. Part of this state duty relating to human rights is to implement fairly and effectively individual criminal legal responsibility and to provide full reparation.

A growing challenge to the effectiveness of the legal concept of due diligence, as women's rights discourse is increasingly accepted, is when a state takes some measures to assist women survivors, but they are not effective. The CEDAW has provided an answer in the case *Ms A.T. v Hungary* particularly in terms of follow-up assessments: that the duty of due diligence is breached until the woman applicant has full remedy.[14] A challenge here for the use of due diligence as a term is that it may be seen as therefore meaningless, as all states are effectively in breach unless and until every person suffering a violation of rights has a full remedy, a state of affairs which is definitely far from reality now. However, as the citation from *Velásquez Rodríguez* shows, as discussed above, the basic requirement to establish state apparatus aimed at enforcing human rights is a reasonable requirement of all states. However, a significant problem is that many women do not feel confident enough to bring their complaints to the state.

Challenges during Women's Journey to Justice

In terms of reparation, in no country Amnesty International has investigated on the issue of domestic violence have women been consistently provided full reparation, including prompt, effective, independent and impartial investigation and access to justice; reparation for harm suffered, including compensation for physical and mental harm, suffering and distress, lost opportunities, and loss of earnings; rehabilitation, including health and social care. While the content of human rights standards and commentary relates mainly to criminal justice processes, these wider requirements for remedy are given very little attention; nor are the deeply linked concerns, such as social ostracism, denial of economic and social rights, and rights to a family life with their children, which affect women's decisions to participate in criminal justice processes.

13 Article 27 of the Vienna Convention on the Law of Treaties.

14 Committee on the Elimination of Discrimination against Women, Communication no. 2/2003, *Ms A.T. v Hungary*, View adopted on 26 January 2005.

Criminal Law

Research by Amnesty International and other commentators has shown that in many states, there is either an absence of laws, or profoundly flawed substantive definitions of criminal laws, relating to violence against women, whether these acts are committed by state or non-state actors. The administration of criminal justice generally fails through lack of professionalism of staff, who frequently display discriminatory attitudes against women, and ineffective procedural laws. These two factors lead to impunity. Commonly, practical problems for women on their journey to justice show a consistent failure to ensure respect for women's right to equality before the law.

Substantive criminal laws

In many countries, it is assumed that violence within the family is not a crime. Frequently, substantive laws on domestic violence do not exist, and police and prosecutors refuse to accept that ordinary laws on assault and murder apply. It is assumed that an intimate relationship negates any criminal responsibility because of the privileged position of a husband or other male relative, or doctrines of privacy of the home.

In some countries, new specific domestic violence criminal law is enacted to emphasise and make clear that the family environment or intimate relationships do not negate the legal character of assaults. The effectiveness of such laws depends on the drafting, particularly ensuring that intimate and familial relationships in all their various forms, not just married persons, are subject to the law. Laws against forced and early marriage should be just as much a part of domestic violence legislation, as this is a significant cause and manifestation of domestic violence.

There is a close relationship between domestic violence legislation and sexual assault laws, particularly marital rape, which is persistently condoned in many countries, through the explicit exemption of husbands from any possible criminal liability for rape of their wives. The attitudes underlying the definitions of rape and sexual assault laws, whether the assault takes place between spouses or otherwise, rely often on force as an element of the crime and play to attitudes and assumptions that women consent to sexual contact unless they reject it absolutely with utmost physical resistance. An equality approach, as confirmed by the European Court of Human Rights, identifies rape as a violation of sexual autonomy, which can be committed using coercion alone, without use of physical force.[15] Generally, laws against harassment and stalking and other forms of psychological violence are not common.

15 European Court of Human Rights, *M.C. v Bulgaria*, Application no. 39272/98, Judgment of 4 December 2003. This case related to a situation where a young girl was lured to an isolated area by acquaintances and raped without the use of physical force, but in a coercive environment.

Administration of criminal law

In the investigation of domestic violence cases, women complainants are often treated with negligence, scepticism or outright disbelief or contempt by police, who refuse to investigate complaints or say there is nothing they can do about a 'family' problem. Police often attempt to mediate between an attacker and a complainant, rather than arresting the perpetrator or otherwise securing the safety of the complainant. Medico-legal evidence may be unavailable due to lack of access to doctors or user charges, or inexpertly noted and presented.

Procedural criminal law relating to assessment of evidence also discriminates against women. In some jurisdictions, evidence relating to rape and sexual violence is subject to the 'cautionary rule', i.e., judges warn juries that women's testimony on such issues should not be relied on without corroboration. Evidence is frequently given in open court, leading to a frightening and humiliating experience for the woman giving evidence, particularly if her alleged attacker chooses to cross-examine her. Cross-examination by lawyers is frequently aimed at undermining a complainant's credibility in an aggressive and humiliating manner.

Protection of Civil Laws

In some countries, there is a mix of specific criminal laws and civil protection orders or injunctions. While looking impressive on paper, often their effectiveness in protecting women is stymied by poor response to breaches of civil injunction, caused by police indifference, failures of coordination between courts, or lack of resources to respond promptly to calls.

Not Even Starting the Journey: Obstacles to Women Seeking Justice

An important fact that Amnesty International has learned in its work on domestic violence so far is that most women come nowhere near approaching the criminal justice system for assistance, although it is this system on which human rights standards currently focus. In addition to social attitudes, several practical issues frequently act together to make women unwilling to seek the assistance of the state, all of which are underpinned by legal issues requiring reform at the same time as any criminal or civil domestic violence law: housing law, family law, employment and social security law and immigration status law. However, women's unwillingness to approach the state, and therefore a relative ignorance of women's experiences on the part of the state, is no excuse for states to fail to act; the standards impose an active duty to take positive measures to eradicate discrimination against women, which includes violence.[16]

16 Article 2 of the CEDAW Convention contains the commitment: 'States Parties condemn discrimination in all its forms, agree to pursue *by all appropriate means and without delay* a policy of eliminating discrimination…[author's italics for emphasis].'

Social Attitudes

Social attitudes are one significant reason why women are unwilling to approach the state for assistance. Women are often too ground down by attitudes of those around them, in society as a whole, but particularly their own immediate families, which assert that men have a right to use violence, or that the use of violence is an inevitable part of human relationships. This is compounded by similar police attitudes, as women often find that they will not be taken seriously when they make complaints. Although the requirement to 'modify the social and cultural patterns of conduct of men and women, with a view to achieving the elimination of prejudices and customary and all other practices which are based on the idea of the inferiority or the superiority of either of the sexes or on stereotyped roles for men and women' is a key obligation in the CEDAW Convention,[17] there need to be more studies and practical guidance on how discriminatory attitudes can be changed. They can be assisted by more attention from the various forms of media in all contexts, as well as from civil society organisations: however, the key legal obligation to undertake this social transformation is on states. Failure to address social attitudes means that other initiatives fail[18] – i.e., reform of the police to improve interviewing of complainants and improve evidence-gathering is pointless if social and economic pressures on women require them to keep families together at all costs, and make life independent of a man impossible.

Housing

Often women are too afraid to seek any kind of assistance for a domestic violence problem; either because they are dependent on the violent man to maintain legal tenure of their home, or out of fear of being made homeless because they cannot

17 Article 5 of the CEDAW Convention provides:
'States Parties shall take all appropriate measures:
(a) To modify the social and cultural patterns of conduct of men and women, with a view to achieving the elimination of prejudices and customary and all other practices which are based on the idea of the inferiority or the superiority of either of the sexes or on stereotyped roles for men and women; (b) To ensure that family education includes a proper understanding of maternity as a social function and the recognition of the common responsibility of men and women in the upbringing and development of their children, it being understood that the interest of the children is the primordial consideration in all cases.'
See Rikki Holtmaat, 'Preventing Violence against Women: The Due Diligence Standard with Respect to the Obligation to Banish Gender Stereotypes on the Ground of Article 5 (a) of the CEDAW Convention,' in this book.

18 'A Gap or a Chasm? Attrition in Reported Rape Cases,' UK Home Office Research Study 293, February 2005, describes how reforms in the criminal justice system to improve treatment of rape cases have been undermined by the failure to address persistent discriminatory social attitudes of those working in the criminal justice system.

afford housing on their own income. Therefore, housing, land tenure and inheritance laws also need reform where they discriminate against women. When seeking injunctions, courts should consider excluding the man from the home to preserve the woman's safety, rather than requiring her to leave the shared home.[19]

Child Custody

Similarly, women often fear seeking assistance because they are afraid of losing custody of their children. In some countries, this is because personal or family legal codes privilege the father's right to maintain custody of children. In other countries, this is because social services may assess a woman living with violence as not being able to care for children, and rather than seeking a holistic solution for the woman and her children to make a new life together away from the violent man, they will simply take the children into care.

Poverty

Women may also be afraid of making a complaint against an abusive partner for fear of poverty if they separate or if he is sent to prison, a problem which is particularly acute when children are involved. Laws allowing women to work, appropriate support if a woman is unable to work because of caring responsibilities, and employment laws allowing part-time and flexible working are important. Sufficient social services support should be available for women in this situation.

Intersectional Discrimination

Migrant women frequently are actively denied services such as housing and social security, even in situations of domestic violence, due to immigration laws. Migrant women may be reluctant to seek assistance for fear of bringing themselves to the attention of the authorities or prejudicing an existing claim. Often immigration laws require a woman's application to be dependent on her husband's, making it impossible to separate from a violent man. Immigration laws therefore require particular attention.

Conclusion and Proposals for Improved Fulfilment of Human Rights Obligations

The elements of due diligence 'respect, protect and fulfil' and 'prevent, investigate, punish' encapsulate a complex system of requirements, all inter-linked, all significant and necessary. The overall prevention strategy incorporates criminal investigation and punishment, both to signify the unacceptability of domestic violence, and to sanction perpetrators. Other strategies are to offer reparation to women, to put them in a position of entitlement rather than shame. Implement-

19 *Ms A.T. v Hungary*, see note 14 above.

ing effective measures to secure women's rights not to suffer violence requires substantial political, economic and sociological knowledge of how the contributing factors influencing the prevalence of domestic violence operate in each state, plus detailed studies of the processes and institutions dealing with women complainants.

More work needs to be done by states, working in cooperation with women's rights non-governmental organisations (NGOs), to listen directly to women living with and recovering from violence. States need to learn from women's analysis of how violence was used against them and in which circumstances. They also need to consider women's views of what decisions were open to them and whether the solutions proposed to them were genuine remedies.

NGOs working to advocate for women's rights, particularly those providing direct services to women seeking assistance with domestic violence problems, should be consulted by states as a part of this. A significant problem for enforcement of the standards within states exists when those human rights defenders are limited in their freedom of action. Often these women human rights defenders are working under conditions of political repression, often of the most egregious gender-based kind. Even where women's human rights defenders can operate without harassment, the struggle to survive financially, the risk that 'mainstreaming gender' leads to invisibility of women's rights issues, and pressures of funding and demands of donors mean that women's human rights defenders, especially service providers, are struggling to maintain services and without the energy or time to look at broader policy issues.[20] The political pressures of being reliant on a state for funding, or on good relationships with ministries in order to implement even the most limited improvements – with the pressure of needing to improve the practical situation for women even in small ways making it harder to ask for the larger transformations which are necessary – all underscore the difficulty of speaking truth to power for these women human rights defenders. That states ensure freedom of action and support for women's human rights defenders is a bedrock requirement for implementing solutions to domestic violence.

In the cases of all types of domestic legal reform, training and funding to support proper implementation of the law is always required, as well as legislation requiring coordination and cooperation between the various agencies (criminal and civil courts, health and social security services, education and housing) to ensure an appropriate and integrated response.

Reform of domestic law is an important step, but is not an end in itself: monitoring its effectiveness in protecting women and providing a remedy is a long-term task. Monitoring is also required to ensure that minority groups do not receive disproportionate attention from the authorities leading not just to individual injustice, but also playing to ideas that domestic violence is a problem only in poor, marginalised, or immigrant families (or 'the other', however perceived).

20 Association for Women's Rights in Development, *Where is the Money for Women's Rights? Assessing the Resources and the Role of Donors in the Promotion of Women's Rights and the Support of Women's Rights Organizations*, February 2006.

The state must publicise two facts: not only that violence against women is unacceptable, but that it is prevalent in all sectors of society.

Due diligence is a facet of state responsibility, but to ensure that states live up to their obligation to pursue a policy to eradicate violence and other forms of discrimination without delay,[21] those working directly with survivors and civil society as a whole must bring their experiences and the need for action to the state consistently. This includes those working in the criminal justice system, health services, and other state functions assisting women, which should all honestly examine their own practices and level of service to women, and act accordingly. The expertise of the women's rights advocates and service providers should be used to shape all state interventions. Sharing an understanding of women's realities is required to ensure states' adherence to international human rights law; and this requires that everyone challenges gendered assumptions that domestic violence is an inescapable part of 'how things are', so that all women can live their lives in dignity, safety, and full enjoyment of autonomy and human rights.

21 Article 2 of the CEDAW Convention, see note 8 above.

Spain: More Rights, but the Obstacles Remain

*María Naredo Molero**

Introduction

> *'I regret having filed a complaint, because my family would not have found out and I would still be in the position I am in now: alone, without any help, working like a Trojan so that my children and I can get by'.*
>
> Testimony of Laura (real name withheld), interviewed by Amnesty International in April 2006.

Since 2002, Amnesty International has produced a series of reports seeking to encourage the Spanish government to address the issue of gender-based violence from a human rights perspective and to bring its legislation and policies into line with United Nations standards. The organisation has taken a keen interest in the drafting and progress of the *Ley Orgánica de Medidas de Protección Integral contra la Violencia de Género*[1] (Basic Law on Comprehensive Protection Measures to Tackle Gender-Based Violence, hereafter referred to as Comprehensive Law) and has made recommendations during its passage through parliament.

Despite the improved protection of rights of women facing gender-based violence, Amnesty International has also observed several shortcomings of the Comprehensive Law, such as the limited protection afforded by the Law in cases of gender-based violence within intimate relationships; the failure to include a provision on the right of victims to obtain redress; the failure to review the *juicios rápidos* (fast-track trials), a type of proceeding that could foster impunity; and the failure to include an explicit provision on the victims' right not to be present on police or court premises at the same time as their assailants.

---

* This article is based on a report of Amnesty International entitled: *España: Más derechos, los mismos obstáculos* published in June 2006 (*Spain: More Rights, but the Obstacles Remain*).

1 Basic Law 1/2004 of 28 December (BOE no. 313 of 29 December 2004).

C. Benninger-Budel ed., Due Diligence and Its Application to Protect Women from Violence
 ISBN 978 90 04 16293 8. pp. 185-190

On the first anniversary of the full entry into force of the Comprehensive Law (the law came into force on 29 January 2005 with the exception of the sections relating to *Tutela penal y judicial* (criminal protection and judicial protection), which came into force on 29 June 2005), Amnesty International was interested to see how the measures introduced by this law had been effectively implemented. During the first year, some of the measures provided for in the Comprehensive Law have been adopted, including the creation of the *Delegación Especial del Gobierno contra la Violencia sobre la Mujer* (special government office dealing with violence against women), the establishment of *Juzgados sobre violencia contra la Mujer* (courts specialising in cases of violence against women) and the *Observatorio Estatal de Violencia sobre la Mujer* (National Observatory on Violence against Women), and the appointment of a *Fiscalía contra la Violencia sobre la Mujer* (Public Prosecutor's Office dealing with Violence against Women).

Amnesty has also identified several obstacles that women who are victims of gender-based violence face in defending their rights. As mentioned above, there are some very important issues not covered by law, but there is also a lack of territorial uniformity in the institutional response to gender-based violence. Examples are: the continuing difficulty of early detection of violence, the lack of assistance for women in the area of health, the lack of accessibility and quality control of resources to provide victim support and the patchy provision of comprehensive assessment units to serve the administration of justice. These problems will be discussed below in more detail.

In a report entitled *España: Más derechos, los mismos obstáculos* published in June 2006 (*Spain: More Rights, but the Obstacles Remain*),[2] Amnesty International – using the testimonies of women who are victims of gender-based violence, professionals in the field and representatives of organisations working with these women in eight autonomous communities – has analysed how Spain's response to gender-based violence has changed since this law came into force, in a year which has produced more murders than the year before: in 2006, 67 women died at the hands of their partner or ex-partner. It is important to underline that the responsibility of states to exercise due diligence in defending women's rights does not stop at the legislative stage, but continues until such rights become a reality.

Continuing Inadequacies in Spain's Response to Gender-Based Violence

After the adoption of the Comprehensive Law, there continues to be a *lack of territorial uniformity* in institutional response to gender-based violence. This has serious consequences for the guaranteeing of minimum standards of assistance, protection and justice for victims.

The *lack of material and human resources* is an enduring factor in every link of the chain of agencies responsible for assistance, protection and justice in the face of gender-based violence. The budgetary allocation to enable the measures

2 The complete report is available in Spanish at www.es.amnesty.org/nomasviolencia.

set out in the Comprehensive Law to be put into practice is insufficient and inadequate to guarantee the protection of women.

One major shortcoming identified in every field subjected to analysis concerns compulsory, adequate *training*, sensitive to gender issues and which probes deep into the roots of violence, designed for all professionals working with victims of gender-based violence. For example, less than 10 percent of health professionals, both men and women, benefit from any training, though this is an area of vital importance in dealing with physical and psychological consequences to victims of gender-based violence and early detection of this kind of violence. In spite of the commitments made in the Comprehensive Law, violence against women does not appear to be a priority in the health sector: it is not included in the health indicators for the population, nor in the current draft Mental Health Strategy.

The resources available for *integrated assistance* for victims of gender-based violence continue to be inadequate and unevenly distributed. Not all the autonomous communities have an integrated support centre, although it was provided for in the 'financial planning' of the Comprehensive Law that integrated assistance centers must be implemented in the short term. As a result, boarding houses and hostels are still being used to accommodate women in emergency situations. Women who are illegal immigrants are not entitled to the assistance provided under the Comprehensive Law. This situation has been condemned by the Spanish Economic and Social Council, which has called for it to be remedied.[3]

Every year an increasing number of women are filing complaints; in 2005 the number of complaints was 73,109. In 49,657 of these cases a protection order was requested. In 38,409 the protection order was granted. In 22.7 percent of the cases that order was refused, sometimes without stating the grounds for the refusal.[4] Amnesty International is concerned that, by way of the Comprehensive Law, the 'protection order' has become a requirement for access to basic resources such as financial aid, housing aid and even, depending on the territory concerned, psychological aid, contravening the recommendations of the Council of Europe.[5]

3 Economic and Social Council, *Report 08/2005 on the Royal Decree Regulating the Economic Aid Established in Article 27 of the Organic Act 1/2004 of 28 December on Integrated Protection Measures against Gender Violence*, adopted by the plenary in extraordinary session on 28 September 2005.

4 Protection orders. Percentage of adoption/rejection. Year 2005

Initiated	Adopted	percent of total	Rejected	percent of total
49,657	38,409	77.3	11,248	22.7

Source: General Council of the Judicial Power, *Domestic Violence in Judicial Statistics* (2005) and *Protection Orders of the Courts on Violence against Women* (second semester of 2005). The percentage of rejection is an average between the rejection rate of the courts on violence against women and the rejection rate of the remaining courts that process protection orders.

5 Committee of Ministers to Member States on the Protection of Women against Violence, Recommendation (2002), 5.

With regard to *policing*, although there has been an increase in numbers of specialist units in the national security forces, the number of such units is still insufficient. There continues to be a need for training initiatives not only for members of specialist units, but for police officers in general.

Although the Comprehensive Law establishes the right to free access to justice for women when required, lawyers' associations, including those in Madrid, Vitoria and throughout Andalusia, have no service providing a presence for victims at police stations, with the result that women may have no legal assistance when they file a complaint. On the other hand, this procedure – as a result of Instruction 14/2005 issued by the Secretariat of State for Security 'on the police treatment of foreign women victims of domestic or gender-based violence whose presence in the country is illegal' – may expose foreign women whose presence in the country is illegal to the *risk* that *expulsion* proceedings might be initiated against them if their attempt to obtain a protection order and conviction of the assailant is unsuccessful. In addition, there is a dissuasive effect on these women when they come to file a complaint.

The road to *obtaining justice* is also still barred by obstacles. The courts blame lack of resources to guarantee victims some privacy and security, excessive workload, delays in processing the civil cases they also have to deal with and, above all, lack of training for their staff.

Amnesty International is concerned that the specialist courts dealing with cases of violence against women are dealing with no more than the tip of the iceberg of violence (incidental injuries, as occurs in 77.4 percent of cases), without addressing previous case histories of violence. Moreover, there are still some provinces, including Álava, Valencia, Ciudad Real and Madrid, where there is no forensic assessment unit to assess victims' injuries.

With regard to victim *compensation*, which is one of the continuing deficiencies of the Comprehensive Law, no simple or accessible solution has yet been found. What is required is fair compensation, especially in cases where the state has not exercised due diligence.

Indicators to Measure the Success of the Comprehensive Law and Compliance with the Due Diligence Standard

Amnesty International has proposed in the report *Spain: More Rights, but the Obstacles Remain* the following 18 minimum indicators for assessing, in 2008, when the term of the present legislature comes to an end, the extent to which the institutional response to gender-based violence by the Spanish government, the governments of the Autonomous Communities, the *Fiscalía contra la Violencia sobre la Mujer* and the *Consejo del Poder Judicial* (General Council of the Judiciary) has been successful and has complied with the due diligence standard.

- An integrated national health programme has been drawn up which establishes minimum standards for first-rate training for all health professionals, designed to guarantee a uniform, quality response across all Autonomous Communities.

- The National Mental Health Strategy includes measures to address the impact of gender-based violence on the mental health of women.
- Public health studies undertaken by the National Health System include indicators relating to gender-based violence.
- The short-term forecasts laid down in the financial element of the Comprehensive Law have been met, so that there is at least one integrated support centre in each Autonomous Community and no victim of gender-based violence in need of emergency housing is accommodated in a hostel or boarding house.
- In all Autonomous Communities, women who are drug addicts, have problems with alcohol, mental illness, are working prostitutes, suffer from some disability or have children over 12 years of age have access to specialist gender-based violence resources.
- No reception centre will deny residence to women fleeing violence in another Autonomous Community on the grounds that they have not been referred officially.
- Undocumented women migrants have access to financial assistance designed to support victims of gender-based violence when they break away from their assailant, on an equal footing with other women.
- The Secretariat of State for Security's Instruction 14/2005 has been withdrawn and substituted by clear guidelines for avoiding any discriminatory treatment of undocumented women migrants when they report gender-based violence.
- There is a compulsory training programme on gender-based violence for all members of the national security forces.
- Lawyers' associations in all provinces have a duty shift, with sufficient resources, to assist women at the time they file a complaint and continue to defend them throughout the proceedings.
- All professionals working in courts dealing with violence against women receive compulsory, first-rate training.
- All courts processing protection orders receive compulsory training in gender-based violence.
- All Institutes of Forensic Medicine have a Forensic Assessment Unit with sufficient resources to carry out their work.
- All courts specialising in gender-based violence have facilities to permit the separation of victims and assailants and provide privacy for victims.
- An assessment has been carried out of the extent to which courts dealing with violence against women have met their objectives, with the participation of victims, personnel assigned to these courts and members of the legal profession with experience of them.
- Judicial statistics on gender-based violence includes data on acquittal and conviction rates according to type of proceedings, paying special attention to data relating to *juicios rápidos* (fast-track trials), as well as data on acquittal/conviction rates in proceedings brought on the grounds of a breach of judicial measures to protect victims.

- State legislation enacts provisions for flexible and effective means of guaranteeing that women victims of gender-based violence obtain fair and adequate redress, including adequate compensation and full rehabilitation. Redress is guaranteed, in particular in cases where the state has not exercised due diligence.
- Associations and collectives of victims of gender-based violence are involved in discussions and participate in the process of ascertaining the suitability of the institutional response to this type of violence.

Trafficking in Women

Human Trafficking: A Brief Introduction to Issues of Responsibility and Accountability

Anne Gallagher

> *A human rights approach to trafficking...demands that we acknowledge responsibility of governments to protect and promote the rights of all persons within their jurisdiction. This responsibility translates into a legal obligation on governments to work towards eliminating trafficking and related exploitation. Passivity and inaction are insufficient. Tolerance or complicity is inexcusable.*[1]

Introduction

The term 'human trafficking' refers to the trade in human beings, within and between countries, for the express purpose of their exploitation. Trafficking and related exploitation have been standing items on the international agenda for at least a century. However, it is only in the last decade that the international community has begun to take this issue seriously. While concerns about migration and organised crime may have prompted recent changes in law and policy, the human rights violations associated with trafficking have been extensively documented and are well understood. Human rights are implicated in the causes and vulnerability factors that contribute to trafficking as well as in the responses of governments and others at both national and regional levels. Trafficking is also a highly gendered phenomenon and gender affects all aspects of the trafficking process. Women are trafficked in different ways to men and for different reasons. Discrimination and violence have been identified as key factors in increasing the vulnerability of women and girls to trafficking and in shaping the trafficking outcome. Gender and rights are also relevant to the ways in which states deal with the problem: legal and social discrimination against women is a common feature of many national responses to trafficking.

1 Mary Robinson, United Nations High Commissioner for Human Rights, Keynote Address to the OHCHR/Council of Europe Panel Discussion: *Combating Trafficking in Human Beings – A European Convention?*, Palais des Nations, Geneva, 9 April 2002.

C. Benninger-Budel ed., Due Diligence and Its Application to Protect Women from Violence
© Koninklijke Brill NV. Printed in The Netherlands. ISBN 978 90 04 16293 8. pp. 193-202

This chapter provides an introduction to human trafficking from an international legal perspective – with specific emphasis on the issues of state responsibility and accountability. It begins with a short summary of the 'wrong' of trafficking: the primary rules that are implicated in trafficking situations and that provide the starting point for identifying the key obligations of states. The following section outlines the secondary rules of state responsibility applicable in a typical trafficking situation where the state itself is not the direct agent of harm. In the final section, an attempt is made to identify the parameters of a 'state accountability index'[2] for trafficking: a set of criteria, derived from these primary and secondary rules, that could be used to determine the circumstances under which a state is in violation of its international obligations.

The Wrong of Trafficking

Working out the legal 'wrong' of a complex, composite phenomenon such as trafficking is not easy. Human rights law, apart from two solid references in the Convention on the Elimination of All Forms of Discrimination against Women and the Convention on the Rights of the Child, does not contain a comprehensive prohibition on trafficking.[3] The question of whether or not such a prohibition exists, or whether it can be inferred, or whether other prohibitions that *do* exist can be made to fit the trafficking phenomenon can only be provisionally answered with reference to a myriad of human rights instruments and standards.

Analysis of trafficking from the perspective of human rights law is nevertheless a productive exercise. Human rights law contains strong prohibitions on many practices linked to trafficking including slavery, the slave trade, servitude, debt bondage, forced labour and forced marriage.[4] Human rights law outlaws the gender and racial discrimination that is at the heart of many trafficking situations. It prohibits torture and ill-treatment, arbitrary detention and commercial sexual exploitation. It champions the rights of individuals as workers, as women, as children and as migrants. It requires states to protect both citizens and non-

2 The term 'state accountability index' has been borrowed from the UN Special Rapporteur on violence against women who, in the symposium that gave rise to this publication, noted the urgent need to develop a system for measuring the extent to which a state fulfilling its duty to protect the rights of women.

3 Convention on the Elimination of All Forms of Discrimination against Women, 1979. G.A. res. 34/180, 34 UN GAOR Supp. (no. 46) at 193, UN Doc. A/34/46, entered into force 3 September 1981, Article 6; Convention on the Rights of the Child, 1989. G.A. res. 44/25, annex, 44 UN GAOR Supp. (no. 49) at 167, UN Doc. A/44/49 (1989), entered into force 2 September 1990, Articles 32, 34, 35, 39.

4 On the applicability of the prohibition on slavery to trafficking, for example, see Anne Gallagher, 'Using International Human Rights Law to Better Protect Victims of Trafficking: the Prohibitions on Slavery, Servitude, Forced Labor and Debt Bondage' in *Coming of Age in International Criminal Law: An Intellectual Reflection on the Work of M. Cherif Bassiouni*, ed. Leila Sadat and Michael P. Scharf (forthcoming, 2007).

citizens from violations and to provide remedies in cases where prevention does not work.

While there can be no doubt as to the relevance and importance of human rights law for modern-day trafficking, it is important to acknowledge that this branch of law has not been used especially well. Rarely are even the most clear-cut and uncontested provisions (e.g., those relating to debt bondage, forced marriage and forced labour) advanced in relation to a situation of trafficking. Despite the issue being raised with increasing frequency in the context of states parties reports, none of the relevant international human rights treaty-bodies has yet managed to tie trafficking directly to a violation of a specific right in a specific treaty. Perhaps this is because trafficking is just too complicated. Perhaps it is because the norms themselves are devoid of sufficient content to support their real-life application. Perhaps the situation is aggravated by the fact that, as discussed below, traffickers are generally bad people and bad organisations, not bad governments.

The human rights law monopoly on human trafficking was broken and the international legal framework around trafficking substantially strengthened with the adoption of the UN Protocol on the Prevention, Suppression and Punishment of Trafficking in Persons especially Women and Children in December 2000.[5] In addition to articulating the first-ever international legal definition of trafficking, the Protocol sets out, in considerable detail, the steps to be taken by states parties in preventing and dealing with this crime. Some of these are couched in the language of legal obligation. For example, states parties are required to criminalise trafficking when committed intentionally;[6] to establish jurisdiction to investigate, prosecute and punish all relevant offences committed within their territory;[7] and to cooperate in the return of victims.[8] Unfortunately those provisions dealing with victim protection are, by and large, optional, serving to substantially weaken the Protocol in terms of human rights protections.[9] However, the Protocol has since been supplemented by a number and range of international and regional agreements and instruments that, with only a few exceptions, add significantly to our understanding of the 'wrong' of trafficking. The most important treaty-based instrument is a European Convention on Trafficking, adopted in 2002 and po-

5 Protocol to Prevent, Suppress and Punish Trafficking in Persons, Especially Women and Children, Supplementing the United Nations Convention against Transnational Organized Crime, (2000, G.A. Res. 25, annex II, UN GAOR, 55th Session, Supp. no. 49, at 60, UN Doc. A/45/49 (Vol. I) (2001), entered into force 25 December 2003. (Hereafter Trafficking Protocol).

6 Trafficking Protocol, Article 5.

7 Trafficking Protocol, Article 15 (1).

8 Trafficking Protocol, Article 8 (3).

9 For a detailed overview of the Protocol's provisions, see Anne Gallagher, 'Human Rights and the New UN Protocols on Trafficking and Migrant Smuggling: A Preliminary Analysis,' *Human Rights Quarterly* 23 (2001): 975–1004.

tentially encompassing all the member states of the European Union.[10] Individual criminal responsibility for trafficking in certain situations is now a possibility with the inclusion of trafficking and its generally identified associated offences in a number of central provisions of the Statute of the International Criminal Court.[11]

At the national level, many countries have enacted or are in the process of finalising legislation against trafficking. In some cases this has involved amendments to the national criminal code. In other cases new and very detailed laws have been developed, many of these based on the provisions of the Trafficking Protocol. Softer legal and political commitments abound at both the international and regional levels. The most influential of these is the United Nations Principles and Guidelines on Human Rights and Human Trafficking (2002).[12]

Taken together, these developments confirm the existence of a core of obligations, enshrined in and protected by international law.

The Responsibility of States for the 'Private' Harm of Trafficking

Despite their eagerness to enact new and better laws, states continue to deny legal responsibility for trafficking and for the violations of human rights that are integral to the trafficking process. In some cases, this denial is based on the fact that the primary wrong (the trafficking) was committed by a criminal or groups of criminals and not by the state itself. In other cases, responsibility is not acknowledged because the state claims to have done everything reasonably possible to avoid the harm. An understanding of the principles of international legal responsibility as they apply in the trafficking context is an essential prerequisite for examining and, if justified, for rejecting claims of this kind.

In all cases it first becomes a question of working out whether an action or omission, that is itself a breach of an international obligation, can be attributed to the state. In some situations, where the action or omission can be linked directly to state institutions or state officials acting in an official capacity, the question of attribution can be easily settled. The passing of a trafficking law that discriminates against women would be one example of direct attribution. The known,

10 Council of Europe Convention on Action against Trafficking in Human Beings, 2005, (ETS no. 197), Warsaw, 16.V.2005. (Hereafter European Convention). For an analysis of the Convention see Anne Gallagher, 'Recent Legal Developments in the Field of Human Trafficking: A Critical Review of the 2005 European Convention and Related Instruments', *European Journal of Migration and Law* 8 (2006): 163–189. Available online at http://ssrn.com/abstract=954441.

11 The Rome Statute of the International Criminal Court (The Rome Statute), UN Doc. A/CONF.183/9* signed 17th day of July 1998, entered into force on 1 July 2002; Articles 7 (1) (g), 7 (2) (c), 8 (2) (b) (xxii), 8 (2) (e) (vi).

12 *Recommended Principles and Guidelines on Human Rights and Human Trafficking, Report of the High Commissioner for Human Rights to the Economic and Social Council*, 2002, UN Doc. E/2002/68/Add.1. (Hereafter UN Principles and Guidelines).

systematic and reoccurring involvement of law enforcement officials in trafficking operations provides another straightforward example.

In the majority of trafficking situations, however, direct state involvement is either not present or unable to be conclusively established. For example, the trade in women, men and children between Lao PDR and Thailand is largely conducted by individuals and loosely connected criminal groups. While this traffic is facilitated by systemic, low-level public sector corruption there is not a great deal of solid evidence of direct, official involvement in either Lao PDR or Thailand – both of which have taken at least some preliminary steps to outlaw trafficking and to cooperate in its eradication.[13] The trafficking of women from Thailand to Australia is firmly in the hands of highly organised and sophisticated international criminals.[14] The governments of Thailand and Australia have not condoned or otherwise taken steps to adopt the conduct of these groups as their own. As in the previous example, individual officials in both states have undoubtedly facilitated this trade through their inaction, inertia and occasional active involvement. However, the *harm* of trafficking, in terms of both the process and the end result, is very much a direct consequence of actions taken by private entities, not states, their institutions or their representatives.

This is a problem because, as the International Law Commission (ILC) has pointed out: '[a]s a general rule the conduct of private persons or entities is not attributable to the state under international law.'[15] How general is the general rule? Can countries of origin, transit and destination for trafficked persons absolve themselves of any responsibility to these individuals on the basis that the conduct complained of is not directly attributable to them? If this were indeed the case, international rules on state responsibility would appear to offer very little scope for securing the accountability of states for trafficking taking place within their territories or involving their nationals. A rigid application of this standard would, in fact render almost totally ineffective the complex web of international rules that have evolved to protect trafficked and other vulnerable persons from exploitation and abuse. In other words, by holding the state responsible only for the harm that it directly causes, the international legal order would be failing in its greater purpose of securing accountability and justice. It would also be failing to recognise the actual and potential power of states to structure their internal order (including through regulation and control of private conduct) in a way that can either facilitate or obstruct trafficking and related forms of exploitation.

---

13 See further the studies cited at note 16 below.

14 See generally, Parliamentary Joint Committee of the Australian Crime Commission, *Enquiry into the Trafficking of Women for Sexual Servitude,* June 2004. Available online at http://www.aph.gov.au/senate/committee/acc_ctte/completed_inquiries/2002-04/sexual_servitude/report/report.pdf.

15 UN General Assembly, *Draft Articles on State Responsibility for Internationally Wrongful Acts,* extract from the *Report of the International Law Commission on the Work of its Fifty-Third Session,* Supplement no. 10, UN Doc. A/56/10, (2001), chapter 4.E.2, draft Article 8, 103.

Such a result would be contrary to the object and purpose of the human rights system in particular and would serve to remove, from its sphere, an ever-increasing range of conduct that has a direct impact on the enjoyment by individuals of their rights and freedoms. It is therefore not difficult to accept that the general rule of non-attribution of private conduct as articulated by the ILC must be read in light of the relevant primary obligations as well as basic principles of effectiveness.

In determining the responsibility of states for the harm of trafficking, the following summary of the relevant international legal principles and rules could provide guidance:

First: International legal responsibility requires that the act or omission be attributable to the state.

- The 'official' (even if unauthorised) conduct of a state organ or of a state official who violates established primary rules is attributable to the state.
- Whether an act or omission is determined to be 'official' or private depends, to some extent, on whether the conduct in question is systematic or recurrent to the point that the state knew or should have known of it and should have taken steps to prevent it.
- States will generally not be held responsible for the conduct of private entities absent a special circumstance (indicating control and/or approval) linking apparent private behaviour to the state itself.

Second: In addition to being attributable to the state, the act or omission must *also* constitute a breach of an international obligation of the state.

- The question of whether there has been a breach of an obligation depends on the content and interpretation of the primary rule.
- In the area of human rights and trafficking, the general obligations of states extend beyond negative obligations on non-interference to include positive obligations such as legislative reform, provision of remedies and protection from non-state interference. The composite nature of trafficking is reflected in the fact that breaches of obligation will often involve composite acts.

Third: Despite the general rule of non-attribution of private conduct, there are indeed circumstances under which the state can be held responsible for trafficking-related violations originating in the conduct of private persons or entities.

- In cases where responsibility for the initial act does not fall on the state, responsibility could still be imputed through a concomitant or subsequent failure on the part of the state to prevent, respond to or remedy abuses committed by private persons or entities. Whether or not responsibility can be imputed in this way in a particular case will always depend on the content of the relevant primary rule.
- Human rights treaties often impose a general obligation on states to 'respect' and 'ensure'. In other words, states are required to guarantee rights as opposed to merely refraining from interfering with their enjoyment. This will

usually require at least some action on the part of the state party to prevent and respond to non-state interference with established rights.

– In the context of human rights, the standards of 'due diligence' or 'reasonable and appropriate' are becoming the accepted benchmarks against which state actions to prevent or respond to violations originating in the acts of third parties are to be judged. An assessment of whether a state has met such a standard will depend, once again, on the content of the original obligation as well as the facts and circumstances of the case.

In conclusion, in relation to trafficking, states will generally not be able to avoid responsibility for the acts of private persons when their ability to influence an alternative, more positive outcome (judged against the primary rule) can be established. In such cases, the source of responsibility is not the act itself but the failure of states to take measures of prevention or response in accordance with the required standard.

Towards a 'State Accountability Index' for Trafficking[16]

As noted in the introduction, clarifying the rules around trafficking is an essential undertaking. States must understand what is required of them before it becomes possible for these same requirements to influence their decision-making. The more precise and action-oriented the identified norms are the better. It is not good enough for us to say that trafficking is prohibited under international law – or that states should help victims. At a practical level, that means next to nothing. To be effective, the rules around trafficking must be able to answer the basic questions that are asked everywhere, every day in the context of real situations: Do states have to criminalise trafficking? If so, does this obligation extend to related conduct such as forced labour, debt bondage and exploitative prostitution? Do states have to provide for appropriate penalties and what does this actually mean? Are states under an obligation to either extradite or prosecute suspected traffickers? Do they have to investigate trafficking and, if so, to what standard?

The list of basic questions includes many that relate to the treatment of victims: Are states actually required, by law, to protect the rights and welfare of victims? If so, which rights and to what extent? Is detention of trafficked persons (including so-called protective detention by governmental or non-governmental welfare agencies) permissible and, if so, under what circumstances? Is there a different

16 This section summarises an obligations framework developed by the author that has been explored in depth and in relation to specific countries in several publications including: Anne Gallagher, 'A Shadow Report on Human Trafficking in Lao PDR: The US Approach vs. International Law', *Asian and Pacific Migration Journal* 15 (2006): 525–552, available online at http://ssrn.com/abstract=954428; and Anne Gallagher, 'Human Rights and Human Trafficking in Thailand: A Shadow TIP Report' in, *Trafficking and the Global Sex Industry*, ed. Karen Beeks and Delila Amir (Lanham, MD: Lexington Books, 2006).

standard of care for child victims of trafficking? Can states force victims to return home even if this is manifestly unsafe? Can they be forced to accept returning victims? Do victims have an enforceable right to remedies? What limits, if any, does international law place on the *response* of states to the crime of trafficking? To what extent can they pressure or coerce other states into action?

These questions cannot, of course, be answered fully within the scope of the present study. However, tentative responses to at least some of them are now more than possible thanks to recent developments in the applicable legal framework. A 'state accountability index,' of the kind proposed by the UN Special Rapporteur on violence against women, may, in relation to trafficking, include the following core obligations of states:

The obligation to criminalise trafficking and related offences

The obligation to criminalise trafficking when committed intentionally is a central and mandatory provision of every international and regional agreement on trafficking.[17] In terms of what is to be criminalised, the definition contained in the Trafficking Protocol, representing, as it does, the general legal consensus, is an essential aspect of this obligation for all states.

The obligation to quickly and accurately identify victims of trafficking

The obligation to actively identify victims of trafficking is the foundation upon which all other obligations with respect to victims rest. It is also essential when it comes to ending impunity for traffickers because of the critical importance of victim cooperation and testimony in facilitating investigations, prosecutions and convictions.

The obligation to investigate and prosecute trafficking cases with due diligence

The due diligence standard has been directly linked to the investigation and prosecution of trafficking cases.[18] In determining whether or not a state has met this standard it is necessary to evaluate whether the steps taken evidence a seriousness on the part of the state to investigate and prosecute trafficking. This could involve consideration of a range of factors such as the extent to which the legal framework supports effective investigation and prosecution; the adequacy of human and material resource allocation; and the existence or absence of a specialist law enforcement response.

The obligation to provide victims with support and protection

Taking the various international, regional and national instruments together, and drawing strength from a perceptible trend towards detailed articulation of vic-

17 E.g., Trafficking Protocol, Article 5; European Convention, Article 18; and the UN Principles and Guidelines, Principles 12–17 and Guideline 4.

18 The UN Principles and Guidelines declare unequivocally that: 'States have a responsibility under international law to act with due diligence to...investigate and prosecute traffickers,' Principle 2.

tims' rights and concomitant state duties,[19] it is possible to identify several core obligations when it comes to protecting and supporting victims of trafficking. These include: protection from further harm; provision of emergency shelter, primary health care and counselling; assistance with legal proceedings; safe, and where possible, voluntary return; and access to remedies.

The obligation to provide special protection for child victims including girls
It is widely accepted that the particular physical, psychological and psychosocial harm suffered by trafficked children including girls and their increased vulnerability to exploitation requires that they be dealt with separately from adult trafficked persons in terms of laws, policies and programmes. This approach is validated by international human rights law that explicitly recognises the special position of children and thereby accord to them special rights.

The obligation to prevent trafficking
International human rights law recognises a legal obligation on states to act with due diligence to prevent human rights violations. Every major international and regional instrument on trafficking specifies an obligation of prevention.[20] In determining whether or not a state has met the due diligence standard of prevention it is necessary to consider the circumstances of that state and its place on the trafficking chain. In relation to any state, failure to take known preventive measures when this is both possible and practical should be considered sufficient grounds for establishing a violation of the obligation of prevention.

The obligation to cooperate across national borders
International cooperation is essential for the successful repatriation and reintegration of victims of trafficking who have been transported across international borders. In addition, the successful investigation and prosecution of trafficking cases will, in most cases, require cooperation between national criminal justice authorities in countries of origin and destination. All key legal agreements and policy documents on trafficking recognise the critical importance of internation-

19 See, for example, UN Commission on Human Rights, *Basic Principles and Guidelines on the Right to a Remedy and Reparation for Victims of Gross Violations of International Human Rights Law and Serious Violations of International Humanitarian Law*, C.H.R. res. 2005/35, UN Doc. E/CN.4/2005/L.10/Add.11 (19 April 2005). Note that the Rome Statute (see note 11 above) requires the International Criminal Court to 'protect the safety, physical and psychological well-being, dignity and privacy of victims' as well as to permit the participation of victims at all stages of the proceedings as determined to be appropriate. The Statute also includes provisions on reparation, including restitution, compensation and rehabilitation.

20 See, for example, Trafficking Protocol, Articles 1, 9, 11, 12; European Convention, Articles 1 (1), 29, 32; and the UN Principles and Guidelines, Principles 2, 4–6 and Guideline 7.

al cooperation.[21] The failure of any state to engage in meaningful cooperation with other states on the issue of trafficking should be seen as a failure of a legal duty that is part of a broader obligation to prevent and work against trafficking in persons.

Conclusion

The key message of this chapter is the critical importance of the state responsibility framework in terms of ending impunity for traffickers and securing justice for victims. Clarity and precision with regard to legal obligations is an essential aspect of identifying and attaching responsibility. Despite the promising developments of the past decade, there remains a great deal of uncertainty as to what states must do – or not do – when it comes to human trafficking. This lack of certainty serves reluctant governments well: permitting them to deny responsibility for the harms caused by human trafficking. It also prevents effective monitoring of state performance by international human rights mechanisms and marginalises law as a tool of change. The international legal framework around trafficking has traditionally been too weak to support detailed, measurable obligations that go beyond vague rules and commitments. That situation has now changed. The new obligations must now be articulated as clearly as possible and applied to specific situations. It is only then that concepts such as due diligence will have real impact and meaning. It is only then that states will be held accountable for their role in human trafficking and related exploitation.

21 Trafficking Protocol, Articles 2, 9, 10, 13; the United Nations Convention Against Transnational Organized Crime (adopted 15 November 2000, UN GAOR, 55th Session, Annex 1, Agenda Item 105, at 25, UN Doc. A/55/383 (2000), entered into force 29 September 2003), Articles 16, 18; European Convention, Articles 18, 33, 34); and the UN Principles and Guidelines, Guideline 11.

Problems with the Implementation of the Due Diligence Standard from the Perspective of Countries of Origin in the OSCE Region

*Shivaun Scanlan**

I will aim to describe the broad trends in countries of origin by way of due diligence measures taken to address trafficking. By countries of origin I will be referring to those countries of origin in South Eastern Europe and the Commonwealth of Independent States (CIS) from which much of the experience of the Organisation for Security and Co-operation in Europe (OSCE) in anti-trafficking derives.[1]

The Standards of Due Diligence in Trafficking

Under international law states have a responsibility to act with due diligence to (i) prohibit or prevent trafficking and related acts; (ii) investigate, prosecute and punish traffickers; and (iii) protect victims.[2] A number of international instruments reflect these specific obligations. Some of these key instruments are summarised below.

* This chapter is based on my presentation at the Workshop on Trafficking at the Symposium on *Due Diligence: The Responsibility of the State for the Human Rights of Women* (Bern, 21–23 September 2005). The comments made in this overview are those of the author and do not necessarily reflect the views of the Organisation for Security and Co-operation in Europe (OSCE).

1 It is of course recognised that many countries of origin of trafficking victims may also act as destination countries for trafficking victims from other countries or equally suffer from internal trafficking of both its own or other nationals. This chapter, however, focuses only on the measures taken to address trafficking as a country of origin.

2 See also principle 2 of the *Recommended Principles and Guidelines on Human Rights and Human Trafficking, Report of the High Commissioner for Human Rights to the Economic and Social Council*, 2002, UN Doc. E/2002/68/Add.1.

C. Benninger-Budel ed., Due Diligence and Its Application to Protect Women from Violence

ISBN 978 90 04 16293 8. pp. 203-211

(i) Obligations to Prohibit or Prevent Trafficking and Related Acts
Article 6 of the Convention on the Elimination of All Forms of Discrimination against Women of 1979 provides that 'States Parties shall take all appropriate measures, including legislation, to suppress all forms of traffic in women and exploitation of prostitution of women.' In relation to children, Article 35 of the Convention on the Rights of the Child of 1989 states: 'States Parties shall take all appropriate national, bilateral and multilateral measures to prevent the abduction of, the sale of or traffic in children for any purpose or form.' Regarding instruments specifically on trafficking in human beings, Article 5 (1) of the Protocol to Prevent, Suppress and Punish Trafficking in Persons, especially Women and Children, Supplementing the United Nations Convention against Transnational Organized Crime (hereafter Trafficking Protocol) and Article 18 of the Council of Europe Convention on Action against Trafficking in Human Beings (hereafter Council of Europe Convention on Trafficking) require that states adopt legislative measures to establish trafficking as a criminal offence in its internal law. In addition to trafficking, other related acts are also prohibited under international human rights law, including slavery and forced labour. For instance, Article 4 of the European Convention on Human Rights stipulates that '1. No one shall be held in slavery or servitude. 2. No one shall be required to perform forced or compulsory labour.'[3] In further developing this obligation, the European Court of Human Rights recently held in *Siliadin v France* that member states have a positive obligation to penalise slavery and forced labour.[4]

To prevent trafficking, Article 9 of the Trafficking Protocol and Article 5 of the Council of Europe Convention on Trafficking require that states take very general measures relating to research, awareness-raising and socio-economic initiatives 'to alleviate the factors that make persons, especially women and children, vulnerable to trafficking, such as poverty, underdevelopment and lack of equal opportunity' (Article 9 (4), Trafficking Protocol).

(ii) Obligations to Investigate, Prosecute and Punish
Obligations to investigate, prosecute and punish non-state actors with due diligence have been affirmed by the European Court of Human Rights in such cases

3 Other relevant instruments include the Slavery Convention of 1926, the ILO Forced Labour Convention no. 29 of 1930 and the ILO Convention no. 183 (Worst Forms of Child Labour Convention) of 1999 and the International Covenant on Civil and Political Rights of 1966.

4 *Siliadin v France*, Application no. 73316/01, Judgement of 26 July 2005, para. 112. The case concerned a Togolese national who was forced to work as a domestic servant on very low wages and in harsh living and working conditions. The Court found that there had been a violation of France's positive obligations under Article 4 of the European Convention on Human Rights.

as *Osman v United Kingdom*[5] and *Z and Others v United Kingdom*.[6] Article 10 of the Trafficking Protocol also requires international cooperation to strengthen law enforcement and Article 23 (1) of the Council of Europe Convention on Trafficking provides that '[e]ach Party shall adopt such legislative and other measures as may be necessary to ensure that the criminal offences...are punishable by effective, proportionate and dissuasive sanctions.'

(iii) Obligations to Protect Victims

A number of human rights instruments including the Optional Protocol to the Convention on the Rights of the Child on the Sale of Children, Child prostitution and Child Pornography contain provisions on the protection of victims.[7] With respect to trafficking-related instruments, pertinent provisions include Articles 6 to 8 of the Trafficking Protocol and chapter 3 of the Council of Europe Convention on Trafficking. In contrast to the Council of Europe Convention, which places the human rights of trafficked people at the centre of anti-trafficking strategy,[8] the Trafficking Protocol is essentially focused on the criminal justice aspects of trafficking. Its provisions on protecting victims of trafficking are not mandatory and are decidedly weak. States parties 'shall consider implementing measures' to provide victims with protection, support and remedies but are not required to do so. They are also encouraged to avoid involuntary repatriation of victims but are under no legal obligation in this regard. The Protocol also provides no guidance on the identification of trafficking victims, which is seen as the starting point for the provision of protection to trafficking victims.

The Council of Europe Convention on Trafficking on the other hand includes mandatory measures on protection. It has also developed detailed requirements to ensure that victims are rapidly and accurately identified. Article 10 (2) of the Council of Europe Convention on Trafficking obliges states to 'adopt such legislative or other measures as may be necessary to identify victims as appropriate in collaboration with other Parties and relevant support organizations.' Some commentators have considered this aspect of the Convention a 'landmark develop-

5 *Osman v United Kingdom,* Application no. 23452/94, Judgement of 28 October 1998, paras. 115–116. The case involved a claim by the applicant that the UK authorities had failed to protect her husband and son from a school teacher who developed an obsession with her son.

6 *Z. and Others v United Kingdom,* Application no. 29392/95, Judgement of 10 May 2001, para. 109. Z and others, who were minors, successfully argued that the local authority had failed to protect them when they were subjected to ill-treatment and neglect at home in violation of Article 3 of the European Convention on Human Rights.

7 Articles 8, 9 and 10 of the Optional Protocol on the Sale of Children, Child Prostitution and Child Pornography.

8 See Explanatory Report of the Convention, at http://www.coe.int/t/dg2/trafficking/campaign/Docs/Convntn/explanreport_en.asp.

ment' recognising that a failure to correctly identify will lead to the denial of that person's rights.[9]

If there are reasonable grounds to believe that a person is a victim of trafficking, the competent authorities are to refrain from removing or deporting that person until the identification process is complete. At this stage the state must also provide the basic assistance provided for under Article 12 (1) of the Council of Europe Convention on Trafficking, which is not only reserved for those agreeing to act as witnesses, as is the position under EU law.[10]

Article 12 (1) includes detailed measures of protection to be implemented by states. Measures to be taken include, but are not limited to, secure accommodation, access to emergency medical assistance, translation and interpretation services, counselling and provision of information in languages victims can understand, assistance during judicial proceedings, and access to education for children. Victims lawfully residing in destination states can receive wider protection than those residing illegally, including additional medical assistance and access to employment, vocational training and education.[11]

Further important provisions in the Council of Europe Convention on Trafficking from the perspective of destination countries include Article 13 (recovery and reflection period) and Article 14 (residence permit). Article 13 obliges states to provide a recovery and reflection period of at least thirty days where there are reasonable grounds to believe that a person is a victim of trafficking. The grant of a recovery and reflection period is not conditional on victims cooperating with prosecution authorities and during the period it is not possible to enforce any expulsion order against the person. Once the thirty-day period is up, states parties are to issue a renewable residence permit to victims if, in their opinion, an extended stay is necessary owing to the victim's personal situation or for the purposes of their cooperation in an investigation or prosecution. This provision has the practical effect of ensuring that states parties retain the right to grant residence permits to those victims cooperating with the authorities or those who can show a fear of persecution or are likely to face ill treatment or torture on return.[12]

9 See Anne Gallagher, 'Recent Legal Developments in the Field of Human Trafficking: A Critical Review of the 2005 European Convention and Related Instruments', *European Journal of Migration and Law* 8 (2006): 163–189.

10 See EU Council Directive 2004/81/EC on the residence permit issued to third-country nationals who are victims of trafficking in human beings or who have been the subject of an action to facilitate illegal immigration and who cooperate with the authorities. The Directive seeks to prevent illegal migration and trafficking by providing victims with incentives, including assistance and temporary residence permits, to come forward and cooperate with authorities in the detection and prosecution of smugglers and traffickers. See for further discussion Gallagher (2006), ibid., 168.

11 Articles 12 (3) and 12 (4).

12 See for further discussion Gallagher (2006), note 9 above, 180.

An effective investigation into cases of trafficking and the victim's participation in the criminal justice process can also be regarded as a form of redress for victims. To secure the right of victims to participate, states need to provide effective witness protection to protect the identities of victims and access to information about the proceedings, interpretation and legal advice. These measures are stipulated in Articles 6 (1) and 6 (2) of the Trafficking Protocol and Articles 12 (1) (e) and 15 of the Council of Europe Convention on Trafficking.

Trafficked persons are entitled to compensation for the damage suffered through trafficking. Both the Trafficking Protocol and the Council of Europe Convention on Trafficking require states to provide in their internal law for the right of victims to compensation 'from the perpetrators' (Article 15 of the Council of Europe Convention) or more generally 'for damage suffered' (Article 6 (6), Trafficking Protocol). The Council of Europe Convention also goes further, requiring states to take steps to guarantee compensation of victims through, for example, the establishment of a special fund (Article 15 (4)).

Finally, although the Trafficking Protocol was considered a disappointment when it came to the rights of children, the Council of Europe Convention on Trafficking is extremely detailed with respect to the protection of child victims of trafficking. Key measures include the benefit of special measures where a victim of trafficking is presumed to a be a child (Article 10 (3)); the appointment of a representative to act in the best interests of the child (Article 10 (4) (a)); access to education (Article 12 (1) (f)); special protection of the right to privacy (Article 11 (2)); special protection measures during a trafficking investigation taking into account their best interests (Article 28 (3)); no repatriation of child victims if a risk assessment indicates that repatriation would not be in a child's best interests (Article 15 (7)) and considerations of the best interests of the child victim to govern the issuing and renewal of residence permits (Article 14 (2)).

The OSCE has a different role to play in terms of generating measures 'to pour into the empty vessel that is due diligence', to paraphrase the words of Professor Andrew Clapham at the opening evening of the symposium on due diligence in Bern. As a political organisation, it has developed numerous 'political commitments', adopted by consensus, relevant to tackling trafficking which sometimes go further in reach than the international legal standards. These commitments have been given very detailed content and form under the OSCE Action Plan to Combat Trafficking in Human Beings, adopted in 2003.[13] The Action Plan consists of a series of recommendations to the OSCE participating states to help them implement their commitments on trafficking in the areas of prevention, investigation and prosecution and protection, reflected in the international standards.

The recommendations represent a wide-ranging body of measures and good practices that the OSCE participating states have agreed to adopt in the name

13 The *OSCE Action Plan to Combat Trafficking in Human Beings* was adopted by Ministerial Council Decision 2/03 in Maastricht, 2003.

of combating trafficking.[14] Besides the recommendations under the Action Plan, the OSCE's Human Rights Institution, the Office for Democratic Institutions and Human Rights (ODIHR), aims to further assist states by developing guidance on securing protection of trafficked persons rights. In this regard it has developed guidance on the 'national referral mechanism' model (NRM),[15] which the OSCE states have committed to establish. The NRM provides a framework for identifying and protecting trafficked persons and has been recognised as an effective way of ensuring protection of the rights of trafficked persons. I would suggest that all these measures which further develop the international standards outlined above, form part of the due diligence standards to which a state, or those acting on its behalf, should be held accountable.

Situation in Countries of Origin

The countries of origin with which the OSCE/ODIHR is concerned have all been subject to serious transformation in recent years, either as a result of conflict or changing political and economic systems. Nearly all countries of origin for trafficked persons share similar problems which may be seen as root causes of trafficking. These include severe socio-economic decline, non-existent social safety protection, widespread unemployment, corruption, opportunistic/organised crime, violence and discrimination against women and limited legal migration channels, amongst other issues.

Preventive Measures

The changes in many of these countries of origin, however, is of such a scale that clearly cosmetic anti-trafficking prevention measures designed to address some of these root causes will have little long-term impact on the most vulnerable and marginalised groups at risk of trafficking. Membership in the European Union (EU) for some states might effectively eliminate the incidence of trafficking amongst their nationals, as has already been witnessed in Poland, Hungary, the Czech Republic and Slovakia, where economic opportunities and stability exist at home. For those countries remaining outside the EU, however, problems remain acute, including in Moldova, Albania, Ukraine and Romania,[16] and the measures taken by states to address the root causes of trafficking make slow progress.

Other measures taken as preventive action against trafficking in numerous origin countries include awareness-raising campaigns. These however, have proven

14 It should be noted that the *OSCE Action Plan to Combat Trafficking in Human Beings* integrates many of the recommendations developed by the UNHCHR Principles and Guidelines, see note 3 above, and the *UNICEF Guidelines on the Protection of Child Victims of Trafficking* (New York: UNICEF, 2006).

15 See *National Referral Mechanisms: Joining Efforts to Protect the Rights of Trafficked Persons, A Practical Handbook* (Warsaw/Poland: OSCE/ODIHR, 2004).

16 Note that Romania became a member of the EU on 1 January 2007.

difficult to evaluate in terms of their impact on preventing trafficking, although they continue to receive support from the donor community. On the other hand, many have been criticised for their deliberate 'scare-mongering' to deter would-be migrants. Such campaigns have been seen to pander to the anti-immigration agendas of many western states and have not been pursued solely in the spirit of preventing trafficking.[17]

Investigation and Punishment

In terms of investigation and punishment in countries of origin, major problems remain with the reform of criminal justice systems, rule of law and corruption. Although much police training has been provided in countries aiming to sensitise law enforcement to the issue of trafficking and needs of trafficked persons and specialised anti-trafficking units have been created in certain countries, difficulties are still widespread. Local police, to whom trafficked persons may more frequently turn for assistance, invariably know little of trafficking and are insensitive and discriminatory towards its victims. In other cases police have becoming overenthusiastic in securing evidence of trafficking and some reports indicate that increasingly coercive methods are used by police to win the collaboration of victims in criminal proceedings.

Prosecutors and judges often lack training on new legal provisions on trafficking in domestic legislation, and tending rarely to find the 'textbook' cases of trafficking are reluctant to convict individuals for trafficking offences or rarely hand down recommended sentences for trafficking crimes. Another development in some countries has been the increasing prosecution of young women as recruiters or transporters in the trafficking process, leaving those responsible for the exploitation and arguably profiting the most from the crime at large. At the same time witness protection, although provided in law in many countries of origin, is rarely applied in practice. As a result, victim testimony is frequently withdrawn during judicial proceedings as the traffickers threaten those whom the state is unable to protect.

Assistance and Protection

By way of assistance and protection, most countries offer some form of short-term assistance to returned trafficked victims in terms of social, medical or psychological assistance. Often, however, this assistance is not offered unconditionally, as required both by international human rights law and OSCE commitments, but requires collaboration with law enforcement in proceedings against the perpetrator of trafficking. This conditionality deters many trafficked victims from seeking the assistance to which they are entitled and in the long term may also undermine law enforcement efforts to prosecute the perpetrators, since successful cases are

17 See *Trafficking in South Eastern Europe: Focus on Prevention* (Sarajevo, Bosnia and Herzegovina: UNHCHR, UNICEF, OSCE/ODIHR, 2005).

invariably dependent on good victim testimony. Also in some countries of origin eager to adopt EU-compatible migration policies, returned trafficked victims are subject to punishment in the form of travel bans and fines for their irregular entry into or residence in another country. Such responses are clearly incompatible with notions of assistance and protection to trafficked persons. Finally the absence of long-term solutions to returned trafficked persons in countries of origin is seen to contribute to a possibly growing problem of re-trafficking, whilst destination countries are unable to offer long term solutions including residence permits and therefore continue to repatriate trafficked victims.

Progress on Paper

Another development in certain countries of origin in the OSCE region has been the adoption of particular measures as a means of satisfying different political agendas. For instance, many countries have developed national action plans on trafficking and created national coordination mechanisms. At face value these measures should indicate that the country takes seriously its obligations to address trafficking. In reality many of these developments have been seen to be rather empty, satisfying objectives on the part of the state to appear from the outside as if it is addressing trafficking without necessarily putting such plans into practice. Therefore well crafted national action plans exist without benchmarks for assessing progress towards implementation or resources allocated. Shelters are opened for trafficked victims whose services are of such poor quality that they remain empty. Prosecutions of the perpetrators of trafficking are on the increase but often little is known of how many convictions result in imprisonment or really represent the serious cases. In South Eastern Europe the international community has been seen to have pushed too quickly for structures and systems on paper in the absence of ensuring that individual trafficking cases can be addressed. Also the importance which many countries attribute to the United States Trafficking in Persons Report, which ranks countries in tiers according to the action they take to combat trafficking, has been seen to make countries pander to one country's political agenda on trafficking rather than devoting attention and resources to appropriate responses.

It is also clear that competing political agendas intervene and possibly dominate when states take measures to combat trafficking. So, for instance, the EU's agenda on controlling immigration has meant that many measures that are strictly about immigration control and whose impact on trafficking is unknown are presented as anti-trafficking measures by EU candidate states keen to indicate their compliance with EU migration policy. Therefore many measures may be taken in the 'guise' of anti-trafficking, and might be interpreted by others as doing much, but sometimes these measures conflict with human rights protections. Thus for instance, the provision of protection and assistance does not come first in many states but is conditional on collaboration with law enforcement, because for the state combating organised crime or immigration crime is possibly more important than protecting victims. Also there is a widespread sense that states that do not take measures to reduce their sex industry are possibly penalised in the United States Trafficking in Persons Reports, which promotes the anti-prostitution agenda of the United States.

Conclusion

From the perspective of the OSCE there is no shortage of due diligence measures on trafficking. What is clear, however, is that due diligence measures apart, competing agendas intervene when states take measures to combat trafficking. Therefore due diligence obligations to protect from human rights obligations are not all that states concern themselves with when they act to combat trafficking. Other agendas such as combating organised crime, controlling immigration or eliminating prostitution are all of particular concern to states and the 'measures' resulting are very much influenced by these agendas.

Human Trafficking in Germany

Nivedita Prasad and Babette Rohner

Introduction

The Protocol to Prevent, Suppress, and Punish Trafficking in Persons, especially Women and Children[1] – adopted in Palermo in 2000 and which supplements the United Nations Convention against Transnational Organized Crime – defines human trafficking as follows:

> '"Trafficking in persons" shall mean the recruitment, transportation, transfer, harbouring or receipt of persons, by means of the threat or use of force or other forms of coercion, of abduction, of fraud, of deception, of the abuse of power or of a position of vulnerability or of the giving or receiving of payments or benefits to achieve the consent of a person having control over another person, for the purpose of exploitation. Exploitation shall include, at a minimum, the exploitation of the prostitution of others or other forms of sexual exploitation, forced labour or services, slavery or practices similar to slavery, servitude or the removal of organs[.]'[2]

Under a subsequent European Union (EU) framework directive, all member states were obliged to amend their domestic legislation to bring it into line with the United Nations Protocol. Germany complied with this requirement in February 2005 by amending its criminal law; trafficking in human beings is now defined in Section 18 of the Criminal Code as a crime against personal freedom, and no longer as a crime against sexual self-determination. § 232 of the Criminal Code covers human trafficking for the purpose of sexual exploitation, while § 233 deals with human trafficking for the purpose of the exploitation of labour. Following the amendment of the Criminal Code, it is now also a punishable offence to en-

1 See at www.uncjin.org/Documents/documents.html#convention.

2 Article 3 (a).

C. Benninger-Budel ed., Due Diligence and Its Application to Protect Women from Violence
 Printed in The Netherlands. ISBN 978 90 04 16293 8. pp. 213-221

courage trafficking.[3] This means, for example, that drivers can now be prosecuted under criminal law for aiding and abetting human trafficking as a result of having knowingly transported trafficked people.

What is clear is that human trafficking is no longer defined solely in relation to prostitution. Instead, emphasis has been given to the fact that trafficking can occur in all branches of industry, and even in the context of a marriage or partnership. Trafficked persons may be found in the sex trade, but they may also be domestic workers or wives. Even if the laws are drafted in such a way as to be *gender neutral, de facto,* at least in the sex trade, the victims of trafficking are women,[4] and it has to be assumed that this is also the case when trafficking occurs within marriage. No data are currently available regarding trafficking for the purpose of labour exploitation.

Migration Routes

All non-EU nationals require a visa before they can enter or cross Germany or stay in the country for any length of time. To obtain a visa they must apply in person to the German Embassy or Consulate in their country of origin. Foreigners travelling on a tourist or visitor visa are not authorised to take up employment in Germany. If they do, their presence in the country is deemed unlawful.

There is no legal right to obtain a visa. The restrictions applied by German embassies are so strict that most women who want to migrate have to assume that without outside help they stand no chance of obtaining a visa. Consequently, most women from Central and Eastern Europe enter Germany illegally. Generally, however, they do not realise this before they travel, because they assume that the money they need to pay back to the traffickers would include the cost of a visa.

Trafficking and Marriages of Convenience

When entry by land is not possible (e.g., from Thailand), the women travel legally by air, but the amount of money they have to pay back in return is much higher. Initially, they are authorised to stay in the country for a maximum of three months, and an extension of this initial period is generally only possible if they get married. Trafficked women are therefore often married before they start working, although in many cases the only purpose of the marriage is to make their presence in Germany appear to be lawful. As a result, and like women entering the country illegally, these women are likely to be blackmailed for violating immigration laws. This vulnerability to blackmail is a core element of human trafficking.

Married women hope that after a period of working under slavery-like conditions they will be able to stay in Germany and pursue their own goals. What they generally fail to realise is that in marrying only on paper they have already broken

3 § 233 (a) of the German Criminal Code.

4 Federal Crime Office, *Human Trafficking Situation in 2003* (Wiesbaden, 2004).

the law. They first get a visa for three years, but after this period, their residence permit can only be extended when they are able to prove that the marriage lasted at least two years (§ 31 of the Residence Act) – which is particularly difficult in the case of a marriage of convenience. Even when obtaining a further residence permit, the women have to make sure the authorities do not find out that they were initially in a paper marriage, because if so they would lose their residence permit. Thus if these women turned to the authorities to complain about their exploitation, their 'sham' marriages would be exposed and they would lose their residence permits. Consequently, women with no other prospects in terms of the laws on residence are clearly not prepared to testify against those who exploit them. Because their papers seem to be correct, they do not come to the attention of the police – even during a raid, since one of the main signs the police usually look for as evidence of trafficking is the lack of a residence permit. This makes the identification of trafficked women very difficult.

§ 31 of the Residence Act is not only used as a means of exerting pressure in relation to trafficking in the sex industry. Unscrupulous matrimonial agencies also refer to the possibility of quick deportation, at no cost to the husband, should a separation occur within two years – because if the marriage does not last at least two years, the non-German spouse will have to leave the country. The only exception is when the woman is able to prove that a continuation of the marriage would have represented a hardship for her: for example, because her children had been sexually abused by the husband. In practice, this is very difficult to prove.

Trafficked People

In addition to vulnerability to extreme exploitation, the living and working environment of trafficked people is such that they have to put up with conditions akin to slavery. They have little or no influence over their working conditions. They can be mercilessly exploited and serve only to satisfy someone else's search for gain. Trafficked people who work in the sex industry for example, are not in a position to refuse either clients or sexual practices. Nor can they insist on the use of condoms. Their earning capacity, insofar as it exists at all, bears absolutely no relation to the money they actually receive from clients. Any fictitious or real debts they have must be paid off according to unilaterally imposed terms and interest rates. Many of them are deprived of their freedom and subjected to violence. None of this bears any resemblance to a freely entered upon occupation in the sex industry.

Human trafficking implies therefore that there are elements of contemporary forms of slavery, debt bondage, serfdom, or forced labour.[5] Even if not all forms of human trafficking currently found in Europe resemble traditional systems of serfdom or debt bondage, core elements of such systems are usually involved and

5 Slavery is defined in Article 1.1 of the 1926 Slavery Convention; debt bondage and serfdom are defined in Article 1 (a) and (b) of the 1956 Supplementary Convention on the Abolition of Slavery; forced labour is defined in the 1930 ILO Convention 29.

can also be proven in law. Examples may be the fact of regarding another person as property, selling that person, restricting his or her freedom, creating a state of *de facto* rightlessness, or exercising deception or force. So it is possible for a person to be willing to migrate – even without the necessary documents – and to work as a prostitute and yet still be trafficked. A person may be willing to work in conditions tantamount to exploitation, but, by definition, they cannot give their consent to forced labour and/or practices akin to slavery. Conversely, of course, not all poorly paid irregular labour migrants – including those working in the sex trade – are trafficked.

Psychosocial Assistance to Trafficked Persons

The opportunities for receiving psychosocial assistance by trafficked people depends on several different factors. Residence status is of particular importance, as it also determines a person's official access to the welfare system. It is extremely difficult to assist trafficked people without residence status. For women who agree to testify in court the situation is slightly easier, insofar as they are granted a temporary residence permit and access to basic care under the Asylum Seekers Act. Those trafficked women who are married are the ones with the best access to medical and psychosocial care.

Status of Witnesses

In Germany, trafficked people who agree to testify in court against their traffickers are granted a temporary visa. In this particular context, it is not only their willingness to testify that counts but also the extent to which the police and public prosecution service will be able to use their evidence. Once the persons concerned have been granted temporary leave to remain, they also have access to the following rights:

- The right to a renewable six-month residence permit by virtue of § 25 (4) of the Residence Act; after 18 months the permits are granted for a renewable period of one year.
- If they so wish, they can be housed in a women's shelter.
- Under the Asylum Seekers Act, they are entitled to benefit payments in the form of a subsistence allowance (194 Euros per month).
- They are also authorised to receive medical care, although they must submit a special request for any treatment not deemed absolutely necessary, e.g., psychotherapy. The authorities do not have to give a reason for refusing such requests.
- They have a right to their own legal representative, which means to be represented by a lawyer as a joint plaintiff in court. Lawyers' costs are generally borne by the state.
- Theoretically, they have the right to work, but in practice, and notably because they only have a six-month residence permit, it is very difficult for them to find employment.

They are not able to see their children or other members of their family during this time. Nor are they allowed to enrol for any training. Three years can elapse from the time they first give evidence to the moment the court delivers its verdict. For the women, not being able to see their family for so long is a great strain, especially as they are worried, and with good reason, that their family is particularly endangered as a result of their having given evidence in court. The fact that witnesses are unable to work during this period also makes the situation very difficult, as it means they have no means of earning any money during this period even though the financial pressure on them in such a situation is enormous. The time it takes for the case to come to court also means that a lot of time important to them and that they desperately need to plan for the future is wasted. During this time, the women are not entitled to receive any psychological support. As mentioned above they can apply for this support – but have no guarantee that they will receive it. After the court case, at the latest, the women must leave Germany. Theoretically, if a return to their country of origin would be dangerous for them, they may be granted leave to remain once the court case is over; in practice, this option proves very difficult given that since the Immigration Act came into force the Federal Office for Migration and Refugees[6] has to be consulted on such cases.

The Italian Model

In our opinion, Italy has the best legislative framework in Europe for trafficked people, since under Italian legislation their residence permit is kept as separate as possible from their potential status as witnesses in a court case brought against their perpetrators.

The basis for this is Article 18 of Legislative Decree no. 286/98. In order to obtain a residence permit for an initial period of six months, the persons concerned must make a basic statement to the police so that the police can investigate their claim that they have been trafficked. They must provide information about the people who have exploited them and must stop working as prostitutes. If the police are able to establish that they have indeed been trafficked, they are granted a temporary residence permit, which is extended after six months if they take part in an integration course. If they manage to find employment, they are granted permanent residence. Once in possession of a permanent residence permit, trafficked people are covered by the same laws as other migrants.

The women can choose between the *social route* and the *legal route*. If a trafficked person files an official complaint and agrees to give evidence in court, s/he is granted a residence permit via the legal route. This is comparable to the proce-

6 The Federal Office for Migration and Refugees was actually set up as the body responsible for deciding on the return of refugees. It describes itself as an expert on state persecution in many countries. Trafficked people however, are not usually victims of state violence. Instead, they tend to come under threat from individuals, but frequently live in countries where there are no adequate protection measures.

dure in Germany according to which women willing to testify are granted a temporary residence permit. The big difference is that in Italy the permit by law can be granted permanently – whereas in Germany this is not the case. Sometimes there will be a pre-trial hearing, attended by both the judge and the accused. This dispenses with the need for a court hearing. The police or the public prosecutor is responsible for the remaining prosecution, and the immigration bureau is responsible for issuing the residence permit.

As far as the Italian social route is concerned, trafficked people can contact an authorised counselling centre, even without filing an official complaint. As outlined above, all they must do is make a statement to the police. Only certain bureaus are authorised for this purpose, and they must be specially registered. With the legal route, it is the public prosecutor who decides whether or not a woman can stay in the country, whereas with the social route, it is the *Questura*. The only difference is that with the social route the opinion of the public prosecutor is totally irrelevant.

Obviously any information provided in connection with the social route is dealt with via the official police channels, since Italy applies its own legality principle. If the information is used to bring a trial, the women are still expected to take the witness stand should the court so require. In that case, however, they are subject to the same rules as Italian nationals, who also have an obligation to give evidence. Like Italians, if the women fail in this obligation, they can be punished, but they cannot be deported.

Possibility of Applying the Italian Model in Germany

On the whole, trafficked people in Italy must comply with similar requirements to obtain a residence permit under Article 18 to those applicable to the women in Germany who are willing to testify. If a woman in Germany makes a statement that cannot be substantiated she too will be refused witness status and consequently will not be granted a residence permit.

An important difference between the two systems is that in Italy the women are not automatically required to give evidence in court. Also, once they have made their initial statement they are left in peace. No pressure is placed on them, their safety is guaranteed and they can make up their minds as to whether they wish to give evidence in court or not. Women who have suffered trauma are generally more willing and able to testify if given time to think. In theory, the women can also opt initially 'only' to make a statement, then be reunited with their children once they have a permanent residence permit and take the witness stand later.

Lawyers defending traffickers in Germany always try to accuse court witnesses of agreeing to testify only in order to 'wangle' a residence permit. In a system where all trafficked people – regardless of whether they give evidence in court – are granted a residence permit, defence lawyers are no longer able to use these tactics against witnesses, whose credibility is so vital.

Some countries reject such a system for fear that some migrants will use it to legalise their situation. According to the organisation Anti-Slavery International, however, this is not what has happened in Italy, Belgium, or the Netherlands.[7] Even now it is the police in Germany who decide whether a woman is trafficked or not, and were we to apply the Italian model that would still be the case. The 'only' difference would be that if there were a clear separation between the residence procedure, on the one hand, and participation in the court case brought against those accused of trafficking, on the other hand, the emphasis would be on the victims' needs, rather than, as now, on the need to have them as witnesses in court.

Outlook

The debate surrounding human trafficking is high on the agenda in nearly all EU countries. Unfortunately, however, it is our impression that trafficked people stand to gain nothing from the debate since the sole focus is on the migration process. From a human rights standpoint, this is not acceptable. An EU report is also heavily critical of this approach:

> 'From a human rights perspective, the primary concern is to combat the exploitation of human beings under forced labour or slavery like conditions, no matter whether such exploitation involves a victim of trafficking, a smuggled person, an illegal migrant or a lawful resident. In the application of the UN Trafficking Protocol, policies should therefore focus on the forced labour and slavery like outcomes of trafficking, rather than on the process through which people arrive in such conditions.'[8]

Unfortunately, there is good reason to fear that the trafficking debate will be used to limit immigration. Take, for example, the debate surrounding the liberalisation of the German visa policy in Ukraine. Even to this day, there is no proof that the policy really did encourage human trafficking, and yet, despite all the expert statements to the contrary, this is what is so vehemently claimed. All that has been shown is that a few labour migrants used the visas as a way of securing their safe entry into Germany so that they could work there, of their own free will, without the necessary papers. There is no proof, however, of an increase in trafficking from Ukraine. As far as we know, there is only one (!) trafficked person in Germany who entered the country on such a visa. It is this case that is always quoted in the press.

In our opinion, the best prevention against trafficking would, on the contrary, be to make it possible for migrants to find regular employment. It has been argued that immigration restrictions are even responsible for the increase in human trafficking. For example, according to the EU Experts Group against Trafficking in Human Beings:

---

7 Elaine Pearson, *Human Traffic Human Rights: Redefining Witness Protection* (London: Anti-Slavery International, 2002).

8 EU Experts Group against Trafficking in Human Beings (Brussels, 2004), 8.

> 'State policies in promoting immigration restrictions and reducing opportunities for regular migration have not been effective in preventing migration. Rather they have created a market for irregular migration, often as organised serious crime, through trafficking and smuggling of people.'[9]

We believe that enabling migrant women and men to work legally should also mean enabling them to work as sex workers, since there is a need for this work, just as there is a need for workers in other branches of industry. On the other side we have people who are keen to migrate and who are willing to perform these jobs – so we fail to understand why Western states do not allow it. The German Immigration Act would have established an adequate framework for responding to this need, but unfortunately the government did not use this opportunity. Admittedly, migration channels have been created for highly qualified workers, but no channel has been established for other potential categories of workers.

If such possibilities were to be created, however, steps would have to be taken at the same time to ensure the workers cannot be exploited. There is a need therefore for minimum labour standards so that everyone knows where they stand. Here, too, we think the trafficking debate offers a good starting point because, as well as critical voices, there are also those who regard the trafficking debate as very helpful for discussing labour laws. According to the International Labour Office, for example: '...the global movement against trafficking has certainly given an impetus to the understanding of, and action against, forced labour...'[10]

We agree with this view because it has shown itself to be true in practice. We have succeeded, for example, in pushing through minimum standards for domestic employees of diplomats.[11] This category of labour migrants live and work in situations of considerable precariousness, insofar as their stay is tied to their work in the employment of individual diplomats. Moreover, on account of their diplomatic immunity their employers are not accountable to the German courts. If a domestic worker in this situation falls prey to trafficking, she is particularly vulnerable and without protection. Authorities are now more aware of the problem thanks to the trafficking debate, and so the situation of domestic employees has slightly improved.

Introducing the Italian model in Germany would obviously have meant a real improvement in the living conditions of those affected by trafficking. Migrants unable or unwilling to contact the authorities, however, would still be without protection. Because no residence permit is available to them, or because their residence status is so precarious, they are denied access to basic human rights – and no western European country seems to be giving any thought to changing this situation. Otherwise, why is it that none of these countries is considering ratifying the 1990 International Convention on the Protection of the Rights of

9 Ibid., 11.

10 International Labour Office, *A Global Alliance Against Forced Labour* (Geneva, 2005), 7.

11 Ban Ying, *Information for Domestic Workers Working for Diplomats* (Berlin, 2003).

All Migrant Workers and Members of Their Families, which is the only convention where access to basic rights is not dependent on residence status and which provides that even people without the necessary papers have the *right to rights.* We believe ratification of this Convention to be essential from a human rights perspective.

Ratification of the Convention would obviously also benefit those affected by trafficking – but it is simply not a realistic option in the short term. At the moment, in nearly all European countries, trafficked people can only obtain a temporary residence permit – and hence access to minimum healthcare – if they are prepared to take the witness stand. We believe that in that case the destination countries are failing in their responsibility to prevent and address human rights violations related to trafficking with due diligence.

Violence against Women Legitimised with Arguments of 'Culture'

Violence against Women, Cultural/Religious Traditions and the International Standard of Due Diligence

Judith Wyttenbach

Violence against Women and International Human Rights Instruments

In the context of the fight against religiously/culturally motivated violence against women, a distinction must be made between two categories of international instruments: on the one hand, women-specific treaties and, on the other, general non-women-specific human rights treaties.

Women-Specific Instruments

The promotion and protection of women's human rights are addressed in the 1979 Convention on the Elimination of All Forms of Discrimination against Women (the CEDAW Convention), the 1994 Inter-American Convention on the Prevention, Punishment and Eradication of Violence against Women (the so-called Convention of Belém do Pará) and the 2003 Protocol to the African Charter on Human and Peoples' Rights on the Rights of Women in Africa.

The CEDAW Convention contains no explicit provision requiring states to counteract violence against women. Hence, special weight is attached to interpretative statements about the Convention by international bodies, the most important in relation to the CEDAW Convention being the comments of the UN Committee on the Elimination of Discrimination against Women (the CEDAW Committee), which monitors the CEDAW Convention, and the declarations of the UN General Assembly. To compensate for this shortcoming of the CEDAW Convention through teleological interpretation, the CEDAW Committee has made clear in its General Recommendation no. 19 (1992)[1] that:

1 Committee on the Elimination of Discrimination against Women, General Recommendation no. 19, Violence against Women (eleventh session, 1992), UN Doc. A/47/38.

C. Benninger-Budel ed., Due Diligence and Its Application to Protect Women from Violence
© *Koninklijke Brill NV. Printed in The Netherlands. ISBN 978 90 04 16293 8. pp. 225-239*

> 'Gender-based violence, which impairs or nullifies the enjoyment by women of human rights and fundamental freedoms under general international law or under human rights conventions, is discrimination within the meaning of article 1 of the Convention.'[2]

According to the Committee, states can also be responsible for private acts if they fail to act with due diligence.[3] In the same comment the Committee held that attempts to justify violence against women on religious or cultural grounds are a major obstacle in the fight against discrimination:

> 'Traditional attitudes by which women are regarded as subordinate to men or as having stereotyped roles perpetuate widespread practices involving violence or coercion, such as family violence and abuse, forced marriage, dowry deaths, acid attacks and female circumcision. Such prejudices and practices may justify gender-based violence as a form of protection or control of women. The effect of such violence on the physical and mental integrity of women is to deprive them of the equal enjoyment, exercise and knowledge of human rights and fundamental freedoms. While this comment addresses mainly actual or threatened violence the underlying consequences of these forms of gender-based violence help to maintain women in subordinate roles and contribute to the low level of political participation and to their lower level of education, skills and work opportunities.'[4]

States parties are called upon to identify and take action against these practices and patterns of justification and to present an account of the measures taken in their state reports.

In 2003 the CEDAW Committee ruled on the first individual complaint relating to domestic violence. It criticised Hungary for failing to provide protection and held that unduly long criminal and civil proceedings violated women's right to immediate and effective protection. It was inadmissible to give precedence to a man's ownership and access rights to the family home over protection of a woman's integrity. The Committee also addressed the issue of traditional stereotyped roles as causes of violence against women:

> 'The Committee addresses articles 5 and 16 together in its general recommendation 19 in dealing with family violence....It has stated on many occasions that traditional attitudes by which women are regarded as subordinate to men contribute to violence against them. The Committee recognized those very attitudes when it considered the combined fourth and fifth periodic report of Hungary in 2002, and was concerned

2 Ibid., para. 7.

3 Ibid., para. 9.

4 Ibid., para. 11.

about "the persistence of entrenched traditional stereotypes regarding the role and responsibilities of women and men in the family…."'[5]

Article 1 of the 1993 Declaration on the Elimination of Violence against Women[6] calls on states to counter violence against women occurring in public and in private:

> 'For the purposes of this Declaration, the term "violence against women" means any act of gender-based violence that results in, or is likely to result in, physical, sexual or psychological harm or suffering to women, including threats of such acts, coercion or arbitrary deprivation of liberty, whether occurring in public or in private life.'

According to Article 2 of the Declaration, violence against women includes, in particular, dowry-related violence, female genital mutilation (FGM), other practices harmful to women, physical, sexual, and psychological violence in the family and society, at work or in educational institutions, as well as trafficking in women and forced prostitution. The Declaration further states explicitly that states may not invoke any custom, tradition, or religious consideration to avoid their obligations with respect to the elimination of all forms of violence against women (Article 4). Other international human rights documents refer to the abortion of female foetuses, female infanticide, forced marriage and child marriage as further examples of religiously/culturally motivated violence against women.[7]

In the Inter-American Belém Convention, states parties agree to undertake progressively specific measures to:

> 'modify social and cultural patterns of conduct of men and women, including the development of formal and informal educational programs appropriate to every level of the educational process, to counteract prejudices, customs and all other practices which are based on the idea of the inferiority or superiority of either of the sexes or on the stereotyped roles for men and women which legitimize or exacerbate violence against women.'[8]

The 2003 Protocol to the African Charter on Human and Peoples' Rights on the Rights of Women in Africa also addresses the issue of violence against women. States parties are required under Article 4 to take appropriate and effective

5 Committee on the Elimination of Discrimination against Women, Communication no. 2/2003, *Ms A.T. v Hungary*, View adopted on 26 January 2005, para. 9.4.

6 Declaration on the Elimination of Violence against Women, UNGA Res. 48/104 of 20 December 1993.

7 See, inter alia, Committee on the Elimination of Discrimination against Women, General Recommendation no. 14, Female Circumcision (1990), UN Doc. A/45/38, 80, according to which states parties should take appropriate and effective measures with a view to eradicating the practice of female circumcision.

8 8. Article 8 (b).

measures to 'eradicate elements in traditional and cultural beliefs, practices and stereotypes which legitimise and exacerbate the persistence and tolerance of violence against women' and under Article 5 to 'prohibit and condemn all forms of harmful practices which negatively affect the human rights of women and which are contrary to recognised international standards'.

General Regional and International Human Rights Treaties

The core regional and international conventions such as the European,[9] African,[10] and Inter-American human rights conventions,[11] the two UN Human Rights Covenants[12] and the Convention on the Rights of the Child[13] contain a prohibition of gender-based discrimination and enshrine the right (not formulated in women-specific terms) to life and to protection against torture and cruel, inhuman, and degrading treatment. The Convention against Torture[14] and the Geneva Conventions on international humanitarian law[15] also contain norms protecting physical and sexual integrity. The Convention on the Rights of the Child furthermore requires states to protect children against violence in the family and sexual exploitation and to take measures against traditional practices that are prejudicial to health. International jurisprudence on states' obligations to protect in the context of private acts of violence is based for the most part on these treaties and is reflected, in particular, in the interpretative statements of monitoring bodies and the jurisprudence of the UN Human Rights Committee, the European Court of Human Rights and the Inter-American Court of Human Rights.

Several UN human rights monitoring treaty bodies have commented on the subject of violence against women in a number of documents. In its General Comment no. 28,[16] the Human Rights Committee, which monitors the UN International Covenant on Civil and Political Rights of 1966 (ICCPR), condemned various forms of violence against women as violations of ICCPR guarantees. In its General Comment no. 16,[17] the Committee on Economic, Social and Cultural

9 European Convention for the Protection of Human Rights and Fundamental Freedoms, 1950.

10 African [Banjul] Charter on Human and Peoples' Rights, 1981.

11 American Convention on Human Rights, 1969.

12 International Covenant on Economic, Social and Cultural Rights, 1966; International Covenant on Civil and Political Rights, 1966.

13 Convention on the Rights of the Child, 1989.

14 Convention against Torture and Other Cruel, Inhuman or Degrading Treatment or Punishment, 1984.

15 In particular Convention (IV) relative to the Protection of Civilian Persons in Time of War, 1949.

16 General Comment no. 28, Equality of Rights Between Men and Women (Article 3) (2000), UN Doc. CCPR/C/21/Rev.1/Add.10.

17 General Comment no. 16, The Equal Right of Men and Women to the Enjoyment of All Economic, Social and Cultural Rights (2005), UN Doc. E/C.12/2005.4, para. 27.

Rights, which monitors compliance with the UN International Covenant on Economic, Social and Cultural Rights (ICESCR), highlighted the importance of gender equality in marriage and the family as a basis for the elimination of discrimination. In its General Comment no. 14 (para. 21),[18] it stressed that the realisation of women's economic and social rights is a fundamental means of combating domestic violence and other forms of violence against women.

Religiously/Culturally Motivated Violence Against Women

Levels of Justification

Attempts at religious/cultural justification occur at a number of different levels.

(a) Treaty ratification level: Religiously/culturally motivated *reservations or interpretative declarations* at the time of ratification of international and regional human rights treaties (e.g., 'the obligations assumed under this treaty in respect of equal rights of women and men in the family shall apply only where such obligations are compatible with the religious laws in force').

(b) Level of state reporting to human rights bodies: Invocation of religious/cultural impediments to the *implementation* of human rights obligations.

(c) Domestic implementation level: *State reluctance to intervene in the private sphere* or the *religious/cultural attitudes of police officers and members of the judiciary* frequently give rise to negligence in dealing with violence against women, ranging from unduly protracted proceedings to complete inaction or even active shielding of the perpetrators.

Who Defines Religious or Cultural Rules?

There is no really clear-cut distinction between attempts at religious justification of violence against women and *culturally* and *traditionally* motivated considerations, inasmuch as religion, culture, and tradition are polymorphous constructs which can be defined, used and (re)interpreted depending on the interests involved. Moreover, the authority of 'custom and morality', 'religious law', or 'customary law' is usually invoked in opposition to state law and international standards. In her report of 2006, the UN Special Rapporteur on violence against women stated that the oppressive nature of certain practices pursued in the name of culture has to be addressed within the human rights discourse. This requires, in her words:

> '(a) drawing on positive elements within culture to demystify the oppressive elements of culture-based discourses; (b) demonstrating that culture is not an immutable and homogenous entity; and (c) identifying and contesting the legitimacy of those who monopolize the right to speak on behalf of culture and religion. In this context, hegemonic

18 Committee on Economic, Social and Cultural Rights, General Comment no. 14, The Right to the Highest Attainable Standard of Health (2000), UN Doc. E/C.12/2000.4.

interpretations of culture must be challenged by uncovering the power dynamics that underlie these…'.[19]

Religious/cultural considerations are invoked to 'justify' not only honour killings, widow burning, female genital mutilation, and forced marriage, but also domestic violence. Routine violence in the family and in couple relationships is or has been accepted in almost all countries as a fact of social life. To a large extent, this acceptance and the related leniency towards perpetrators are (also) rooted in every society in traditional cultural practices.

Challenging the Universality of Women's Rights: Freedom of Religion and Minority Rights

Religious sensitivities and religious customs and traditions are protected by international and regional human rights treaties. A common stipulation of these freedom of religion provisions is that the practice of religious customs and traditions can be limited in the interest of the rights of others. Article 18 (3) ICCPR states this principle in the following terms: 'Freedom to manifest one's religion or beliefs may be subject only to such limitations as are prescribed by law and are necessary to protect public safety, order, health, or morals or the fundamental rights and freedoms of others.'[20] These fundamental 'rights of others' include, first and foremost, the rights protected by the two UN Human Rights Covenants and the other core international treaties: the prohibition of gender-based discrimination, the prohibition of slavery, protection of physical and mental integrity, freedom to marry and the right to health and education. The terms of Article 18 (3) ICCPR further cover legal standards that have fundamental status in the domestic legal order and generally enjoy constitutional protection.[21] States are thus justified in taking action against religious customs and traditions that threaten or violate these fundamental legal entitlements of women and girls.

It has frequently been argued that the right of peoples to self-determination and the rights of minorities to preserve their cultural identity give cultural or religious groups the right to take autonomous decisions regarding religious or cultural rules and customs in their community. This is held to include freedom to determine the status of women and their rights in society.

The right of peoples to self-determination in Article 1 ICCPR and Article 1 ICESCR accords *peoples* the right freely to determine their political status and to pursue their economic, social and cultural development. Unlike the other rights

19 Report of the UN Special Rapporteur on violence against women, its causes and consequences, *The Due Diligence Standard as a Tool for the Elimination of Violence against Women*, UN Doc. E/CN.4/2006/61, 20 January 2006, para. 85.

20 Article 9 of the European Convention on Human Rights contains an almost identical provision regarding the limitation of freedom of religion.

21 Manfred Nowak, *U.N. Covenant on Civil and Political Rights. CCPR Commentary*, 2nd rev. ed., (Kehl/Strassbourg/Arlington: Engel Publishers, 2005), 430f.

under the two UN Human Rights Covenants, the right to self-determination has a pronounced collective dimension. It belongs to the group of so-called 'third generation' human rights and is not an individual right.[22] It should not be confused with the rights of minorities under Article 27 ICCPR. The precise meaning of the term 'peoples' is still a moot question. According to a widely held view, it protects national or ethnic groups who, as part of a multinational state, are identified with a particular territory as well as peoples under foreign occupation.[23] While the UN Committee on the Elimination of Racial Discrimination has noted in its General Recommendation no. 21,[24] para. 5, that 'governments should be sensitive towards the rights of persons of ethnic groups, particularly their right to lead lives of dignity, to preserve their culture...', the focus is on their right freely to determine their political system and freely to dispose of their own natural resources and their land rights. So far, cultural or religious issues in the narrow sense, that are not connected to land use rights or the political system, have been of secondary importance.[25]

The invocation of minority rights in Article 27 ICCPR is potentially of greater importance in the context of violence against women. Article 27 is an individual right; it stipulates:

> 'In those States in which ethnic, religious or linguistic minorities exist, persons belonging to such minorities shall not be denied the right, in community with the other members of their group, to enjoy their own culture, to profess and practise their own religion, or to use their own language.'

However, the jurisprudence of the Human Rights Committee on this Article deals primarily with linguistic rights, land rights, and land-use rights and only marginally with the preservation of religious minority culture.[26] In contrast to many other individual rights under the Covenant – and in particular the provision concerning freedom of religion in Article 18–Article 27 is silent on the question of limitations on this right. It has been inferred from this omission that higher standards are applicable to limitations on freedom of religion in dealing with minorities than in dealing with the 'majority culture or religion'. However, the fact that the exercise of minority rights is constrained by the need to protect

22 Human Rights Committee, *Mikmaq v Canada*, Communication no. 78/1980, 30 September 1980, or *Lubicon Lake Band v Canada*, Communication no. 167/1984, 26 March 1990.

23 Sarah Joseph, Jenny Schultz, and Melissa Castan, *The International Covenant on Civil and Political Rights. Cases, Materials and Commentary* (Oxford: Oxford University Press, 2000), 100, paras. 7.06f.

24 UN Doc. HRI/GEN/1/Rev.6 (2003), 210.

25 See Nowak (2005), see note 21 above, 24ff; Joseph et al. (2000), see note 23 above, 106f.

26 See Joseph et al. (2000), see note 23 above, 582 and 591, with the Human Rights Committee communications cited therein.

the rights of others flowing from the Covenant is uncontested.[27] Religious/cultural practices which violate the right to life or the right to physical integrity cannot be justified by invoking Article 27 ICCPR.[28] In its General Comment no. 28, the Human Rights Committee states in connection with the prohibition of gender-based discrimination that states parties should 'ensure that traditional, historical, religious/cultural attitudes are not used to justify violations of women's right to equality before the law and to equal enjoyment of all Covenant rights'.[29] Attempts to use considerations of freedom of religion or 'cultural minority rights' to justify violence against women thus run up against the human rights principle of protection of the integrity of women and girls.

The fact that the issue of violence against women is interdisciplinary and touches on issues of freedom of religion and minority rights is demonstrated by the comments of human rights mechanisms concerned with freedom of religion. Thus, the report of the UN Special Rapporteur on freedom of religion or belief stated explicitly that the universality of women's rights could not be challenged by reference to religion or culture:

> '29. ...[t]he notion of the universality of human rights is today fully accepted as an established norm that can no longer be challenged. This tenet is derived from the human person and from the fact that women's rights, even where they have a bearing on cultural and religious questions, form part of the fundamental rights of the human person....Where a woman's dignity is undermined, there can be no further question of invoking either sovereignty or cultural or religious specificities....'[30]

Implementation of Human Rights Obligations: Effective Protection against Violence

Levels of Obligation

The concept of due diligence denotes the minimum amount of state action that is required to implement the human rights embodied in international and regional treaties. On ratifying international human rights treaties, states undertake to respect, to protect, and to fulfil the guarantees they contain:

(a) The obligation to respect women's rights means that the state must itself refrain from behaving in a manner that is contrary to human rights. This obligation is immediate and direct. Example: police officers/soldiers are prohibited from raping women.

---

27 Patrick Thornberry, *International Law and the Rights of Minorities* (Oxford: Oxford University Press, 1991), 203; Nowak (2005), see note 21 above, 666.

28 See also Nowak (2005), see note 21 above, 667.

29 UN Doc. HRI/GEN/1/Rev.6 (2003), 179, para. 5.

30 UN Special Rapporteur on freedom of religion or belief, *Étude sur la liberté de religion ou de conviction et la condition de la femme au regard de la religion et des traditions* (2002), UN Doc. E/CN.4/2002/73/Add.2.

(b) The state must further afford women effective protection against violence by private actors. Here again there is a direct obligation where the state is aware of violations and in a position to take action against them. Example: the duty of police intervention in cases of domestic violence and the obligation to conduct a judicial investigation of violent crimes against women.

(c) Lastly, the guarantees entail an obligation to facilitate the full realisation of women's rights through the provision of appropriate state services (duty to fulfil). Example: adoption and implementation of socio-political measures aimed at enhancing assistance for women victims of violence.

Domestic Implementation

Private actors are far more frequently responsible for violence against women than state agents. The discussion therefore focuses in such cases on the state's *due diligence* in fulfilling its *obligation to protect and to provide* vis-à-vis women. States have a relatively wide margin of discretion when it comes to deciding how to discharge their human rights obligations. The most important types of action include:

(a) *Preventive measures:* The three core regional conventions, the two UN Human Rights Covenants, the Convention against Torture and the CEDAW Convention require states to take all necessary measures to enact and implement legislation aimed at *preventing violations.* Some countries still allow religiously/culturally motivated justificatory defences that afford perpetrators privileged treatment, for instance in the case of honour killings. The elimination of such criminal law provisions constitutes an urgently necessary step that would also have a preventive impact.

Moreover, preventive action can be taken not only in criminal law but also in civil law, for instance through the establishment of appropriate general principles of family law, which play a more effective role than criminal law in shaping the future. The CEDAW Convention further requires states to take preventive measures against discrimination by educating public opinion. In addition, social policy measures such as health promotion, family education and social assistance are envisaged as preventive public-law measures under the ICESCR Covenant and in the area of social rights under the CEDAW Convention.

(b) *Immediate protective action:* Police intervention against perpetrators and other direct protective measures such as restraining orders may be characterised as positive *protection in the narrow sense* inasmuch as their purpose is to bring about the immediate cessation of an ongoing violation. Efforts are currently under way in Switzerland to introduce a civil expulsion and restraint procedure at the federal level for cases of domestic violence. To protect victims, the courts would be empowered to order violent persons to leave the shared place of residence and keep away from it for a specific period of time. Measures to protect children also fall into the category of immediate protective action in the narrow sense. Religiously/culturally motivated genital mutilation of girls also occurs in Switzerland. Parents and performers of FGM are liable to prosecution under Swiss criminal law for causing grievous bodily harm. Child protection measures may be ordered to protect the girls concerned.

(c) *Indirect protective action*: Women victims of violence can be adversely affected (indirectly) by existing legislation. The following example comes from Switzerland: a migrant woman may in certain circumstances lose her Swiss residence permit if she leaves her violent husband and moves out of the family residence. In such cases, it is for legislators to work out solutions that enable migrant victims of violence to obtain protection without endangering their immigration law status.

(d) *Repressive action*: Repressive measures include, for example, punitive criminal and civil measures aimed at punishing misconduct. They comprise criminal penalties and, where prescribed by law, awards of punitive damages against private offenders. In many countries offences such as marital rape and domestic violence are punishable only on the basis of a complaint by the victim. This used to be the case also in Switzerland, where violent acts in the context of marriage and partnerships have been prosecutable ex officio (i.e., without an application by the victim) only since 1 April 2004.

Although 'honour killings' are rare in Switzerland, they have occurred from time to time. The perpetrators' defence counsel occasionally attempt in cases of honour killings or domestic violence to invoke their clients' religious or cultural origin as a ground for mitigation of sentence. In a judgment of 14 December 2000, the Swiss Federal Court held that a father who had murdered his daughter could not derive any significant mitigating effect from his cultural origin. While views held in the defendant's home country had to be taken into account in the overall assessment of his motives, the Court was required to adjudicate an act and not a culture.[31] One canton recently expelled a young woman's male relatives from Switzerland for allegedly subjecting the young woman to a forced marriage; there was furthermore clear evidence that the woman faced an acute and real risk of being subjected to honour killing because she refused to cohabit with her husband.[32]

(e) *Obligation to investigate*: The obligation to undertake a police or judicial investigation of private acts of violence involving violations of the right to life, the prohibition of cruel, inhuman, or degrading treatment or punishment and the right to privacy has been expressly confirmed both by the European Court of Human Rights and by the UN Human Rights Committee.[33]

---

31 BGE 127 IV 10; the reasoning in BGE 117 IV 7 is more ambivalent.

32 *Neue Zürcher Zeitung*, report dated 23 May 2006.

33 See, among many other examples, European Court of Human Rights, *Yasa v Turkey*, Reports 1998–IV, 2 September 1998, 100; Human Rights Committee, *Villafañe*

(f) *Compensatory provisions* are designed to restore the imbalance caused by the misconduct, particularly through awards of civil damages and satisfaction against the offender.

(g) The Convention on the Rights of the Child and the Convention against Torture contain an additional category of rehabilitative obligations, which extend beyond the payment of pecuniary damages by the wrongdoer (Article 39 Convention on the Rights of the Child; Article 14 Convention Against Torture).

(h) *Organisational and procedural obligations*: Fundamental rights and human rights must be exercisable in an effective and non-discriminatory way through procedures based on the rule of law and through properly functioning judicial and administrative authorities. In this context, organisational and procedural obligations are of dual importance. On the one hand, they constitute interests that enjoy human rights protection in their own right. On the other, they are a basic prerequisite for the enforcement of substantive claims arising from other human rights guarantees. Due process guarantees are to be found primarily in Articles 5, 6 and 13 of the European Convention on Human Rights and in Article 14 (1) ICCPR.

The UN Special Rapporteur on violence against women has suggested specific measures in her reports to counter religiously motivated violence. They include public awareness campaigns, training and further training for police and health personnel, the enactment of appropriate legislation to prevent and counteract violence against women by means of civil and criminal law, the abolition of religious justificatory defences and other religiously motivated discrimination in civil and criminal law,[34] dialogue with religious communities and their leaders, transparency of religious instruction, action against extremism, and ensuring non-discriminatory access to judicial proceedings.[35]

Chaparro et al. v Colombia, Comm. no. 612/1995, para. 8.8, 29 July 1997 (right to life); European Court of Human Rights, *Ilhan v Turkey*, Reports 2000–VII, 27 June 2000; *X. and Y. v the Netherlands*, Ser. A, 91, 26 June 1985; Human Rights Committee, *Mónaco de Gallicchio v Argentina*, Comm. no. 400/1990, para. 10.5, 3 April 1995 (right to privacy); *Santullo v Uruguay*, Comm. no. 7/1977, para. 12, 26 October 1979 (prohibition of cruel and inhuman treatment, prohibition of torture).

34 Perpetrators of honour killings still receive privileged treatment in, for example, Lebanon, Jordan, Kuwait, Egypt, Iraq, the United Arab Emirates, Iran, Morocco, Sudan and Pakistan.

35 Report of the Special Rapporteur on violence against women, its causes and consequences, *Violence against Women in the Family*, UN Doc. E/CN.4/1999/68, 10 March 1999; and Report of the Special Rapporteur on violence against women, its causes and consequences, *Trafficking in Women, Women's Migration and Violence against Women*, UN Doc. E/CN.4/2000/68, 29 February 2000.

What Has the International Human Rights Protection Achieved in the Fight against Religiously/Culturally Motivated Violence against Women?

Achievements

(a) The fact that private gender-based violence has been recognised as a violation of women's rights and as a crosscutting issue in the context of international human rights protection must be rated as a positive achievement. This approach is clearly reflected in the human rights bodies' reports and interpretative comments, recommendations and other communications.[36]

(b) A consensus is slowly emerging among states on individual aspects of violence against women. Important steps have included, for example, the subsumption of rape under the definition of torture and its recognition as a crime against humanity[37] and the action taken against female genital mutilation.

(c) A number of international legal documents emphasise the universality of women's rights. At the same time, the justification of violence against women on religious/cultural grounds has been recognised as a problem and categorically rejected.[38] Importance is attached, in particular, to the condemnation of individual practices that affect the right to life or severely impair the physical integrity of girls and women and that have a clearly identifiable religious/cultural basis (such as widow burning). However, domestic violence is also eliciting more and more comment. This type of violence is also increasingly perceived as a widespread culturally motivated phenomenon and as a historically rooted characteristic of all societies, i.e., including contemporary Western societies.

(d) In the reporting procedure before the human rights treaty monitoring bodies, states parties are required to describe in their reports on implementation of the CEDAW Convention, the Convention on the Rights of the Child, the Convention against Torture, and the two Human Rights Covenants the advances they have made in protecting the integrity of women and girls.

36 Impressive examples are to be found in the collection of declarations and resolutions of various human rights bodies contained in the Report of the Secretary-General to the General Assembly, *Working Towards the Elimination of Crimes against Women Committed in the Name of Honour*, 2002, UN Doc. A/57/169.

37 International Criminal Tribunal for the former Yugoslavia (ICTY), *Kunarac, Kovać and Vuković* case, 22 February 2001 (IT-96-23 and IT-96-23/1), confirmed by the Appeals Chamber, 12 June 2002.

38 E.g., General Assembly Resolution 58/147, *Elimination of Domestic Violence against Women*, 22 December 2003, UN Doc. A/RES/58/147; General Assembly Resolution 59/165, *Working Towards the Elimination of Crimes against Women and Girls Committed in the Name of Honour*, 20 December 2004, UN Doc. A/RES/59/165. See also Commission on Human Rights Resolution 2004/36, *Elimination of All Forms of Religious Intolerance.*

The evolution of the CEDAW Committee's jurisprudence will be important in the future. It is about to address the task of specifying the content of CEDAW Convention guarantees in terms of issues relating to violence against women.

Challenges for the Future

At the state level

(a) Religious/cultural practices and codes of conduct play a role primarily in the private sphere – in marriage, the family and childrearing. Hence a major obstacle in the fight against religiously/culturally motivated violence against women consists in *states' traditional reluctance to intervene in the private sphere* and the widely held view that a high value must be placed on the *privacy* of marriage and the family, so that women's individual rights should take second place in these spheres.

(b) States are often reluctant to become involved in confrontations with religious/cultural values and social structures, and tend to give precedence to religious morality over women's rights. The problem may be partly due to the coexistence of *customary, tribal, or religious law* with state (constitutional) law, a coexistence that is all too often interpreted to the detriment of women.[39]

(c) Both broad-based social discrimination against women and religious/cultural traditions are deeply rooted in society. The fight against 'culturally' motivated violence against women is therefore a *long-term programme* for the state and civil society. Unless society engages in an in-depth analysis of the religious/cultural background to social discrimination against women in the family, at work and in politics, even the soundest state legislation is doomed to founder on existing congealed structures.

(d) An important prerequisite for effective protection is a *properly functioning state* with sound law enforcement structures. Where these are lacking, as in failed states or states in transition, women tend to be the first victims of private acts of violence.[40] Thus, when islands of lawlessness emerge during armed conflicts or civil-war-type situations, local law, including religiously imbued tribal or customary law, may gain ground. This can lead to an upsurge in practices such as honour killings as well as forced marriages which remain unpunished. At the same time, a state with weak law enforcement structures (a corrupt and short-staffed police force, lack of jurisdiction) has far-reaching consequences for women, since there is no effective system of protection.

39 See, for example, Committee on the Elimination of Discrimination against Women, General Recommendation no. 21, Equality in Marriage and Family Relations, UN Doc. A/49/38 (1994), 1.

40 See the observations of the Human Rights Committee, General Comment no. 28, note 16 above, para. 8.

(e) A further problem is the close link between the realisation of women's *social and economic rights* and the fight against traditionally motivated violence against women. The implementation of women's rights depends on the availability of material resources. This is particularly true of domestic violence, which tends to be justified by the traditional cultural subordination of women in the family. Women are often in a situation of total material dependency on male family members owing to their lack of or lower level of education and vocational training or because of discriminatory inheritance and divorce law provisions. Where, in addition, the state is unwilling or unable to offer women effective assistance, the prospect of escape from oppressive circumstances must remain a mere fantasy for most women.

At the level of international law

(f) The fight against religiously/culturally motivated violence against women is currently based on a wide range of international norms, some of which fail to do justice to the issues involved. With the exception of the regional Inter-American Belém Convention, there is no *explicit* and binding obligation on states to take action against violence in the private sphere. Instead, this obligation must be derived from the state obligations to protect flowing from traditional non-women-specific human rights guarantees, which are not always uniformly defined in doctrinal terms. This has both advantages and disadvantages. The advantage consists in the fact that it is correct in theory to interpret and apply the treaties also in terms of the realisation of women's rights (women's rights are human rights – human rights include women's rights). In practice, however, this system takes a very long time to generate a stronger commitment on the part of states to ensuring protection against violence.

(g) Many states have made *religiously motivated interpretative declarations and reservations* on ratifying CEDAW Convention and other human rights treaties (e.g., Bahrain, Egypt, Iraq, Libya, Kuwait, Morocco, Saudi Arabia, Syria). Most of these reservations concern women's rights under marriage and divorce law, i.e., in the private sphere.

(h) Quite frequently *arguments based on cultural relativism* are invoked to challenge the universality of women's rights to protection of their integrity or to water down obligations.

(i) *Weaknesses in international enforcement mechanisms* make it easier for states to shirk their responsibility.

Areas of Conflict: Women's Rights – Cultural Traditions – State Intervention

universality of human rights (women's rights)	↔	cultural relativism reservations to human rights treaties by individual states
protection of fundamental rights and human rights in the private sphere against private oppression	↔	dichotomy public – private sphere state restraint in the private sphere primacy of 'religion and morals' in everyday life
international law/ enforcement of state secular (constitutional) law	↔	primacy of local customary law/primacy of religious law
protection of individual human rights also within groups	↔	religious/cultural 'collective rights' right to religious/cultural identity of a social group, which itself determines the status of individual members of the group

Violence against Women Legitimised by Arguments of 'Culture' – Thoughts from a Pakistani Perspective

Farida Shaheed

Introduction

There is a common misperception that 'cultural' justifications for violence only operate in 'traditional' societies (i.e., those not fully integrated into the global economic and political systems of production and governance), and of such justifications being linked to specific religions or cultures. My contention is that regardless of where or when it occurs or the nature of its manifestation, violence against women is always legitimised by arguments of 'culture' because: (1) no society is devoid of culture; (2) the dominant culture throughout the world is patriarchal; and (3) patriarchal culture inevitably validates violence as an acceptable, even desirable, attribute of masculinity while it simultaneously devalues women and all attributes considered feminine, such as nurturing – not just of persons but also of relationships. If violence is considered legitimate, specific acts of violence against individuals who are socially devalued by the dominant culture (including but not only women) automatically become even more acceptable. Once transformed into 'the norm', these acts remain unquestioned. Consequently, explicit and implicit cultural legitimations for violence against women are to be found both in contemporary political discourses and throughout formal state laws and in 'traditional' societies and practices. In order to overcome violence against women, the general pervasive culture of violence must be replaced by a culture of peace[1] to ensure justice for all and to provide social spaces in which differences are resolved without violence.[2]

1 The United Nations Education, Science and Culture Organisation (UNESCO) started a Culture of Peace Programme in the early 1980s. 2000 was declared the UN International Year for the Culture of Peace and the first decade of the new millennium the UN Decade for a Culture of Peace and Non-Violence for the Children of the World (2001–2010) under UNESCO coordination.

2 Diane Bretherton, 'Education, Training, Socialization and Research – Learning the Tools for Living Together Peacefully and with Respect for Differences', in *Asian*

C. Benninger-Budel ed., Due Diligence and Its Application to Protect Women from Violence
 ISBN 978 90 04 16293 8. pp. 241-248

Cultural Underpinnings of the Law

It is important to understand that the law is no more devoid of culture than it is of biases. 'Culture' is evident in the text of the law through specific legal formulations: through prohibitions or prescriptions and in the severity of punishment prescribed for a particular act compared with greater leniency for another. But culture is also evident in legal silences, in the very differentiation between which acts a society considers to be crimes and which it condones by silence. In terms of gender-based violence, the cultural underpinning of laws is visible in different countries across the world, for example in the absence of legislation criminalising domestic violence or marital rape; in what constitutes sufficient proof to establish forced intercourse; and in the text of legal provisions that reduces culpability for murder in cases considered to be '*crimes passionelles*'. In today's context, in which so much attention in South Asia – as elsewhere – is focused on so-called 'honour crimes', it is worth remembering that it was the British colonial rulers who introduced this concept into South Asian law in the shape of the 'grave and sudden provocation' clause. The clause maintains that men should be dealt with leniently when there is evidence of provocation so acute or 'grave' as to make their subsequent acts of violence excusable and therefore deserving of lesser punishments. The circumstances under which violence is 'understandable' – and therefore to be excused – include acts committed to preserve one's 'honour' even at the expense of a woman's life.

If legal texts are patriarchal, it is simply because laws have traditionally been the prerogative of male legislators so that, as stated by Tove Stang Dahl, it 'is generally men's experiences, opinions and interests that throughout time have been etched into law'.[3] It should also be added that the experience reflected in law is that of only certain men belonging to the dominant class.

Yet laws do not implement themselves. Culture permeates the application and interpretation of laws beyond legal formulations. The law is administered by people – the vast majority being men – who have specific cultural beliefs and understandings that they bring to and apply in their work, consciously or unconsciously. Textual biases against women become reinforced by the cultural beliefs of judges and other concerned officials of the law enforcement and justice system. Indeed in some cases, the cultural considerations and beliefs of sitting judges may be so strong as to overrule the text of the law. In Pakistan, for instance, courts have virtually condoned men for murdering their female relatives when the accused claimed they had acted violently because they suspected their womenfolk of having sexual relationships outside marriage. Using the 'grave and sudden provocation' clause, judges in the Supreme Court of Pakistan have opined that:

Women for a Culture of Peace – Report of the Regional Conference for a Culture of Peace, 6–9 December 2000, Hanoi, 76–80 (UNESCAP-UNESCO, September, 2001).

3 Tove Stang Dahl, 'Women's Law: Methods, Problems, Values', *Contemporary Crises* 10 (1986): 362.

> *'Under village conditions and even in many other parts of society in this country, the right* of the male member of the family to control the actions of their women folk, particularly in the field of sexual relations, *is fully recognized and forcefully maintained. The idea* that a young unmarried girl in a village family is entitled to leave her bed during the night and go where she pleases...*simply cannot be entertained* [emphasis added].'[4]

In another case, the judge, finding no other evidence, nevertheless held that:

> *'The appellant had two children from his deceased wife* and when he took the extreme step of taking her life by giving her repeated knife blows on different parts of her body, *she must have done something unusual to enrage him* to such an extent [emphasis added].'[5]

I have added the emphasis in both statements to underscore the cultural understanding as expressed by the judges in support of their decision, though their cultural beliefs have nothing to do with the provisions of the law or, indeed, with the legal case in hand. In the first case for example, the law does not give a male family member any legal right to control his female relatives; this 'right' is 'fully recognized and forcefully maintained' only culturally and outside the purview of the law. In the second case, the judge's ruling was made on the basis of, at best, a rather naïve belief that unless a woman does something unusually provocative, a man could not possibly murder the mother of his own children. In both judgements cultural beliefs superseded legislative provisions: in neither case was any substantive evidence of 'grave and sudden provocation' referred to.

Culture and Religion

My contention is that culture is not equivalent to religion. Even though religion (as customs and practices) does influence culture, I would posit that patriarchal considerations constitute the prism through which religious interpretation takes place and that it is not a coincidence that across the globe, religious interpretation has been a jealously guarded male monopoly. In the case of Islam this monopolisation has meant that in everyday practice as well as in law, religious tenets supporting women's rights are frequently overlooked, suspended or put into parentheses. Consequently, whenever there is a clash between patriarchal concerns embodied in 'traditional customs' on the one hand and religious tenets on the other, customs almost always override religion.

One small example is that in 1997 Pakistan deleted the provision of 'grave and sudden provocation' from the statute books because it was deemed un-Islamic. Nevertheless, judges continue to refer to this no-longer extant – and now officially un-Islamic – clause to reduce sentences. Experience also shows that when state law, customs and religious tenets provide different options, in practice it is inevitably the one least favourable to women that is actually applied. For example,

4 Supreme Court Judgement, *Mohammed Saleh v The State*, PLD 1965 SC 446 (370).

5 Supreme Court Judgement *Muhammad Younis v The State*, 1989 PCr.LJ (1747).

women have been killed in Pakistan simply for marrying someone of their own choosing even though state laws and Islamic injunctions both unequivocally uphold an adult woman's right to decide.

Hence, it needs to be said that religion per se is not the critical factor determining women's oppression in Muslim societies. The essential components of patriarchy are the same in Muslim societies as elsewhere: women's subordination occurs in the immediate family and in kinship structures, in state-building projects and in international policy-making. But articulations of patriarchy are always culturally specific and, despite the many factors that differentiate and divide women in Muslim societies, the 'Muslimness' of this articulation is similar.[6] Moreover, the influence of religion is not limited either to 'traditional' or 'Muslim' societies as evidenced in the growing strength of the Christian religion as a key reference point in public discourse (that both informs and is informed by culture) in the United States of America, for instance.

Whose Culture and Who Speaks for the Group?

Culture is not a definitive entity frozen in time, but an ever-evolving process. As Ashish Nandy says, the greatest tradition of all is the reinvention of tradition.[7] 'Culture' is continuously being amended as a result of societal contestations and in response to changing circumstances, thereby redefining norms of appropriateness. All change is not necessarily positive: developments may render violence less acceptable, but some developments may promote a greater acceptance of violence against women as, for example, in armed conflict situations. Indeed, changing circumstances may yield both positive and negative results at the same time. For instance, developments may enable women to be more gainfully employed but, at the same time, render women more vulnerable to domestic control within the household.

Today in Pakistan and South Asia as a whole, we face a two-fold challenge: to confront both the traditional patriarchal culture that denies women their rights and the new patriarchal culture that presents itself in religious robes or other forms of identity politics. In Pakistan this latter process started with the dictatorship of General Zia-ul Haq in the 1970s, a dictatorship seemingly bent upon promoting by all means possible an acceptance of all forms of violence against citizens by justifying violence in the name of religion through the introduction of legalised barbaric punishments it claimed were 'Islamic'.[8]

6 See Farida Shaheed, 'Controlled or Autonomous: Identity and the Experience of the Network, Women Living under Muslim Laws', *Signs – Journal of Women in Culture and Society. Feminism and the Law* 19, no. 4 (Summer 1994): 997–1019.

7 Ashish Nandy, *The Intimate Enemy: Loss and Recovery of Self under Colonialism* (Delhi: Oxford University Press, 1983).

8 For example, under the guise of 'Islamisation' the regime's Hudood Ordinances (1979) made the punishments of stoning to death, the amputation of limbs and whipping legal.

Societies never have only one culture. Every society has both a dominant culture and multiple subaltern cultures. The dominant culture reflects the viewpoint and the interests of those in power at a particular time; subaltern cultures represent the viewpoints and perspectives of those who either do not accept or do not live according to the prescribed 'normative' behaviour. Minorities outside the mainstream (e.g., ethnic or religious groups) frequently have their own distinct culture. But subaltern cultures also exist for less defined communities, e.g., individuals living on the periphery of society, such as the homeless, who also evolve their own cultures. Finally, there are the subaltern cultures representing groups who consciously reject the main dominant culture, indicating not only differences within society but also a proactive resistance to the existing norms. In this last category I would include both the historically documented sub-cultures of women as well as subaltern cultures formulated by human rights activists.

Women rarely define the dominant culture, because they do not have the economic, social or political power to do so. Of course women are not a homogenous category and are differentiated by class and other factors of power and powerlessness. Nevertheless, while all men enjoy – in some measure – the advantages of a patriarchal culture and structures of power, all women suffer, albeit to differing degrees, the impositions and constraints of that same culture and structure. In addition to evolving their own subaltern cultures, women are also part of the cultures of resistance. When multiple cultures contend to be heard within a society, a key question is which voice is given or acquires legitimacy as *the* voice of 'the people'. This is equally important for the majority community as for minorities. Where the dominant cultural trend becomes articulated by the state, a critical question for minorities is which voice the state accepts as speaking on behalf of a particular group. Currently, for instance, certain self-proclaimed 'community leaders' in the UK demand to be accepted as *the* voice of all Muslims, or of all Sikhs or of all Hindus, etc. Significantly, these 'leaders' are not elected by the constituency they claim to represent. Another example in South Asia are the forces commonly labelled 'fundamentalists' that deliberately seek to project themselves as the sole authentic spokesperson for a community appropriating for themselves the power to define what are cultural norms: re-writing history or making reference to religion and other sources of 'authenticity' where convenient to advance their essentially political and social agendas as also pointed out by Indian activists examining the Gujrat violence.

So the question is why the state that supports democratic processes in the mainstream should defer to or acknowledge them as 'the authentic voice' merely because they claim religious status. Matters are further complicated by the absence of organised alternative voices from within these communities and the fact that many progressive voices from within the same communities consciously eschew a religious or ethnic basis for their engagements, preferring to identify on other lines such as ideology or class. Surely, it should be the responsibility of the state to elicit a full compendium of voices from within a particular community of citizens as from within the citizenry at large.

This is in no way meant to suggest that the state should overrule the collective rights of minorities. On the contrary, collective rights and special interests of minority communities must be ensured. However, under no circumstances should the collective rights and special interests of any group be promoted at the expense of the fundamental rights and human dignity of individuals within that community. One example of problematic state responses to issues of minorities is the Indian Muslim Women (Protection of Rights on Divorce) Act of 1986. Denying Muslim women the rights conferred on other Indian female citizens to post-divorce maintenance,[9] this Act was passed in deference to those loudly claiming to speak for the Indian Muslim community; notably not taken into consideration was the voice of the concerned female citizens themselves.

Women's Rights: A Western Construct?

A question that is quite often posed is whether the concept and desire for women's self-determination is merely a western construct. The question is especially noticeable in recent times in discussions around Islam and women. It needs to be clearly stated that neither is women's oppression an eastern construct, nor is women's resistance to such oppression a western construct starting in the eighteenth and nineteenth centuries. Women have resisted oppression throughout the ages in every society; for example, Dunja Rihtman-Augustin documented elements of rebellion embedded in 'female sub-cultures' flourishing in many so-called 'traditional societies'.[10] Still, the idea that women's resistance is a western monopoly has gained so much ground that women in Third World countries as a whole and women from Muslim contexts in particular seem to have bought into this myth. Precisely to refute the claim that the struggle for women's rights is alien to women in Muslim societies and contexts, I traced women's assertions for rights from the eighth century to the 1950s, from Indonesia in South East Asia to Nigeria in Africa, in the Arab world and in Central Asia; in South Asia and in China.[11] The answer to whether women's rights is a western construct therefore is no. Women have fought for their rights in every era and society even though the

9 The Act came after the controversial Shah Bano Case (*Mohammed Ahmed Khan v Shah Bano* AIR 1985 SC 945) in which Shah Bano was granted maintenance under Section 125 of the Indian Criminal Procedure Code (CrPC). Controversy led to the 1986 Act that deprived Indian Muslim women the right to post-divorce maintenance under this section. See the special paper commissioned by Women's Research and Action Group (WRAG), *Women, Law and Customary Practice* (Mumbai, 1997).

10 Dunja Rihtman-Augustin, 'The Structure of Traditional Thought', cited in Aleksandra Alund, 'Feminism, Multiculturalism, Essentialism', in *Women, Citizenship and Difference*, ed. Nira Yuval-Davis and Pnina Werbner, 147–161 (London: Zed Books, 1999).

11 Farida Shaheed with Aisha Shaheed, *Great Ancestors: Women Asserting Rights in Muslim Contexts – a Training & Information Kit* (Lahore: Shirkat Gah/WLUML, 2004).

articulation rights, priorities set and strategies adopted differ across both time and space.

Political Use of Religion

Finally it needs to be emphasised that politico-religious parties and militant groups who present their agendas in a religious idiom and project themselves as the only true mantle bearers of Islam are *not* religious movements. These are political movements aiming to gain political power at the community, national or international level. In this power game, a major strategy is to monopolise the religious discourse and impose this as the only legitimate framework for all political and social discourse. This is similar to instances of ethnic-national collectivities formulated in such dichotomous terms that they preclude both dissent and pluralism from within.[12] These actors control people by silencing all dissenting voices, including other religious voices. They do so by blackmailing people into silence by equating any dissent to their proposals with an opposition – even betrayal – of people's religion and faith, and by crushing dissent through violence including against their own community.

From South Asia I can categorically state that the political use of religion is not confined to the Muslim world. I see this as part of a wider global challenge. This is the challenge posed by identity based politics replacing ideological political agendas. Unlike ideological agendas that aim to change underlying structures and systems, identity politics simply promise a better deal for a particular group – defined by religion, ethnicity or language – but only if you give up your agency and let them appropriate your voice, and only if you divest yourself of all other markers of identity, and only if you buy into the proposition that your interests are threatened by other identity-based groups.

Conclusion

In conclusion let me reiterate that to really eliminate violence against women, in my view we need to replace the culture of violence by a culture of peace, starting from the very earliest socialisation that defines cultural notions of gender as well as acceptable and unacceptable practices, acts, and behaviours. What does this mean in terms of due diligence on the part of the state?

At the very least, due diligence should imply that the state provides equal opportunities to different voices in society to articulate their opinions. It should mean actively searching for and listening to the voices of subaltern cultures and opinions within the minorities, and ensuring women's representation.

It also means that just enacting laws to address and prevent violence against women, though necessary, is never going to be enough. Legal provisions need to be accompanied by measures to overturn the culture of violence promoted in news and entertainment media as well as in textbooks. Impunity for acts of vio-

12 Alund (1999), see note 10 above, 147–161.

lence against women rests on the cultural outlook of people in society at large and the cultural perceptions of state agents. Therefore in order to eliminate impunity, all state agents, especially those engaged in any aspect of the justice system, must be sensitised and oriented to uphold the right of women (and other citizens) to be free of violence. In countries like ours where legal systems are challenged by informal dispute resolution forums (some traditional, some new), the state needs to take steps to ensure that informal forums are not allowed to pass rulings and/or take any actions that deny women their legal rights, respect or dignity. After all, these are rights and entitlements enshrined in many constitutions and fall under the responsibility of the state. It would be naïve, however, to expect that the state shall automatically take these steps since those with decision-making powers tend to be precisely those people who benefit from the existing power dynamics, economic structures and political processes. Consequently, the state will only exercise due diligence when enough of a groundswell has been created in society by political and civil society actors.

Controlling Women's Sexuality, Sustaining Dominant Culture(s), Legitimising Gender-Based Violence: The Case for Due Diligence

Susana T. Fried

Introduction: Gender, Culture and Sexuality

> *'One night, not so long ago, a mother was beating her daughter. She was placed in a sack, hung from the ceiling, and beaten by a broom again and again. On other occasions, the daughter was made to kneel on painful rocks or dry mung beans, arms stretched out, both hands holding glasses of water, and told to hold that position for hours on end unless she wanted to be mercilessly beaten again. When she was not beaten, she was forced to do manual domestic labor, often doing 'traditional' male chores like fixing broken pipes or standing near the front door all night long. All this, simply because she is a lesbian.'*

This story comes from a 2004 report on violence against lesbians in the Philippines by Lesbian Advocates Philippines (LeAP!).[1] The abuses it describes could have taken place in nearly any country of the world where countless women face discrimination at work, torture by police and other state officials, rape by male family members, and subject to other forms of violence and inhumane treatment because of their actual and/or perceived sexual orientation and gender expression.[2] While the story above exemplifies some of the brutal reprisals faced by those whose sexuality and/or gender expression transgress cultural standards of appropriate femininity and masculinity – *heteronormativity*[3] – it also represents an activist effort by LeAP! to demand that governments act with due diligence to prevent such violations and to promote and protect human rights.

1 Lesbian Advocates Philippines (LeAP!) Inc., *Unmasked: Faces of Discrimination against Lesbians in the Philippines* (LeAP! 2004), 6.

2 The testimonials also point to the complexity with which we need to understand violence against women – in this case, both the perpetrator and the victim are women.

3 *Heteronormativity* refers to the normative social construction of gender, based on the pairing of male/female, man/woman, husband/wife, among the series of oppositions taken to be 'normal' and 'natural', and includes a variety of forms of coercive and/or compulsory heterosexuality.

C. Benninger-Budel ed., Due Diligence and Its Application to Protect Women from Violence
© *Koninklijke Brill NV. Printed in The Netherlands.* ISBN *978 90 04 16293 8. pp. 249-262*

In this chapter, I argue that accountability using the due diligence standard is a way to make clear that governments are responsible to address and prevent gender-based violence perpetrated in the name of culture, and violence that takes place in the context of family and community. This is particularly important since culture is often used to justify violence against women. The essay emphasises the persistent use of violence to control women's (and men's) sexuality, and the brutal reprisals meted out to gender transgressors and sexual outlaws (persons whose sexual and gender identity and expression do not conform to social and cultural standards of appropriate femininity and masculinity).

The use of the due diligence standard is important since many states are complicit in such violations – either by turning a blind eye to violence against women perpetrated by 'non-state actors'[4] or by maintaining laws and policies that validate or encode cultural excuses for violence against women and girls. As such, these states have failed to follow the standard of due diligence to address violence against women. As the UN Special Rapporteur on violence against women, its causes and consequences, has commented:

> 'Under the due diligence obligation, States have a duty to take positive action to prevent and protect women from violence, punish perpetuators of violent acts and compensate victims of violence. However, the application of the due diligence standard, to date, has tended to be State-centric and limited to responding to violence when it occurs, largely neglecting the obligation to prevent and compensate and the responsibility of non-State actors.'[5]

The due diligence standard demands a nuanced analysis of gender-based violence, where the most common pattern is of a male perpetrator and female victims, but also other scenarios occur, like the one quoted at the outset of this article, where women may be perpetrators of violence, where women refuse the 'victim' identity, or where men are victims. While the due diligence standard is still being elaborated in human rights jurisprudence, governments' obligation to it has been affirmed in a number of consensus documents, including the UN Declaration on the Elimination of Violence against Women, adopted by the UN General Assembly in 1993.[6] Increasingly, advocates for the human rights of women are seeking

---

4 The category of 'non-state' actors is broad and diverse, encompassing family members, private educational institutions, religious groupings, businesses and other private sector institutions, for example. For more information about non-state actors and human rights, see Amnesty International, 2004, *It's in Our Hands: Stop Violence against Women* (AI Doc: ACT 77/003/2004).

5 Yakın Ertürk, Report of the UN Special Rapporteur on violence against women, its causes and consequences, *The Due Diligence Standard as a Tool for the Elimination of Violence against Women,* UN Doc. E/CN.4/2006/61, 20 January 2006.

6 Article 4 of the UN Declaration on the Elimination of Violence against Women states that 'States should condemn violence against women and should not invoke any custom, tradition or religious consideration to avoid their obligations with respect to its

greater specificity to the meaning of due diligence and the substantive and procedural obligations it entails. This essay is part of that collective endeavour.

Controlling Women's Sexuality: Using Dominant Culture(s) to Legitimise Gender-Based Violence

As work on gender-based violence moves through the first decade of the 21st century, efforts to demand and defend the human rights of women – especially by women's rights activists – are taking shape in every country and community in the world. As this work proceeds, it is important to give a focus to the persistent and powerful impact of persecution of women within their families and communities. Attacks against women are justified in the name of 'culture' (or as a colleague recently put it, by the custodians of resistance to the human rights of women[7]). At the same time, 'culture' is defined in terms articulated by those in power who seek to sustain and retain it. As Farida Shaheed of Shirkat Gah in Pakistan has noted, those in power define themselves as the norm, or the representation of what it means to be human (i.e., male, representing the majority group or the group in power, etc.) and everyone else is somehow a little less human, where being a little less human becomes a justification for culturally specific forms of violence.[8] Or, as Susie Jolly notes in her discussion of gender, culture and the development industry, dominant cultures and the norms they express (and enforce) are maintained in the interests of those who dominate. In such circumstances,

> 'Respecting local "culture" can mean "respecting hierarchies". What is "local" is not sealed off from influences from elsewhere, nor is it insulated from change over time. Nor is "local culture" a single body of beliefs and practices that everyone agrees with....[W]ithin families, communities and nations, there are many different and even contradictory ideas of what is "normal", and that these ideas change over time, so there is a choice to be made in deciding which of the "local" cultures to respect and ally with.'[9]

---

elimination. States should pursue by all appropriate means and without delay a policy of eliminating violence against women and, to this end, should: (c) Exercise due diligence to prevent, investigate and, in accordance with national legislation, punish acts of violence against women, whether those acts are perpetrated by the State or by private persons.' See at http://www.unhchr.ch/huridocda/huridoca.nsf/(Symbol)/A.RES.48.104.En?Opendocument.

7 Personal communication, October 2006, name withheld.

8 Farida Shaheed, 'Violence Legitimized with Arguments of "Culture"' (panel presentation at the Symposium *Due Diligence: The Responsibility of the State for the Human Rights of Women*, held 21–23 September 2005, Bern, Switzerland). See generally her contribution 'Violence against Women Legitimised by Arguments of "Culture" – Thoughts from a Pakistani Perspective', in this book.

9 Susie Jolly, in *Gender and Development InBrief*, Issue 10: Culture, 2002, http://www.bridge.ids.ac.uk/dgb10.html.

A growing accumulation of human rights documentation confirms the devastation that patrolling the boundaries of 'culture' has wrought, especially but not solely, on women.[10] Women who challenge these standards may be locked up in their homes, held in so-called 'protective custody', incarcerated in psychiatric institutions, forced into marriage and forced into pregnancy among a host of other abuses. Their offices are attacked, their organisations are tainted in the media, and their family members are refused jobs or terrorised. Take, for example, the case of Elena Urlaeva, who has dared to speak out about the rights of citizens of Uzbekistan. In an action alert about her case, Human Rights First[11] notes that the violence perpetrated against her – forced psychiatric treatment – is often targeted toward women:

> 'Elena Urlaeva, a well-known rights activist and member of the Human Rights Society of Uzbekistan, was detained by security agents on August 27, 2005, while distributing flyers at a peaceful protest in Tashkent, Uzbekistan. Authorities forcibly committed her to a psychiatric hospital – a Soviet-era technique meant to silence dissidents that is used in present day Uzbekistan, particularly against female activists.'[12]

Individuals who are from and/or work for the rights of socially marginalised communities – immigrants, racial/ethnic minorities, lesbian, gay, bisexual and transgender persons, among others – are at an even greater risk for their transgressions of 'cultural' standards.[13] Moreover, when they do seek justice through the police, all too often their charges are met with disinterest, complicity or direct violence by the authorities who are charged with a duty to protect them.

'Sexuality-baiting' is a particularly vicious form of attack. As Cynthia Rothschild has described, 'sexuality-baiting' includes the practices of manipulating ideas or prejudices about sexuality to intimidate, humiliate, embarrass or stifle the work of women who are human rights defenders.'[14] This rhetorical tactic has long been

10 See, in particular, *Challenging Fundamentalisms: A Web Resource for Women's Human Rights* at www.whrnet.org and various of the work produced by Women Living Under Muslim Laws at www.wluml.org.

11 Human Rights First is an international human rights organisation based in the US.

12 Human Rights First, 'Stop Psychiatric Abuse of Women Activists in Uzbekistan', issued 14 September 2005, http://www.humanrightsfirst.org/defenders/hrd_uzbekistan/alert091405_urlaeva.htm (accessed 10 November 2006).

13 See, for example, Amnesty International, *It's In Our Hands: Stop Violence against Women*, AI Index: ACT/77/001/2004; UNIFEM, *Not a Minute More: Ending Violence against Women* (2003), http://www.unifem.org/attachments/products/299_book_eng_01.pdf along with a wide variety of other reports from Amnesty International, Human Rights Watch, the Women's Learning Partnership, Women Living Under Muslim Laws, among others.

14 See Cynthia Rothschild, *Written Out: How Sexuality is Used to Attack Women's Organizing* 'International Gay and Lesbian Human Rights Commission and the Center for Women's Global Leadership, 2005' for an analysis and discussion of lesbian-baiting.

a staple of family and community attacks against women who transgress cultural standards of appropriate femininity. In some contexts, any discussion of 'gender', 'feminism' or 'sexual rights' is taken as evidence of the speaker's 'deviant' sexuality, such as being divorced, marrying against the wishes of the family, refusing to marry or choosing a partner of the same sex. While such charges may be overt or more subtly articulated, such threats are woven into the fabric of daily life, where the simplest of activities can be fraught with risks of exposure and sources of potential humiliation.

Women's sexuality is regulated in all communities and maintained through particular legal responses, strict constraints or even severe punishment and justified as securing social, economic and cultural norms.[15] These include forced marriages and pregnancy, 'corrective rape', so-called 'honour killings', or the perpetuation of beliefs that women, and particularly married women, are always available for sex – with or without their consent.[16] Restraint, control, and punishment – and related coercions – can function in both formal and informal ways, through what a number of authors refer to as the 'honour/shame' complex. The 'honour/shame' complex refers to the fact that in many communities women's chastity is seen to define the honour of their family and community. Any act that challenge a woman's chastity – either through violence perpetrated against her or of her own will – is seen to humiliate the men of her family.[17] It is considered that the men in her family either were unable to protect her, in the case of sexual violence, or they were unable to control her. Whatever the form, this regulation affects not only the sexual and reproductive rights of women but also women's ability to enjoy the full range of human rights, including freedom of movement, their right to information and education and their right to health.

Those who engage in same-sex practices are often the first to be targeted by organised efforts to consolidate or secure power and to maintain control over 'culture' and community. In such cases, it may quickly become clear that the concept of 'dangerous' or 'non-conforming' sexuality can stretch to encompass any act(s) that a government sees as threatening to its power, including single women, men who are not 'masculine enough,' unmarried opposite sex couples and others. Any expression of identity or divergence from cultural norms that require that the expression of gender neatly correspond to biological sex and/or heterosexuality can cause fear and hatred leading to actual violence, threats of violence and psychological harm. Rooted in stereotypes stemming from rigid conceptions

15 Some of the ideas in this paragraph were developed in collaboration with Alice Miller, in a joint submission we made to the UN Special Rapporteur on violence against women in 2001.

16 Susana Fried, Ali Miller, and Cynthia Rothschild, *Lesbians, Gender and Human Rights Violations*, available through Amnesty International at http://www.amnestyusa.org/women/lesbians.html.

17 Lama Abu-Odeh, 'Crimes of Honor and the Construction of Gender in Arab Societies', in *Women and Sexuality in Muslim Societies*, ed. Pinar Ilkkaracan, 363–380 (Istanbul: Women for Women's Human Rights, 2000).

of masculinity and femininity, this violence occurs on many levels ranging from daily torment and harassment in schools to hate-driven murder. The 2005 report of the UN Special Rapporteur on violence against women included information about lesbian women 'being targeted for rape, specifically because of their sexual orientation in order for the aggressor to 'prove the [victim's] womanhood'.[18]

Men who refuse to conform to gender norms of masculinity may also find themselves targeted for violence, as indicated by the persistent harassment and abuse of *metis* (cross-dressing men) reported by the Blue Diamond Society in Kathmandu, Nepal. As former UN Special Rapporteur on violence against women Radhika Coomaraswamy wrote in her 2002 report, women who 'transgress the boundaries of appropriate sexual behaviour', including women who have sex outside marriage, request divorce, choose their own husbands, or choose women as sexual partners, are 'subject to direct violence of the most horrific kind' and can be 'punished severely'.[19] She further wrote that '[t]he killing of women with impunity for these transgressions is perhaps the most overt example of the brutal control of female sexuality'.[20] To a large extent, such violence is justified by family and community in the name of 'protecting their culture'.

Claims of tradition or culture serve to naturalise the notion that women who 'stray' are justifiably punished, first by their family and then by the state standing in for patriarchal authority. Women's agency counts for little, as do girls' and women's claims to liberty or freedom of expression, association, movement and bodily integrity. Yet, even though a significant amount of gender-based violence is justified in the name of culture and tradition (especially when it is paired with controlling women's sexuality), culture is not monolithic, static or immutable. Rather, it is more marked by fluidity and change. As Asma Mohamed Abdel Halim recounts:

> 'traditions are highly sacrosanct and untouchable where women are concerned. Still, I have seen traditions change during my lifetime. The change was so easy and smooth when the men took the initiative. Change, however, requires a lot of pain and hard work when it is initiated by women.'[21]

18 Yakın Ertürk, Report of the Special Rapporteur on violence against women, its causes and consequences, *Intersections of Violence against Women and HIV/AIDS*, UN Doc. E/CN.4/2005/72, 17 January 2005, para. 27.

19 Radhika Coomaraswamy, Report of the UN Special Rapporteur on violence against women, its causes and consequences, *Cultural Practices in the Family that Are Violent Towards Women*, UN Doc. E/CN.4/2002/83, 31 January 2002, paras. 99 and 100.

20 Ibid., para. 100.

21 Asma Mohamed Abdel Halim, 'Tools of Oppression', in *Gender Violence and Women's Human Rights in Africa*, 22 (New Jersey: Center for Women's Global Leadership, 1994).

Moreover, cultures are often (if not always) internally contested. The coherence of 'culture' is often more apparent than real – or as human rights scholar Abdullah An-Na'im puts it, '[o]ne of the apparent paradoxes of culture is the way it combines stability with dynamic continuous change.'[22]

Although the appeal to culture, religion, tradition and customary law can be used to justify human rights violations that take place through the regulation of women's and men's sexuality,[23] for many, they are also sources of strength, community and creativity. Activists in many countries are in the process of adapting cultural mechanisms to combat violence against women. For example, activists in communities as diverse as Bangladesh and Canada's Yukon Territory have adapted traditional systems of local justice, through mediation and conflict resolution, to address domestic violence.[24]

Invoking Due Diligence to Demand Action

The complexity of 'culture' in the context of advancing women's human rights is one of the most significant reasons why it is crucial to invoke and elaborate the due diligence standard, and then hold governments accountable to exercising it. Marital rape, crimes of passion, child marriage, forced marriage, incest and other forms of violence are noted as practices that deny women's sexual rights – and ones for which governments bear responsibility for acting to prevent and address. However, while the state is clearly responsible for violations perpetrated by government authorities or those acting within its auspices, principles of state accountability also concerns accountability for acts perpetrated by non-state actors. At times, the state is responsible for direct abuses, but it is also responsible for failing to respond to abuses by non-state actors – either through tacit approval or through inadequate mechanisms of justice.

One of the ways to explain the nature of a state's human rights obligations is the trio – *respect, protect* and *fulfil*: first, states are required to *respect* rights. That is, government officials, or those acting with the authorisation of the state, must not commit human rights abuses, such as arbitrary arrest and detention; physical, verbal and sexual abuse (which may be considered to be torture or inhuman or degrading treatment and punishment); along with unwarranted restric-

22 Abdullahi Ahmed An-Na'im, 'Toward a Cross-Cultural Approach to Defining International Standards of Human Rights: The Meaning of Cruel, Inhuman, or Degrading Treatment or Punishment', in *Human Rights in Cross-Cultural Perspectives: A Quest for Consensus*, ed. Abdullahi Ahmed An-Na'im, 27 (Philadelphia: University of Pennsylvania Press, 1995).

23 Reprisals against gay men can be particularly severe. Punishments can include stoning, beatings, torture and death. For more information, see Amnesty International, *Crimes of Hate, Conspiracy of Silence: Torture and Ill-Treatment Based on Sexual Identity* (London: Amnesty International Publications, 2000).

24 *Population Reports*, Series L, Number 11 (Takoma Park, MD: Center for Health and Gender Equity), 10.

tions on freedom of movement, association, and expressions. They must respect the human rights of all members of society, even those who are from communities that are, denigrated, deemed dangerous and therefore discriminated against – like sex worker rights activists, HIV/AIDS workers (especially activists who are themselves HIV positive), and lesbian, gay, bisexual and transgender (LGBT) activists, among others.

States are also required to take effective steps to end human rights abuses. Under this obligation, states must not only ensure that their agents don't violate rights – they must also work meticulously to prevent and punish such acts by private actors – as a means of protecting rights. In order to adequately *protect* rights, the government and those acting on its behalf must take steps to prevent other individuals or groups (including private enterprises and corporations) from violating human rights. When police or prosecutors deal with domestic violence as a private or family matter, or consider that the victim must have 'asked for it' and, as a result, allow impunity for the perpetrators, the state has failed to protect the human rights of victims of domestic violence. For example, in their report 'Documenting Human Rights Violations by Non-State Actors: Activist Strategies from Muslim Communities', Bauer and Helie provide the following illustration:

> 'While the defence of honour is not permitted, *per se*, under the law in a number of Western countries, there remains a tendency on the part of some members of the police, of prosecutors and of judges to accept the defence of 'provocation'. By this reasoning, the woman is, essentially, the cause of her own demise because of 'provocative' behaviour of one kind or another. While the defence does not necessarily lead to acquittal in cases of marital rape or spouse murder it does produce reduced sentences. In October 1999, a judge in Texas (United States) sentenced a husband to four months in prison "for murdering his wife and wounding her longtime lover in front of their 10-year-old son".'[25]

So, for example, when states fail to protect women human rights defenders from death sentences imposed on them by extremist groups in the name of 'culture', or when they allow such groups to terrorise women's rights activists with impunity, they have failed in their obligation to protect rights.

The duty to *fulfil* rights requires that the government ensures an infrastructure exists that enables people, including women and women's human rights defenders, to exercise and enjoy their rights to the fullest possible extent. When states fail to act in a persistent and committed fashion to prevent human rights violations, they can be held responsible for the violation. For example, even while some governments have criminalised gender-based violence, few have put sufficient resources and mechanisms in place to make their legislation meaningful. In these cases the state has failed to fulfil the rights of their citizens to be free

25 Jan Bauer and Anissa Helie, *Documenting Human Rights Violations by Non-State Actors: Activist Strategies from Muslim Communities* (Montreal: Rights and Democracy, 2005), 35.

from violence and discrimination.[26] Indeed, the due diligence standard requires that states take effective steps to end human rights abuses. Under this obligation, states must not only ensure that their agents do not violate rights, but they must also work meticulously to prevent and punish such acts by private actors.

The case of so-called honour crimes helps to make these different forms of state responsibility – or the state's failure to act with due diligence – a bit more concrete. In far too many cases, states respond differently to violence against women conducted in the name of 'honour' and violence against women committed by strangers. Impunity for crimes and the differential in state intervention into situations of so-called honour crimes (as opposed to other forms of physical, psychological and sexual abuse) varies among groups and countries depending on the relevant cultural norms. In a comparison, for example, of penal codes and jurisprudence across a number of Arab states, with regard to so-called 'honour' crimes, Abu-Odeh finds two primary areas of variation: first is the question of in which situations can the claim of 'honour' be made (i.e., in some cases it can be applied only in cases of adultery). Second, there are also differences in who can benefit from the excuse used to justify the killing – the husband only, or the husband, the son, the father and the brother.[27] Thus, while the family is always implicated, the specific individuals who are empowered by law to use the 'excuse' depend on the particular legal context.

In each case, the state is implicated. In those cases where the state has crafted formal legal exemptions or reduced sentences for family-member homicides invoking 'honour' concepts,[28] the state has failed in its duty to respect as well as to protect rights. In other cases, the failure to investigate, prosecute or punish (equally applied across ethnic or other cultural differences) indicates a failure to

26 Convention on the Elimination of All Forms of Discrimination against Women, General Recommendation no. 19, Violence against Women, (eleventh session, 1992), at http://www.un.org/womenwatch/daw/cedaw/recommendations/index.html, Article 1 states that '[g]ender-based violence is a form of discrimination that seriously inhibits women's ability to enjoy rights and freedoms on a basis of equality with men.' Article 6 further explains that '[t]he definition of discrimination includes gender-based violence, that is, violence that is directed against a woman because she is a woman or that affects women disproportionately. It includes acts that inflict physical, mental or sexual harm or suffering, threats of such acts, coercion and other deprivations of liberty. Gender-based violence may breach specific provisions of the Convention, regardless of whether those provisions expressly mention violence.'

27 Abu-Odeh (2000), see note 17 above, 365.

28 So-called honour crimes are related to but distinct from other gendered honour systems in criminal law: for example, the 'defense of honour' crimes documented by Human Rights Watch in Brazil, wherein husbands or boyfriends benefited from a judicial doctrine reducing the seriousness with which the crime was considered when the wife/girlfriend was alleged to be sexually active outside the relationship. In these cases, the claim resides in the sexually betrayed husband/lover, not in the natal or marital family; the regulation of sexuality focused on the interpersonal claims of sexual honor as between intimates, not the familial claim to filial chastity.

pursue state obligations because protection is not adequately implemented. One can also point to situations where states ban so-called honour crimes but fail to meet the due diligence standard because they ignore incidences, fail to vigorously prosecute, or fail to proactively educate citizens about the illegality of these practices.

If a state fails to act diligently to prevent and address human rights violations it can be held responsible for the violation. As described elsewhere in this volume, this is the crux of the standard of due diligence.[29] While it does not absolve the actual perpetrators from being prosecuted and punished for the initial acts of violence, it holds that complicity, acquiescence and omission constitute a form of responsibility on the part of the state. In elaborating the due diligence standard, this means that states prevent, investigate and punish acts that impair any of the rights recognised under international human rights law even if these acts are perpetrated by non-state actors (e.g., families, communities, religious institutions, private academic institutions). In addition, the state must provide access to remedy, attempt to restore the right violated and provide reparation or compensation for damages incurred.[30] And, when it fails to do so, it has itself engaged in a violation of human rights.

It is important to remember, however, that access to remedy is always contingent on access to resources, and the ability to speak out publicly or pursue action through the criminal justice system. One's gender, race, class, sexuality, gender identity, and status as migrant or indigenous all matter. Those who come from socially marginalised groups often find their access to remedies blocked by racism, sexism, xenophobia, homophobia and other forms of intolerance. Activists who work at the margins of so-called respectability may also find it difficult to secure access to remedies, because they are blamed for the violations against them. In this context, states have the obligation to ensure that multiple axes of identity do not produce enhanced discrimination. The concept of *intersectionality* captures an understanding of the interplay of gender, race, ethnicity, health status, rural or urban location, and other such characteristics as mutually constituted, not as additive. As a result, the notion of intersectionality suggests that understanding human rights violations requires grappling with the various aspects of identity that bring risk and targeting for violence and violations. The obligation to protect all individuals, regardless of gender, race, ethnicity, class, sexuality, etc., is central to the definition of discrimination in most international human rights treaties as well as to invoking the standard of due diligence to ensure the enjoyment of human rights. As Amnesty International has noted:

29 See generally, Joanna Bourke-Martignoni, 'The History and Development of the Due Diligence Standard in International Law and Its Role in the Protection of Women against Violence', in this book.

30 The doctrine of *due diligence* was set out in Velásquez Rodríguez, Judgement of 29 July 1988, Inter-American Court of Human Rights, Series C, no. 4, paras. 174–175. See http://www1.umn.edu/humanrts/iachr/b_11_12d.htm.

> 'Discriminatory practices and policies have tremendous consequences for targeted groups not only in terms of the nature of their ill-treatment by government agents or society at large, but also in terms of their access to redress and equal protection under the law. Discrimination also often leads to a lack of official action, such as investigations into alleged abuses, which further reinforces impunity.'[31]

A case from the same Amnesty report offers a useful illustration of how state actors' failure to act with due diligence results in impunity for the perpetrators of violence in the community in the specific context of discrimination and violence based on sexual and gender identity:

> 'In Los Angeles, three women attacked an immigrant transgender woman working as a street vendor. The women allegedly surrounded her and began verbally abusing her and threatening her because they did not want her in the neighborhood. When bystanders called the police, the officers reportedly responded, "If they kill her, call us".'[32]

Conclusion: Contesting Violence, Demanding Diligence, Seeking Sexual Rights

Gender-based violence is culturally (i.e., geographically, temporally and locationally) specific, but the standards to guide governments in acting with due diligence and their duty to address gender-based violence is encompassed by the universality of human rights. In this sense, it is more accurate to say that gender-based violence is not so much 'culturally specific' but that its manifestations are anchored in the local realities of gender and sexuality.

Family, kinship-based and community-sponsored crimes serve to patrol the borders of 'culturally appropriate female behaviour' and especially appropriate (hetero)sexuality and female gender expression. States often support these cultural standards, but with differing degrees of alignment: dominant cultural norms about heterosexual, procreative sexuality may be embedded in the legal structure and the state's administrative and policy apparatus in highly visible and more subtle ways. Less dominant cultural practices may not be enshrined in national law and policy, but, in exchange for political accommodation, or as vestiges of colonialist bargains, male elites in minority cultures and religions may succeed in having gendered, male-privileging sexual/marital practices enshrined in personal status laws applicable to that group only.[33] In practice, the objection to women's sexual agency (both the power to say yes, and the power to say no to sex) is re-

31 Amnesty International USA, *Stonewalled: Police Abuse and Misconduct Against Lesbian, Gay, Bisexual and Transgender People in the U.S.* (AI Index: AMR 51/122/2005), 2.

32 Ibid., *SUMMARY,* http://www.amnestyusa.org/outfront/document.do?id=ENGUS20050922002.

33 See the Shah Bano case in Radhika Coomaraswamy, 'To Bellow Like a Cow: Women, Ethnicity, and the Discourse of Rights', in *Human Rights of Women: National and In-*

inscribed through the creation of a multicultural taboo, an unchanging tradition and a legal norm.

In this context, it is useful to consider the emerging concepts of sexual rights and bodily integrity. While there is no single globally agreed definition of sexual rights, there are a number of principles, generally comprising the right of each person to experience her/his sexuality freely, fully and consensually, and with and understanding of sexuality as a realm of experience encompassing sexual orientation, gender identity, sexual and gender expression, desire, pleasure and sexual practices. 'Sexual rights' is now emerging as a term used in the international women's health and women's human rights movements. However, the issues considered under the rubric of sexual rights have a long history in women's (and men's) resistance to the regulation of sexuality.[34]

Claims to sexual rights are claims to a range of protections connected to identities, expressions and practices around gender and sexuality. It includes both positive rights to dignity, autonomy over one's body and sexual life, to privacy (among consenting adults), free expression, assembly, liberty and physical integrity. It also encompasses traditional 'negative' rights such as the right to be free from discrimination, torture, violence and coercion on the basis of sexual orientation, and/or gender identity and expression. Claims to sexual rights are what one activist calls 'the embodiment of an old and general goal: on the one hand, the achievement of substantive equality for all persons; on the other hand, the extension of protections for human freedom and dignity to include the most vulnerable groups, and to publicize and prevent even the least visible and most easily concealed abuses and violations.'[35]

Sexual rights frameworks attempt to speak to the rights of bodily integrity and sexual and gender autonomy and expression, and they can engender advocacy strategies that embrace a diverse community of actors and targets of human rights abuses. Working across these 'borders' whether within or across countries and/or in international arenas necessitates that we build organising strategies that take into account geographically and historically specific concepts of sexuality and gender. This cross border work must give deference to local activists' preferred ways of thinking of and expressing gender which falls outside social and cultural norms; it requires modes of organising that do not reify gender binaries.

In this vein, Sonia Corrêa and Richard Parker comment that the struggle for sexual rights in its diverse and multiple forms 'is among the most important forc-

ternational Perspectives, ed. Rebecca Cook, 39–57 (Philadelphia: University of Pennsylvania Press, 1994).

34 For a discussion about this history, see Susana T. Fried and Ilana Landsberg-Lewis, 'Sexual Rights: From Concept to Strategy', in *Women's Human Rights Reference Guide*, ed. Kelly D. Askin and Dorean M. Koenig, 91–122 (New York: Transnational Press, 2000).

35 Human Rights Watch and International Gay and Lesbian Human Rights Commission, 'Sexual Orientation, Gender Identity and the Human Rights Mechanisms of the United Nations: Examples and Approaches' (unpublished, 2005).

es of change in contemporary society, with key contributions to broader debates related to social development and human security in the contemporary world.'[36] They argue that on a global level, sexuality has become 'a key contested domain or field of struggle [in which] sexuality and sexualities are being reformulated and reframed around the globe today. Highly 'modern' sexualities are being constructed in societies throughout the world, just as diverse forms of fundamentalism and violence have been unleashed in response to such changes.'[37] As a result, they argue, sexuality is a key locus of political and social contestation and conflict, such that '[c]oncrete examples of these struggles are almost endless....'[38]

Thus, a sexual rights framework also creates a space for cross-movement organising, which is crucial for advancing the human rights of all people who are subject to discrimination on the basis of their actual or perceived sexual orientation – for *hijras*[39] in India who have no right to housing, for *metis* in Nepal who are repeatedly abused by the police and arbitrarily arrested and detained, for *travestis*[40] in Argentina who face daily discrimination in the workplace, for *baklas*[41] in the Philippines who don't have access to accurate health information, for butch[42] women in Guatemala who are targeted for rape, for a transgender person in the US who is thrown into jail because she is assumed to be a prostitute or denied a passport because her gender expression doesn't match the sex on her identity documents, or for any woman anywhere who is ridiculed and persecuted by her family, the police and other community members for presuming that she has the right to live free from violence.

In summary, the protection of 'culture' is a pervasive excuse for violence against women. And a significant amount of this violence is perpetrated by non-state actors – in other words, family or community members, in particular. As illustrated, the obligation to respect, protect and fulfil rights requires that states act to address violations perpetrated by family and community members. In particular, the standard of due diligence requires that the state must consider the steps to be taken at all levels – legislative, policy, administrative, service provision

36 Sonia Corrêa and Richard Parker, 'Sexuality, Human Rights, and Demographic Thinking: Connections and Disjunctions in a Changing World,' *Sexuality Research and Social Policy* 1, no. 1 (2004): 19.

37 Ibid.

38 Ibid.

39 *Hijra* communities have existed in India for more than 4000 years. They claim a sacred space and a third gender status and tend to be associated today with transgender communities.

40 *Travesti* is a Latin American term used to refer to males who, often at very young age, adopt female names, clothing styles, hairstyles, and linguistic pronouns.

41 *Bakla* is a Tagalog term used in the Philippines to refer to men who present themselves with real or perceived manifestations of femininity, including cross-dressing and/or sexual or emotional attraction for an individual of the same sex.

42 *Butch* women either present themselves as or are perceived to be more 'masculine' than the prevailing standard of femininity for women in a particular community.

and educative – that will make their obligation to end violence against women meaningful.

Violence in Armed Conflict

Violence against Women in Armed Conflict

Theodor Winkler

Violence against Women Occurs in Peacetime, in Armed Conflict, and after Conflict

Women live in a world that is dominated by male violence, from conception until death. Nobel Prize laureate Amartya Sen estimated in 2003 that there were 101 million 'missing women' worldwide.[1] The word 'missing' is here a euphemism for being killed. Women are killed in gender-selective abortion and infanticide, and by discrimination in access to food and medicine. They are burned in so-called kitchen accidents and in acid attacks, and killed within their homes. Globally, one in four women suffers sexual abuse by an intimate partner in their lifetime; 40 to 70 percent of female murder victims are killed by their husbands or boyfriends.[2] Hundreds of thousands of women and girls are bought and sold into prostitution each year, or subjected to sexual violence in schools, workplaces, and health care institutions.[3]

Violence against women in conflict situations should be understood as part of a *continuum of violence* experienced by women and girls, in times of relative peace, through conflict into post-conflict situations, and as taking place within a broader context of disadvantage and discrimination.[4] Responses to violence

---

1 Amartya Sen, 'Missing Women – Revisited', *British Medical Journal* 327 (December 2003): 1297–1298.

2 World Health Organisation, *Global Campaign for Violence Prevention*, at http://www.who.int/violence_injury_prevention/violence/global_campaign/en/index.html (last visited 31 July 2006).

3 Ibid.

4 The Geneva Centre for the Democratic Control of Armed Forces (DCAF) has published a comprehensive study of violence against women, Marie Vlachová and Lea Biason ed., *Women in an Insecure World: Violence against Women – Facts, Figures and Analysis* (Geneva, 2005), at http://www.dcaf.ch/women/bk_vlachova_biason_women.cfm?navsub1=11&navsub2=3&nav1=3 (last visited 31 July 2006). DCAF

C. Benninger-Budel ed., Due Diligence and Its Application to Protect Women from Violence
 ISBN 978 90 04 16293 8. pp. 265-271

against women must stop the violence, punish the perpetrators and assist and compensate the victims, but should also seek to transform women's inequality into empowerment. Further, responses to violence against women must grapple with the fact that these crimes are *almost always* perpetrated by men. Men must be a part of the response. It follows that obligations of due diligence on the part of the state should not be interpreted narrowly. Protecting women and girls from violence requires security services and governance structures that are participatory and democratic, and that actively promote women's security and empowerment.

During Armed Conflict a State's Capacity to Exercise Due Diligence Is Weak

During armed conflicts, existing inequalities and patterns of discrimination tend to be exacerbated. Whilst the impact of armed conflict on women differs between contexts and between individual women, it is possible to identify common characteristics: widespread violence, and the extreme burden which war places on women to ensure their own survival, and the care of children and the elderly. During conflict, women and girls are particularly vulnerable to sexual exploitation and abuse. The figures are shocking: 20,000 to 50,000 women were raped in the war in Bosnia-Herzegovina;[5] 250,000 to 400,000 Rwandan women were raped in the 1994 genocide;[6] 23,000 to 45,600 women were raped in Kosovo between August 1998 and August 1999;[7] 50 percent of women in Sierra Leone,[8] and 70 percent of women in Liberia[9] were subjected to sexual violence in the conflicts there. Research with rape survivors in the Democratic Republic of Congo be-

promotes good governance and reform of the security sector. The Centre conducts research on good practices, encourages the development of appropriate norms at the national and international levels, makes policy recommendations and provides in-country advice and assistance programmes. DCAF's partners include governments, parliaments, civil society, international organisations and the range of security sector actors such as police, judiciary, intelligence agencies, border security services and the military.

5 Quoted on http://www.irinnews.org/webspecials/GBV/default.asp (last visited 22 August 2006).

6 International Red Cross Report (2002), quoted in: Amnesty International, *Making Violence against Women Count: Facts and Figures – a Summary*, 3 May 2004, at http://news.amnesty.org/index/ENGACT770342004 (last visited 22 August 2006).

7 Michelle Hynes and Barbara Lopes Cardozo, 'Sexual Violence against Refugee Women', *Journal of Women's Health & Gender-Based Medicine* 9, no. 8 (2000): 819–823.

8 During her visit to Sierra Leone in August 2001, the UN Special Rapporteur on violence against women, its causes and consequences, Radhika Coomaraswamy, found that 72 percent of Sierra Leonean women had experienced human rights abuses and over 50 percent had been victims of sexual violence, http://www.womenwarpeace.org/sierra_leone/sierra_leone.htm.

9 Amnesty International, *Liberia: No impunity for Rape – A Crime against Humanity and a War Crime*, December 2004, at http://web.amnesty.org/library/Index/ENGAFR340172004?open&of=ENG-LBR (last visited 22 August 2006).

tween 1996 and 2003 documented that 79.7 percent of victims of sexual violence had been raped by more than one attacker: up to twenty men.[10] These are broad estimates, just a shadow of the hundreds of thousands of women raped in conflicts around the world, in the last decades, last years, today, and tomorrow.

In these conflicts, such levels of violence against women could not have reached had the security structures that protect the population not been eroded or collapsed. A mal-functioning security sector is a recurring factor in internal armed conflicts. We witnessed this in Milosevic's Yugoslavia, where corrupt and bloated security forces were a constant threat to communities. We witnessed it in Somalia's warlord entrepreneurs, in Guatemala's death gangs, in Afghanistan. When the security sector is not under strict civilian and parliamentary control, too often the state monopoly of legitimate force is questioned, under siege, or lost. The state's capacity to exercise due diligence to prevent, investigate, and punish violence against women, and to provide remedies and assistance, is then weak. Violence against women is perpetrated by militias supporting or opposing the state that are beyond the control of state security services. Violence against women may also be perpetrated by and tolerated by state security services themselves, against 'enemy' women or against all women, within a climate of impunity for human rights violations.

During conflict, preventing violence against women is rarely a political priority, whether that violence is being used as a weapon in the conflict, or whether it is 'normal' violence taking place within the woman's own home. In Iraq, for example, the magnitude of sexual violence has reportedly increased sharply during the war and occupation. However, if a victim of sexual violence reports the crime, there are serious barriers to obtaining justice, which include a lack of female police officers and reluctance of police to investigate. Without a referral from the police, a victim cannot receive the forensic examinations that provide legal proof of sexual violence.[11]

The weakness of the state in exercising due diligence to protect women from violence calls for a range of responses from international actors at different stages of the conflict/post-conflict cycle. Some responses attempt to substitute for the state, whilst other responses, of the type in which the Geneva Centre for the Democratic Control of Armed Forces (DCAF) is engaged, seek to enable the state to protect women.

10 Réseau des Femmes pour un Développement Associatif, Réseau des Femmes pour la Défense des Droits et la Paix and International Alert (2005), *Women's Bodies as a Battleground: Sexual Violence against Women and Girls during the War in the Democratic Republic of Congo*, at http://www.eldis.org/static/DOC18757.htm (last visited 22 August 2006).

11 Human Rights Watch, *Climate of Fear: Sexual Violence and Abduction of Women and Girls in Baghdad Iraq* (New York: 2003), at http://hrw.org/reports/2003/iraq0703/ (last visited 31 July 2006).

Substituting for the State to Protect Women from Violence

International humanitarian law contains many provisions that supplement human rights law to protect women from violence during armed conflict.[12] Sexual violence is expressly prohibited. This prohibition has been strengthened by the recognition, in the Statutes and jurisprudence of the International Criminal Tribunal for the former Yugoslavia and the International Criminal Tribunal for Rwanda, as well as the Statute of the International Criminal Court, of rape as a war crime and a crime against humanity, and that acts of sexual violence can constitute torture, inhuman treatment and (in certain circumstances) genocide. International humanitarian law also protects women in detention, as members of the civilian population, when displaced, in relation to shelter, livelihood, health care et cetera.[13]

The 2005 United Nations World Summit confirmed the collective international responsibility to protect populations from genocide, war crimes, ethnic cleansing, and crimes against humanity, and the legitimacy of Security Council-led action to uphold the responsibility to protect when national authorities are manifestly failing to do so.[14] The international community thus has a clear responsibility to step in to protect women from sexual and other forms of violence that may constitute genocide, war crimes, ethnic cleansing, or crimes against humanity. Peace support operations, led by the United Nations or other multilateral organisations such as NATO, the European Union and the African Union, have the potential to play an important role in protecting women from violence in conflict.

The due diligence standard is important not only for measuring the behaviour of a state in protecting its own people, but as a measure for the performance of international actors. The United Nations Special Rapporteur on violence against

12 International humanitarian law should not be understood as replacing women's human rights during armed conflict, as this too must be upheld. Derogations from international human rights law treaties are permitted only in situations of public emergency threatening the life of the nation; they must be proportional to the crisis at hand, they must not be introduced on a discriminatory basis; and they must not contravene other rules of international law – including rules of international humanitarian law – or seek to undermine the prohibitions on torture or cruel, inhuman, or degrading treatment or punishment or slavery of which derogation is under no circumstance permitted. Armed conflict does not release a state from its obligations of due diligence in respect of these fundamental human rights. For further discussion, refer to the website of the International Committee of the Red Cross (ICRC) and to the Human Rights Committee, General Comment no. 29 on Derogations during States of Emergency, UN. Doc. CCPR/C/21/Rev.1/Add.11 (2001).

13 The ICRC Guidance Document, *Addressing the Needs of Women Affected by Armed Conflict,* (2004) systematically examines women's needs in conflict and the relevant international humanitarian law provisions, at http://www.icrc.org/Web/Eng/siteengo.nsf/htmlall/p0840/$File/ICRC_002_0840.PDF!Open (last visited 31 July 2006).

14 2005 World Summit Outcome Document, UN Doc. A/60/L.1.

women, its causes and consequences, has stated that 'where States and/or intergovernmental bodies are deploying military, peace-keeping or civilian policing operations abroad, they must also act with due diligence to ensure that these personnel do not commit acts of violence against women.'[15] The fact that some peacekeeping personnel themselves abuse and exploit women and children is a matter of great shame. The United Nations is responding to this problem in a number of ways, including through efforts to mainstream gender in peace operations, to recruit more female peace-keeping personnel, and through its Comprehensive Strategy on Assistance and Support to Victims of Sexual Exploitation and Abuse by United Nations Staff or Related Personnel.[16]

The challenge to states providing peacekeepers remains: to properly train its military and civilian personnel, to control their behaviour whilst on mission, and to firmly discipline any personnel who commit acts of violence against women. Training must include that rape (and other forms of violence against women) is a war crime, in international law and in the law of their own country. Armed forces personnel who commit acts of violence against women should not be shielded by a military disciplinary system. A soldier who rapes should not be court-martialled – he should go to prison. States should also take steps to address any culture of violence against women within their own armed forces. Peacekeepers who treat women with respect must first be soldiers or civilians who treat women with respect.

Security Council Resolution 1325 on Women, Peace and Security is an important standard in planning and monitoring responses to violence against women in armed conflict. Resolution 1325 both recognises the particular impacts of armed conflict upon women and girls and calls for their protection, and reaffirms 'the important role of women in the prevention and resolution of conflicts and in peace-building.' In urging states 'to ensure increased representation of women at all decision-making levels in…institutions and mechanisms for the prevention, management, and resolution of conflict…' the Security Council reinforces the duty not only to protect women from violence, but to work towards women's equality and empowerment.

Enabling the State to Protect Women from Violence: Building a Democratic and Participatory Security Sector

Violence against women is particularly prevalent in post-conflict situations, due to widespread trauma, disruption of community and family networks, and the

15 Report of the United Nations Special Rapporteur on violence against women, its causes and consequences, Yakın Ertürk, *The Due Diligence Standard as a Tool for the Elimination of Violence against Women*, UN Doc. E/CN.4/2006/61, 20 January 2006.

16 Comprehensive Review of the Whole Question of Peace-keeping Operations in all Their Aspects, Letter dated 25 May 2006 from the Secretary-General to the President of the General Assembly, 5 June 2006, UN Doc. A/60/877.

disarray of pre-war security institutions. Reform (or re-creation) of the security sector will usually be a precondition to recovery: if a state lacks a monopoly of the legitimate use of force, if the security sector is not under civilian and parliamentary control, there can be neither peace, rule of law, nor democracy, and there will likely be little investment or development. Such a state cannot meet its obligations of due diligence in relation to human rights violations.

Security sector reform and governance thus lies at the intersection of security, development, and democracy. A well-functioning security service means police officers on whom you can call for protection, knowing that they will not abuse you, extort money from you, or discriminate against you because you are from a particular social or ethnic group. It means a military that is controlled by a democratically elected parliament, not by private influence, and that is professional and has clear lines of command and strict discipline. It means defence budgets approved by parliament, and funds not being siphoned through paramilitary structures. United Nations agencies such as the United Nations Development Programme, international organisations such as DCAF, and individual donor states can assist states emerging from conflict or undergoing transition to democracy to set up good governance structures, through technical assistance and capacity building. Democratic governance of the security sector must be founded on international human rights and governance standards.

Security sector reform processes should develop structures and mechanisms to prevent and respond to violence against women, to promote gender equality, to recognise women's contributions to peace and stability, and to include women in security sector institutions. This requires that women's needs and experiences be considered at every step, and that women be involved in every step. Constitutional and political reform must ensure women's citizenship, and women's right to vote and stand for public office. Legislation should be reviewed to ensure that it meets international standards for women's human rights. In Guatemala, the peace accords themselves spelt out the government's responsibility to revise national legislation to eliminate discrimination against women, using the Convention on the Elimination of All Forms of Discrimination against Women as a guide. States should consider specialised police response groups to address violence against women. Liberia, for example, has established a Women and Children Protection Section in its police service, made up of officers who have been trained in the handling and management of sexual violence, sexual abuse, and gender-based violence cases. There must be effective prosecution of offenders; training of security personnel regarding gender based violence; and recruitment and personnel practices within the security services that promote women. Questions asked by the first Special Rapporteur on violence against women, Radhika Coomaraswamy, on her field visits to assess state adherence to the due diligence standard, also provide guidance in assessing security sector reform:

> 'Is the criminal justice system sensitive to the issues of violence against women? In this regard, what is police practice? How many cases are investigated by the police? How are

victims dealt with by the police? How many cases are prosecuted? What type of judgements are given in such cases?'[17]

Women's civil society should be included in identification of any community's security needs, and how best to meet them. Women must be actively included in disarmament, demobilisation, and reintegration processes.

A comprehensive response to violence against women must seek to promote human security in a holistic manner. It must include measures to assist reintegration of victims, through assistance and social and psychological support. In many conflict-affected environments, the stigma attached to sexual violence makes victims' recovery near impossible. A state's due diligence obligation might include implementing sensitisation programmes to address this stigma. Truth and justice are also aspects of human security: national and international criminal tribunals, including the International Criminal Court, and truth and reconciliation commissions are important mechanisms to obtain justice for women who have suffered violence in conflict. There must be no more impunity.

Using the Due Diligence Standard in Armed Conflict and in Its Aftermath

Due diligence, as a standard of state responsibility, is challenged by the post-Cold War fragmentation of state authority, and the spreading malaise of corruption and poor governance. However, whilst state capacity might be weak in armed conflict, the international community has developed a more rigorous and coherent concept of intervention to protect human rights. Violence against women should be at the fore in considering whether international intervention is warranted in any situation. The concept of human security, being a broader and less state-centric understanding of security, also offers a framework for understanding violence against women as a security issue demanding an urgent response. In any such international response, states should be held accountable to the due diligence standard to prevent, investigate, and punish violence against women, and to provide remedies and assistance.

In avoiding conflict and in building peace after conflict, building a democratic and participatory security sector is crucial. Security sector reform processes hold the potential to transform security institutions and security governance to equip them to fulfil their obligations under the due diligence standard, and to do so in ways that include and empower women.

17 Report of the Special Rapporteur on violence against women, its causes and consequences, Radhika Coomaraswamy, *Violence against Women in the Family*, UN Doc. E.CN.4/1999/68, 10 March 1999

Table of Cases

African Commission on Human and Peoples' Rights

European Court of Human Rights

Inter-American Commission on Human Rights

Inter-American Court of Human Rights

International Criminal Tribunal for the former Yugoslavia

United Nations Committee on the Elimination of Discrimination against Women

United Nations Human Rights Committee

National Courts

Pakistan

South Africa

Switzerland

United Kingdom

The Contributors

Elizabeth A.H. Abi-Mershed is a Principal Specialist for the Inter-American Commission on Human Rights (IACHR) of the Organization of American States. She provides legal advice to the Commission, serves as desk officer, coordinates the legal team charged with the litigation of cases before the Inter-American Court of Human Rights and provides technical support to the Commission's Special Rapporteurship on the Rights of Women. She received her JD from the Washington College of Law, and an LL.M. in International and Comparative Law from the Georgetown University Law Center.

Carin Benninger-Budel is a researcher at the Interdisciplinary Centre for Gender Studies (ICFG), University of Bern, Switzerland, and a consultant on international human rights with a particular focus on women's human rights, violence against women and the United Nations human rights system. For many years she was the Programme Manager of the Violence against Women Programme at the World Organisation Against Torture (OMCT) in Geneva, Switzerland. She holds a law degree from the Utrecht University in the Netherlands.

Ineke Boerefijn is a senior lecturer at the Netherlands Institute of Human Rights (SIM), Utrecht School of Law, and holds the Opzij Chair on Power and Strategy: Women in Conflict, at the Centre for Gender and Diversity, Maastricht University, the Netherlands. Her main areas of work include the United Nations system of protection of human rights and the human rights of women.

Joanna Bourke-Martignoni has degrees in law and in history (honours) from the University of New South Wales in Sydney, Australia. She also has a Master's in International Relations from the Graduate Institute of International Studies in Geneva and is currently enrolled as a doctoral student in international law at the University of Fribourg, Switzerland. She has held positions as a legal advisor to the International Committee of the Red Cross, as a project officer on the Violence against Women Programme at the World Organisation Against Torture (OMCT), as a consultant to the trafficking advisor at the UN Office of the High Commissioner for Human Rights and as a teaching and research assistant in the law faculty at the University of Fribourg. Her main areas of research interest are international human rights and humanitarian law, feminist legal theory and the philosophy of law.

Yakın Ertürk has been on the faculty of the Department of Sociology since 1986 and the Gender and Women's Studies Programme since 1994 at the Middle East Technical University in Ankara, Turkey. She also taught at the Centre for Girls, at King Saud University in Riyadh (1979–1982) and from 1979 to 1981 served as its Chair. Between 1997 and 2001 she joined the United Nations, serving first as Director of the International Research and Training Institute for the Advancement of Women (INSTRAW) in Santo Domingo, Dominican Republic (October 1997–February 1999), then as Director of the Division for the Advancement of Women (DAW) at UN Headquarters in New York (March 1999–October 2001). She has worked for various national and international agencies on rural development and women in development projects. Her academic areas of interest are international human rights regimes; identity politics, conflict and violence against women; globalization and population movements; household labour use patterns and women in development.
On 1 August 2003, Yakın Ertürk was appointed as the United Nations Special Rapporteur on violence against women. Within this context, she undertakes fact-finding missions to various countries; receives complaints regarding violations of women's human rights from around the world; and prepares thematic reports on violence against women, its causes and consequences. She submits annual reports on all her activities and findings to the Human Rights Commission, which has been the Human Rights Council since 2006.

Susana T. Fried is a consultant on gender, sexuality and human rights advocacy, research, training and program development. She was formerly the Program Director at the International Gay and Lesbian Human Rights Commission (IGLHRC). She has worked for many years on social and economic justice issues from a feminist perspective. For the past 15 years, her focus has been on gender and human rights with an emphasis on sexuality and rights, ending violence against women and developing intersectional human rights advocacy and practices. She has written, spoken, trained and published extensively on a range of human rights concerns and has been closely affiliated with the Global Rights, Partners for Justice (Washington, DC, USA), Center for Women's Global Leadership at Rutgers University (USA), Amnesty International, and UNIFEM (UN Development Fund for Women). Fried holds a PhD in Political Economy/Gender and Development from Rutgers University, and is an adjunct Assistant Professor at the School of International and Public Affairs at Columbia University. She is a member of the coordinating team of Amnesty International's intersectional LGBT network.

Anne Gallagher (PhD, M.Int,L, LLB, BA) is an international lawyer specialising in human rights and criminal justice. She worked on human rights in the UN for over 10 years and served as Special Adviser on Human Trafficking to the United Nations High Commissioner for Human Rights from 1999 to 2002. Since 2003 she has led an intergovernmental initiative aimed at developing more effective criminal justice responses to human trafficking within the ASEAN region. Anne Gallagher has taught at academic institutions throughout the world including the NATO Staff College, the European Institute for Human Rights and Universities in Australia, Finland, Switzerland and Thailand. She has published extensively in the areas of policing, human rights and human trafficking.

Lisa Gormley is a solicitor, and received an LLM in International Human Rights Law in 2000 from the University of Essex, UK. Since 2000, she has been a Legal Advisor at Amnesty International's International Secretariat in London, focusing on women's rights and international law, particularly providing legal advice for the Amnesty International campaign 'Stop Violence against Women' and assisting regional research departments with their work on women's human rights.

Rikki Holtmaat (Professor) holds a Chair in International Non-Discrimination Law at the University of Leiden, the Netherlands, Department of Public Law. She has published a great deal on the content and scope of the CEDAW Convention, on the European Union and Dutch equal treatment and non-discrimination legislation, concerning a wide range of non-discrimination grounds. In 2003–2006 she was involved in a project on the use of international human rights standards when combating domestic violence in the Western Balkans. For a full list of publications, see www.rikkiholtmaat.nl.

Eva Naezer studied International Public Law in Utrecht and graduated in July 2006. In September and October of that same year, she was an intern at the Netherlands Institute of Human Rights (SIM). She is currently following a Master's Programme in International Relations at the University of Groningen (RUG), the Netherlands.

María Naredo Molero works as a lawyer and scientific researcher. She focuses on questions concerning gender and criminality issues of socially discriminated groups and examines public authorities' responses to gender violence and the criminalisation of gypsy women. She also works as a trainer on gender and human rights. Maria Naredo Molero was formerly in charge of the campaign 'Stop Violence against Women' at the Spanish section of Amnesty International. Currently, she is an external expert to the Spanish section of Amnesty International and contributes to research missions on violence against women of the International Secretariat of Amnesty International.

Helen O'Connell is Head of Policy at One World Action, a British NGO based in London. She has worked in the UK NGO sector since 1980. Her advocacy and policy change work focuses on democracy, governance, human rights and gender issues in the context of British and European Union aid, trade and political relations with southern countries. Women's rights, women's political participation and gender and development issues are a particular focus of her advocacy, campaigning and writing. She was one of the founder members of Network Women in Development Europe (WIDE). She is active within BOND (the British NGO Platform) particularly on EU policy issues. She is Irish and has lived and worked in London since 1973.

Nivedita Prasad is Project Coordinator and researcher at Ban Ying, a counselling and coordination centre against human trafficking based in Berlin, Germany. She teaches antiracist and human rights-based social work at various universities.

Lisa Pusey is the Programme Officer for the Violence Against Women and Women's Human Rights Programmes at Asia Pacific Forum on Women, Law and Development (APWLD) which is a regional women's network committed to enabling women in the region to use law as an instrument of change for the empowerment of women in their struggle for justice, peace, equality and development. She has an Arts/LLB degree from the University of New South Wales, Australia, in which she focused on women's human rights, human rights law and social justice issues. She is a solicitor who before joining APWLD worked in the Community Legal Centre sector in Sydney, Australia.

Babette Rohner is a sociologist and social worker assisting trafficked women at Ban Ying, a counselling and coordination centre against human trafficking based in Berlin, Germany. She teaches gender issues and child rights issues at the Free University in Berlin.

Originally trained as a UK lawyer, **Shivaun Scanlan** has been working on human rights issues with regard to refugees, discrimination and trafficking for over ten years. She holds a Master's in International Law from the Graduate Institute for International Relations in Geneva and wrote her research thesis on state responsibility for trafficking in human beings. She worked for the International Labour Organisation between 2001 to 2004, focusing on trafficking, forced labour and migrant workers. Since January 2005 she has been working as the senior adviser on anti-trafficking for the OSCE Office for Democratic Institutions and Human Rights in Warsaw. She is responsible for developing and implementing an anti-trafficking programme in the OSCE region and providing support to OSCE States in addressing trafficking.

Farida Shaheed, a sociologist, is a Coordinator of Shirkat Gah – Women's Resource Centre in Pakistan. She developed and runs Shirkat Gah's legal consciousness programme that seeks to change laws and policies while simultaneously building grassroots capacity through legal awareness, paralegal trainings, legal counselling/assistance and networking. A founding member of Pakistan's national lobby, Women's Action Forum, which led women's resistance under a decade of martial law (1977–88), she is one of the coordinators of the international network for information, solidarity and support: Women Living Under Muslim Laws. Her extensive publications focus on intersecting issues of women's rights, customs and religion, state, governance and development. In 1989 her co-authored book *Two Steps Forward One Step Back? Women of Pakistan* won the Prime Minister's award. In 1997 she received the Second Annual Women's Human Rights Award of the Women Law & Development International. Farida Shaheed is currently the Deputy Director of a multicountry research programme supported by DFID: Women's Empowerment in the Muslim World: Poverty, Gender and Democratization from the Inside Out.

Dee Smythe is Chief Researcher at the Gender, Health & Justice Research Unit in the Faculty of Health Sciences at the University of Cape Town, South Africa. She holds political science and law degrees from the University of Cape Town and a JSM degree from Stanford Law School, which she attended as a Fulbright Fellow. Dee Smythe's research focuses on violence against women, human rights and development.

Born on 6 June 1951, **Theodor H. Winkler** studied political sciences and international security at the Universities of Geneva and Harvard University and at the Graduate Institute of International Studies in Geneva. He obtained, in 1981, a PhD in political sciences with a thesis on nuclear proliferation. Winkler joined the Swiss Department of Defence in late 1981 as an international security expert. In 1985 he was appointed Representative of the Chief of Staff for Politico-Military Affairs and in 1995 became Head of the newly created Division for International Security Policy. In 1998 he was promoted to the rank of Deputy Head, Security and Defence Policy. On 13 June 2000, the Swiss Federal Council appointed Winkler to be the Director of the Geneva Centre for the Democratic Control of Armed Forces (DCAF) and promoted him to the rank of Ambassador. Winkler's professional affiliations include membership in the Council of the International Institute for Strategic Studies (London), the PfP Consortium of Defence Academies and Security Studies Institutes, the Geneva Centre for Security Policy, DCAF Brussels, the Centre for Applied Studies in International Negotiations and the International Coalition Women Defending Peace as well as membership in the international Advisory Boards of the Bonn International Centre for Conversion, the Centre for International Security Studies Hungary, and several other academic and international bodies.

Judith Wyttenbach (PhD), born 1968, works as a lecturer at the University of Bern, Switzerland, Department of Public Law. She has published various papers on human rights in general and children's rights and gender issues in particular. Latest publications: *Rebuilding Lives, 25 Years United Nations Voluntary Fund for Victims of Torture*, Baden 2006/translated into French and Spanish (together with Walter Kälin/Lars Müller, by order of United Nations High Commissioner of Human Rights); *Grund- und Menschenrechtskonflikte zwischen Kindern, Eltern und Staat. Schutzpflichten des Staates gegenüber Kindern und Jugendlichen aus dem internationalen Menschenrechtsschutz und aus Art. 11 BV*, Basel 2006; *Menschenrechte von Mädchen aus Einwandererfamilien*, in Eidgenössische Kommission für Frauenfragen, F – Frauenfragen 1/2006; *The Face of Human Rights*, Baden 2004 (together with Lars Müller und Walter Kälin).

The Supporting Organisations

Amnesty International is a worldwide movement of people who campaign for internationally recognised human rights. Amnesty International's vision is of a world in which every person enjoys all of the human rights enshrined in the Universal Declaration of Human Rights and other international human rights standards. Its mission is to undertake research and action focused on preventing and ending grave abuses of the rights to physical and mental integrity, freedom of conscience and expression, and freedom from discrimination, within the context of its work to promote all human rights.

Amnesty International's global *Stop Violence against Women Campaign* was launched on 5 March 2004 and will continue until 2010. Its long-term goals are to:

- Abolish laws that support impunity for violence against women and that discriminate against women
- Enact and implement effective laws and practices to protect women from violence
- Hold states individually and collectively accountable to their obligations under international law to prevent, investigate, punish and redress all acts of violence against women
- Secure effective action to stop violence against women at the community level by local governments and civil society, including religious bodies, traditional and informal authorities

The *Stop Violence against Women Campaign* focuses on various forms of violence: Violence in times of war and armed conflict, violence in the family, sexual violence, violence against girls and violence against women in the workplace. It also focuses on the support of women human rights defenders. For more about Amnesty International and the *Stop Violence against Women Campaign* see www.amnesty.org/actforwomen.

The organisation **Humanrights.ch/Menschenrechte Schweiz** MERS was founded in 1999. Its aim is to better guarantee human rights in Switzerland by means of:

- Promoting human rights in Switzerland
- Raising awareness of public opinion on human rights issues
- Organising projects in the field of education on human rights
- Giving information to non-governmental organisations (NGOs)
- Coordinating and compiling complementary NGO reports on the implementation of human rights conventions

The website – *www.humanrights.ch* – offers a comprehensive source of information on human rights issues related to Switzerland in three languages (English, German and French). This information platform includes precise essential information about international protection of human rights and diverse related human rights themes as well as current news on national and foreign Swiss human rights policy. The English version of the website is the most recent (September 2006) and aims to enable the English-speaking user to better understand human rights policy in Switzerland and, accordingly, to find appropriate information (e.g., on women's rights, gender equality and domestic violence).

The **Interdisciplinary Centre for Gender Studies (ICFG)** offers and coordinates teaching and research in gender studies at the University of Bern. The centre focuses on issues of human rights, sustainable development, governance, globalisation and feminist movements in a transnational perspective. In particular, ICFG:
- Offers teaching in cooperation with the faculties and enhances the implementation of gender studies in the curricula of the affiliated departments
- Engages in inter- and transdisciplinary research in accordance with its profile
- Promotes excellent young researchers in gender studies by means of a doctoral school Pro Doc in Gender Studies
- Holds various mandates for consulting and training from research networks, departments, state affiliated organisations, NGOs and private institutions
- Is part of a national network for gender studies and cooperates with international partners
- Operates the virtual communication and information platform for gender studies and equality in higher education www.gendercampus.ch

The ICFG hosts a number of conferences, colloquia and seminars that are open to students, faculty members, professionals and staff from our partner institutions. The ICFG activities are published twice a year in the Centre's magazine *genderstudies*. For more details on the ICFG please visit our website at http://www.izfg.unibe.ch/

The **World Organisation Against Torture** (OMCT) is the largest coalition of non-governmental organisations (NGOs) fighting against torture, summary executions, forced disappearances and all other forms of cruel, inhuman or degrading treatment. The International Secretariat of OMCT coordinates the SOS-Torture network composed of 282 national, regional and international NGOs in 92 countries. In answer to the increasing number of cases on gender-based specific forms of violence coming from the members of the SOS-Torture network and other sources, OMCT decided in 1996 to establish the Violence against Women Programme, which addresses and analyses the gender-related causes and consequences of torture and other forms of violence against women.

The objectives of the Violence against Women Programme are to:

- Prevent and respond to acts of torture or other forms of violence against women with a focus on the gender dimensions of the causes and consequences of this violence
- Contribute to a more effective integration of gender issues into the considerations of the United Nations (UN) treaty monitoring bodies and increase the capacity of local NGOs to make effective use of the international human rights mechanisms relevant to women's rights.
- Draw attention of state representatives to their obligation of due diligence to protect the human rights of women where the perpetrator of the violence is a private actor
- Draw attention to the issue of violence against women perpetrated by state officials within the framework of the UN Committee on the Elimination of Discrimination against Women (CEDAW) and among women human rights NGOs in order to lobby governments and other relevant actors to take steps to better promote and protect the human rights of women against acts of violence
- Evaluate the overall progress made in the implementation of international commitments aimed at preventing and combating violence against women

For more information about the Violence against Women programme, see www.omct.org.

Index

Nijhoff Law Specials

60. S. Skaale (ed.): *The Right to National Self-Determination: The Faroe Islands and Greenland*. 2004 ISBN 90 04 14207 X

61. E. McWhinney: *The September 11 Terrorist Attacks and the Invasion of Iraq in Contemporary International Law: Opinions on the Emerging New World Order System*. 2004 ISBN 90 04 14143 X

62. B.G. Ramcharan, *The Protection Role of National Human Rights Institutions*. 2005. ISBN 90 04 14526 5

63. C. de Cooker, *Accountability, Investigation and Due Process in International Organizations*. 2005. ISBN 90 04 14793 4

64. P. S. Jones & K. Stokke, *Democratising Development: The Politics of Socio-Economic Rights in South Africa*. 2005. ISBN 90 04 14821 3

65. R. S. Lee (ed.): *Swords Into Plowshares: Building Peace Through the United Nations*. 2005. ISBN 90 04 15001 3

66. J.A. Bovenberg, *Property Rights in Blood, Genes & Data: Naturally Yours?* 2006 ISBN 90 04 15053 6

67. F. Hoffmeister: *Legal Aspects of the Cyprus Problem. Annan Plan and the EU Accession*. 2006 ISBN 978 90 04 15223 6

68. R. Bredel: *The Ethical Economy of Conflict Prevention and Development*. 2006 ISBN 978 90 04 15305 9

69. P. Nedergaard: *European Union Administration: Legitimacy and Efficiency*. 2007 ISBN 978 90 04 15573 2

70. L.G. Loucaides: *The European Convention on Human Rights*. 2007 ISBN 978 90 04 15883 2

71. F. Falcón y Tella: *Challenges for Human Rights*. 2007 ISBN 978 90 04 16022 4

72. A. Vedder (ed.): *NGO Involvement in International Governance and Policy: Sources of Legitimacy*. 2007 ISBN 978 90 04 15846 7

73. Carin Benninger-Budel (ed.), *Due Diligence and Its Application to Protect Women from Violence*. 2008 ISBN 978 90 04 16293 8

For more titles in this series, consult our web site: **http://www.brill.nl/nlsp**

MARTINUS NIJHOFF PUBLISHERS – LEIDEN • BOSTON

www.ingramcontent.com/pod-product-compliance
Lightning Source LLC
Chambersburg PA
CBHW061201240926
51846CB00006B/1076
* 9 7 8 9 0 0 4 1 6 2 9 3 8 *